Birnbaum's 94
Boston

A BIRNBAUM TRAVEL GUIDE

Alexandra Mayes Birnbaum
EDITORIAL CONSULTANT

Lois Spritzer
Executive Editor

Laura L. Brengelman
Managing Editor

Mary Callahan
Senior Editor

Patricia Canole
Gene Gold
Jill Kadetsky
Susan McClung
Beth Schlau
Associate Editors

 HarperPerennial
A Division of HarperCollinsPublishers

To Stephen, who merely made all this possible.

FIRST EDITION

ISSN 0749-2561 (Birnbaum Travel Guides)
ISSN 1056-4357 (Boston)
ISBN 0-06-278119-7 (pbk.)

94 95 96 97 CC/CW 10 9 8 7 6 5 4 3 2 1

Cover design © Drenttel Doyle Partners
Cover photograph © Tom Bross/Stock Boston

BIRNBAUM TRAVEL GUIDES

Bahamas, and Turks & Caicos
Berlin
Bermuda
Boston
Canada
Cancun, Cozumel & Isla Mujeres
Caribbean
Chicago
Disneyland
Eastern Europe
Europe
Europe for Business Travelers
France
Germany
Great Britain
Hawaii
Ireland
Italy
London

Los Angeles
Mexico
Miami & Ft. Lauderdale
Montreal & Quebec City
New Orleans
New York
Paris
Portugal
Rome
San Francisco
Santa Fe & Taos
South America
Spain
United States
USA for Business Travelers
Walt Disney World
Walt Disney World for Kids, By Kids
Washington, DC

Contributing Editors
Brad Durham
Sara Laschever
Nancy Roosa
Tracy Smith
Peter Tietjen

Maps
Mark Carlson
Susan Carlson
B. Andrew Mudryk

Contents

Getting Ready to Go

Practical information for planning your trip.

The City

Thorough, qualitative guide to Boston that offers a comprehensive report on the city's most compelling attractions and amenities — highlighting our top choices in every category.

Diversions

A selective guide to a variety of unexpected pleasures, pinpointing the best places in which to pursue them.

Exceptional Experiences for the Mind and Body

Directions

Seven of the most delightful walks through Boston,
plus a great driving tour.

Foreword

My sister-in-law lives in Boston — well, actually in Watertown, a suburb. This suggests at least two significant ramifications: First is the fact that as a result of her residence my husband, Steve Birnbaum, and I spent a fair amount of time in New England's most important urban enclave. Second is the dramatic endorsement that her presence implies: My sister-in-law is a charter member of the 1960s flower child generation, educated (at least in part) at the fount in Berkeley, and determined to live in only the most convivial of environments.

I can't tell exactly why my husband's youngest sibling finds Boston and its environs so appealing, but I do know that I think of it as a small town. From a third generation Manhattan dweller that's a meaningful compliment, incorporating concepts of both friendliness and escape. For visitors, Boston has a certain pervasive coziness that is very desirable, an accessibility that makes a traveler feel warmly welcome and at home.

With this sense of well-being very much in the air, it is more than normally nice to explore the historic sites and colonial corners that are Boston's signature. Add the host of truly topnotch hotels and savory restaurants that Boston has spawned in abundance, and you begin to get the impression that this is a town really worth exploring. Where once Boston took a backseat to more exotic urban locales, travelers (like me) have more recently grown up enough to appreciate this marvelous metropolis.

Obviously, any guidebook to Boston must keep pace with and answer the real needs of today's travelers. That's why we've tried to create a guide that's specifically organized, written, and edited for the more demanding modern traveler, one for whom qualitative information is infinitely more desirable than mere quantities of unappraised data.

For years, dating back as far as Herr Baedeker, travel guides have tended to be encyclopedic, much more concerned with demonstrating expertise in geography and history than with a real analysis of the sorts of things that actually concern a typical modern tourist. I think you'll notice a different, more contemporary tone to our text, as well as an organization and focus that are distinctive and more functional. Early on, we realized that giving up the encyclopedic approach precluded our listing every single route and restaurant, a realization that helped define our overall editorial focus. Similarly, when we discussed the possibility of presenting certain information in other than strict geographic order, we found that the new format enabled us to arrange data in a way that best answers the questions travelers typically ask.

Travel guides are, understandably, reflections of personal taste, and putting one's name on a title page obviously puts one's preferences on the line. But I think I ought to amplify just what "personal" means. I don't believe in the sort of personal guidebook that's a palpable misrepresentation on its face. It is, for example, hardly possible for any single travel writer to visit thousands of restaurants (and nearly as many hotels) in any given year and provide accurate appraisals of each. And even if it were physically possible for one human being to survive such an itinerary, it would of necessity have to be done at a dead sprint, and the perceptions derived therefrom would probably be less valid than those of any other intelligent individual visiting the same establishments. It is, therefore, impossible (especially in a large, annually revised and updated guidebook *series* such as we offer) to have only one person provide all the data on the entire world.

I also happen to think that such individual orientation is of substantially less value to readers. Visiting a single hotel for just one night or eating one hasty meal in a random restaurant hardly equips anyone to provide appraisals that are of more than passing interest. We have, therefore, chosen what I like to describe as the "thee and me" approach to restaurant and hotel evaluation and, to a somewhat more limited degree, to the sites and sights we have included in our text. What this really reflects is a personal sampling tempered by intelligent counsel from informed local sources, and these additional friends-of-the-editor are almost always residents of the city and/or area about which they are consulted.

In addition, very precise editing and tailoring keep our text fiercely subjective. So what follows is the gospel according to Birnbaum, and represents as much of our own taste and instincts as we can manage. It is probable, therefore, that if you like your cities stylish and prefer small hotels with personality to huge high-rise anonymities, we're likely to have a long and meaningful relationship.

I also should point out something about the person to whom this guidebook is directed. Above all, he or she is a "visitor." This means that such elements as restaurants have been specifically picked to provide the visitor with a representative, enlightening, stimulating, and above all pleasant experience. Since so many extraneous considerations can affect the reception and service accorded a regular restaurant patron, our choices can in no way be construed as an exhaustive guide to resident dining. We think we've listed all the best places, in various price ranges, but they were chosen with a visitor's enjoyment in mind.

Other evidence of how we've tried to tailor our text to reflect modern travel habits is most apparent in the section we call DIVERSIONS. Where once it was common for travelers to spend an urban visit seeing only the obvious sights, the emphasis today is more likely to be directed toward pursuing some special interest. Therefore, we have collected these exceptional experiences so that it is no longer necessary to wade through a pound or two of superfluous prose just to find unexpected pleasures and treasures.

Finally, I also should point out that every good travel guide is a living enterprise; that is, no part of this text is carved in stone. In our annual revisions, we refine, expand, and further hone all our material to serve your travel needs better. To this end, no contribution is of greater value to us than your personal reaction to what we have written, as well as information reflecting your own experiences while using the book. Please write to us at 10 E. 53rd St., New York, NY 10022.

We sincerely hope to hear from you.

Alexandra Mayes Birnbaum

ALEXANDRA MAYES BIRNBAUM, editorial consultant to the *Birnbaum Travel Guides,* worked with her late husband, Stephen Birnbaum, as co-editor of the series. She has been a world traveler since childhood and is known for her lively travel reports on radio on what's hot and what's not.

Boston

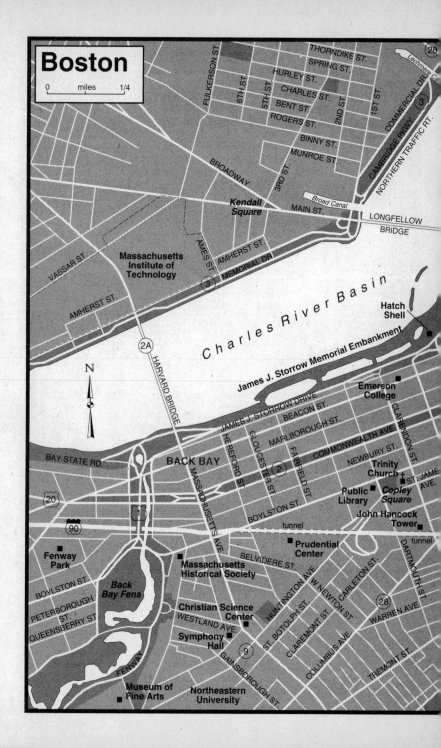

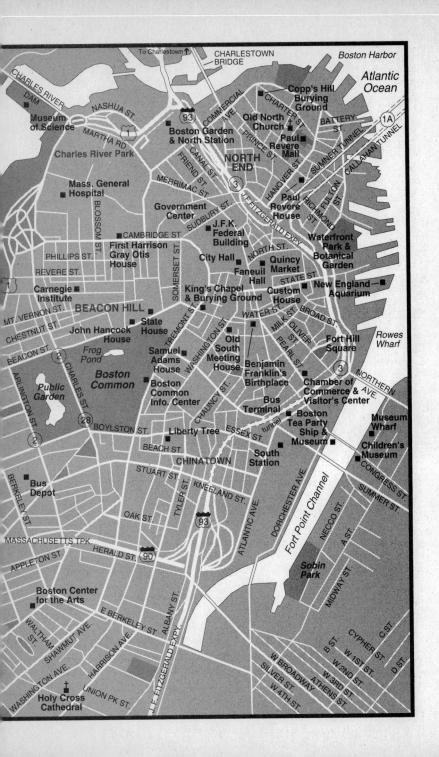

How to Use This Guide

A great deal of care has gone into the special organization of this guide-book, and we believe it represents a real breakthrough in the presentation of travel material.

Our text is divided into four basic sections in order to present information in the best way on every possible aspect of a vacation to Boston. Our aim is to highlight what's where and to provide basic information — how, when, where, how much, and what's best — to assist you in making the most intelligent choices possible.

Here is a brief summary of what you can expect to find in each section. We believe that you will find both your travel planning and en route enjoyment enhanced by having this book at your side.

GETTING READY TO GO

A mini-encyclopedia of practical travel facts with all the precise data necessary to create a successful trip to Boston. Here you will find how to get where you're going, plus selected resources — including useful publications, and companies and organizations specializing in discount and special-interest travel — providing a wealth of information and assistance useful both before and during your trip.

THE CITY

This individual report on Boston offers a short-stay guide, including an essay introducing the city as a historic entity and a contemporary place to visit; *Boston At-a-Glance* material is actually a site-by-site survey of the most important, interesting, and sometimes most eclectic sights to see and things to do; *Local Sources and Resources* is a concise listing of pertinent tourism information, such as the address of the local tourist office, which sightseeing tours to take, where to find the best nightspot or hail a taxi, which shops have the finest merchandise and/or the most irresistible bargains, and where the best museums and theaters are to be found. *Best in Town* lists our choices of the best places to eat and sleep on a variety of budgets.

DIVERSIONS

This section is designed to help travelers find the best places in which to engage in a variety of exceptional — and unexpected — experiences, without having to wade through endless pages of unrelated text. In every case, our particular suggestions are intended to guide you to that special place where the quality of experience is likely to be highest.

DIRECTIONS

Here are seven walks that cover the city, along its main thoroughfares and side streets, past its most spectacular landmarks and magnificent parks, and one drive to the nearby, history-rich towns of Cambridge, Lexington, Concord, and Lincoln.

To use this book to full advantage, take a few minutes to read the table of contents and random entries in each section to get a firsthand feel for how it all fits together. You will find that the sections of this book are building blocks designed to help you put together the best possible trip. Use them selectively as a tool, a source of ideas, a reference work for accurate facts, and a guidebook to the best buys, the most exciting sights, the most pleasant accommodations, and the tastiest foods — *the best travel experience* that you can possibly have.

Getting
Ready to Go

When to Go

Although the most popular vacation period traditionally is June to September, the best time to visit Boston may be autumn. During autumn, the days are most pleasant in New England, generally clear and brisk — although nights can be cold. Winter can be formidable, with icy winds, snow, and sleet; spring is brief and cool; and summers are warm to hot, with breezy and cooler nights.

Travel during the off-season (fall through spring) and shoulder seasons (the months immediately before and after the peak months) offers relatively fair weather and smaller crowds. During these periods, travel also is less expensive. Exception are the peak of fall foliage (mid-September through October) and college graduation time (late May), when bargains disappear and reservations may be required as early as 6 months in advance.

The *Weather Channel* (2600 Cumberland Pkwy., Atlanta, GA 30339; phone: 404-434-6800) provides current weather forecasts. Call 900-WEATHER from any touch-tone phone in the US; the 95¢ per minute charge will appear on your phone bill.

Traveling by Plane

SCHEDULED FLIGHTS

Leading airlines offering flights to Boston include *American, American Eagle, America West, Continental, Delta, Delta Connection, Delta Shuttle, Midwest Express, Mohawk, Northeast Express, Northwest, NW Airlink, TWA, United, United Express, USAir,* and *USAir Shuttle.*

FARES The great variety of airfares can be reduced to the following basic categories: first class, business class, coach (also called economy or tourist class), excursion or discount, and standby, as well as various promotional fares. For information on applicable fares and restrictions, contact the airlines listed above or ask your travel agent. Most airfares are offered for a limited time period. Once you've found the lowest fare for which you can qualify, purchase your ticket as soon as possible.

RESERVATIONS Reconfirmation is not generally required on domestic flights, although it is wise to call ahead to make sure that the airline has your reservation and any special requests in its computer.

SEATING Airline seats usually are assigned on a first-come, first-served basis at check-in, although you may be able to reserve a seat when purchasing your ticket. Seating charts often are available from airlines and are included in the *Airline Seating Guide* (Carlson Publishing Co., PO Box 888, Los Alamitos, CA 90720; phone: 310-493-4877).

SMOKING US law prohibits smoking on flights scheduled for 6 hours or less within the US and its territories on both domestic and international carriers. A free wallet-size guide that describes the rights of nonsmokers is available from *ASH* (*Action on Smoking and Health;* DOT Card, 2013 H St. NW, Washington, DC 20006; phone: 202-659-4310).

SPECIAL MEALS When making your reservation, you can request one of the airline's alternate menu choices for no additional charge. Call to reconfirm your request 24 hours before departure.

BAGGAGE On a major airline, passengers usually are allowed to carry on board one bag that will fit under a seat or in an overhead bin. Passengers also can check two bags in the cargo hold, measuring 62 inches and 55 inches in combined dimensions (length, width, and depth) with a per-bag weight limit of 70 pounds. There may be charges for additional, oversize, or overweight luggage, and for special equipment or sporting gear. Note that baggage allowances may vary for children (depending on the percentage of full adult fare paid). Check that the tags the airline attaches are correctly coded for your destination.

CHARTER FLIGHTS

By booking a block of seats on a specially arranged flight, charter operators frequently offer travelers bargain airfares. If you do fly on a charter, however, read the contract's fine print carefully. Charter operators can cancel a flight or assess surcharges of 10% of the airfare up to 10 days before departure. You usually must book in advance (no changes are permitted, so invest in trip cancellation insurance); also make your check out to the company's escrow account. For further information, consult the publication *Jax Fax* (397 Post Rd., Darien, CT 06820; phone: 203-655-8746).

DISCOUNTS ON SCHEDULED FLIGHTS

COURIER TRAVEL In return for arranging to accompany some kind of freight, a traveler may pay only a portion of the total airfare and a small registration fee. One agency that matches up would-be couriers with courier companies is *Now Voyager* (74 Varick St., Suite 307, New York, NY 10013; phone: 212-431-1616).

Courier Companies

Courier Travel Service (530 Central Ave., Cedarhurst, NY 11516; phone: 516-763-6898).

Discount Travel International (169 W. 81st St., New York, NY 10024; phone: 212-362-3636; and 940 10th St., Suite 2, Miami Beach, FL 33139; phone: 305-538-1616).

Excaliber International Courier (c/o *Way to Go Travel,* 6679 Sunset Blvd., Hollywood, CA 90028; phone: 213-466-1126).

F.B. On Board Courier Services (10225 Ryan Ave., Suite 103, Dorval, Quebec H9P 1A2, Canada; phone: 514-633-0740).
Halbart Express (147-05 176th St., Jamaica, NY 11434; phone: 718-656-8279).
International Adventures (60 E. 42nd St., New York, NY 10165; phone: 212-599-0577).
Midnight Express (925 W. High Park Blvd., Inglewood, CA 90302; phone: 310-672-1100).

Publications
Insider's Guide to Air Courier Bargains, by Kelly Monaghan (The Intrepid Traveler, PO Box 438, New York, NY 10034; phone: 212-304-2207).
Travel Secrets (PO Box 2325, New York, NY 10108; phone: 212-245-8703).
Travel Unlimited (PO Box 1058, Allston, MA 02134-1058; no phone).
World Courier News (PO Box 77471, San Francisco, CA 94107; no phone).

CONSOLIDATORS AND BUCKET SHOPS These companies buy blocks of tickets from airlines and sell them at a discount to travel agents or to consumers. Since many bucket shops operate on a thin margin, before parting with any money check the company's record with the Better Business Bureau.

Bargain Air (655 Deep Valley Dr., Suite 355, Rolling Hills, CA 90274; phone: 800-347-2345).
Council Charter (205 E. 42nd St., New York, NY 10017; phone: 800-800-8222 or 212-661-0311).
International Adventures (60 E. 42nd St., New York, NY 10165; phone: 212-599-0577).
Travac Tours and Charters (989 Ave. of the Americas, New York, NY 10018; phone: 800-872-8800 or 212-563-3303).
Unitravel (1177 N. Warson Rd., St. Louis, MO 63132; phone: 800-325-2222 or 314-569-0900).

LAST-MINUTE TRAVEL CLUBS For an annual fee, members receive information on imminent trips and other bargain travel opportunities. Despite the names of these clubs, you don't have to wait until literally the last minute to make travel plans.

Discount Travel International (114 Forest Ave., Suite 203, Narberth, PA 19072; phone: 215-668-7184).
Last Minute Travel (1249 Boylston St., Boston, MA 02215; phone: 800-LAST-MIN or 617-267-9800).
Moment's Notice (425 Madison Ave., New York, NY 10017; phone: 212-486-0500, -0501, -0502, or -0503).
Spur-of-the-Moment Cruises (411 N. Harbor Blvd., Suite 302, San

Pedro, CA 90731; phone: 800-4-CRUISES in California; 800-343-1991 elsewhere in the US; or 310-521-1070).

Traveler's Advantage (3033 S. Parker Rd., Suite 900, Aurora, CO 80014; phone: 800-548-1116 or 800-835-8747).

Vacations to Go (1502 Augusta, Suite 415, Houston, TX 77057; phone: 713-974-2121 in Texas; 800-338-4962 elsewhere in the US).

Worldwide Discount Travel Club (1674 Meridian Ave., Miami Beach, FL 33139; phone: 305-534-2082).

GENERIC AIR TRAVEL These organizations operate much like an ordinary airline standby service, except that they offer seats on not one but several scheduled and charter airlines. One pioneer of generic flights is *Airhitch* (2790 Broadway, Suite 100, New York, NY 10025; phone: 212-864-2000).

BARTERED TRAVEL SOURCES Barter is a common means of exchange between travel suppliers. Bartered travel clubs such as *Travel World Leisure Club* (225 W. 34th St., Suite 909, New York, NY 10122; phone: 800-444-TWLC or 212-239-4855) offer discounts to members for an annual fee.

CONSUMER PROTECTION

Passengers with complaints who are not satisfied with the airline's response can contact the US Department of Transportation (DOT; Consumer Affairs Division, 400 7th St. SW, Room 10405, Washington, DC 20590; phone: 202-366-2220). Also see *Fly Rights* (publication #050-000-00513-5; US Government Printing Office, PO Box 371954, Pittsburgh, PA 15250-7954; phone: 202-783-3238).

On Arrival

FROM THE AIRPORT TO THE CITY

Logan International Airport is located 3 miles from the center of Boston. The ride from the airport to downtown can take from 10 to 30 minutes, depending on the time of day and traffic. *Airways Transportation Co.* (phone: 617-267-2981) charges $7.50 for bus service to major hotels in downtown Boston, $8.50 for those farther afield. Buses run hourly from 8 AM to 10 PM (Saturdays, until 8 PM).

The most practical means of getting from Logan Airport to almost anywhere in the Boston area (if you aren't carrying much luggage) is by *MBTA* (*Massachusetts Bay Transportation Authority*) *Blue Line* trains, which cost 85¢ and run from 6 AM to 12:45 AM. From the train stop at the airport (served by free shuttle buses) to the Government Center station at City Hall Plaza downtown, travel time is no more than 30 minutes. (Note that a Boston Passport, sold by the Greater Boston Convention and Visitors Bureau, permits unlimited travel on the subway and bus lines and includes other discounts.)

A water shuttle operated by *Massport* (phone: 800-235-6426) connects Logan Airport with Rowes Wharf (400 Atlantic Ave.) downtown on weekdays from 6 AM to 8 PM and Sundays from 12:15 to 8 PM (no Saturday service). The trip takes about 7 minutes and costs $8 ($4 for seniors; $3 for children under 12). Shuttle vans link airport terminals and the water shuttle dock.

RENTING A CAR

You can rent a car through a travel agent or national rental firm before leaving home, or from a regional or local company once in Boston. Reserve in advance.

Most car rental companies require a credit card, although some will accept a substantial cash deposit. The minimum age to rent a car is set by the company; some impose special conditions on drivers above a certain age. Electing to pay for collision damage waiver (CDW) protection will add to the cost of renting a car, but releases you from financial liability for the vehicle being rented. Additional costs include drop-off charges or one-way service fees.

Car Rental Companies

Advantage Rent-A-Car (phone: 617-783-3825).
Agency Rent-A-Car (phone: 800-321-1972).
Alamo (phone: 800-327-9633).
Avis (phone: 800-331-1084).
Brodie Auto Rental (phone: 617-491-7600).
Budget (phone: 800-472-3325).
Dollar Rent A Car (phone: 800-800-4000).
Enterprise Rent-A-Car (phone: 800-325-8007).
Excell Car & Van Rental (phone: 800-894-3923 or 617-864-4801).
Hertz (phone: 800-654-3001).
National (phone: 800-227-3876).
Sears Rent-A-Car (phone: 800-527-0770).
Snappy Car Rental (phone: 617-924-7147).
Thrifty (phone: 800-367-2277).

NOTE *Rent-a-Wreck* (phone: 617-254-1900) rents cars that are well worn but (presumably) mechanically sound. *Exotic Rentals* (phone: 617-279-0181) rents luxury models — but not in winter.

Package Tours

A package is a collection of travel services that can be purchased in a single transaction. Its principal advantages are convenience and economy — the cost is usually lower than that of the same services bought separately. Tour programs generally can be divided into two categories: escorted or locally hosted (with a set itinerary) and independent (usually more flexible).

When considering a package tour, read the brochure *carefully* to determine what is included and other conditions. Check the company's record with the Better Business Bureau. The *United States Tour Operators Association* (*USTOA;* 211 E. 51st St., Suite 12B, New York, NY 10022; phone: 212-944-5727) also can be helpful in determining a package tour operator's reliability. As with charter flights, always make your check out to the company's escrow account.

Many tour operators offer packages focused on special interests such as the arts, nature study, sports, and other recreations. *All Adventure Travel* (PO Box 4307, Boulder, CO 80306; phone: 800-537-4025 or 303-499-1981) represents such specialized packagers; some also are listed in the *Specialty Travel Index* (305 San Anselmo Ave., Suite 313, San Anselmo, CA 94960; phone: 415-459-4900 in California; 800-442-4922 elsewhere in the US).

And for additional organized touring, contact *Brush Hill Tours* (439 High St., Randolph, MA 02368; phone: 617-236-2148), which offers half-and full-day tours of the city and operates the *Beantown Trolley* along the freedom trail — visitors can get on and off all day. *Sleuth & Company* (1 Bryant St., Cambridge, MA 02138; phone: 617-542-2525) features a twilight trolly tour of Boston's "mysteries, criminals, and infamous characters." *Uncommon Boston* (address below) also offers a selection of theme-oriented sightseeing tours.

Package Tour Operators

American Express Vacations (offices throughout the US; phone: 800-241-1700 or 404-368-5100).

Continental Grand Destinations (phone: 800-634-5555).

Corliss Tours (436 W. Foothill Blvd., Monrovia, CA 91016; phone: 800-456-5717 or 818-359-5358).

Domenico Tours (751 Broadway, Bayonne, NJ 07002; phone: 800-544-8687 or 201-823-8687).

Jefferson Tours (1206 Currie Ave., Minneapolis, MN 55403; phone: 800-767-7433 or 612-338-4174).

Marathon Tours (108 Main St., Charlestown, MA 02129; phone: 800-783-0024 or 617-242-7845)

Maupintour (PO Box 807, Lawrence, KS 66044; phone: 800-255-4266 or 913-843-1211).

New England Vacation Tours (PO Box 560, West Dover, VT 05356; phone: 800-742-7669 or 802-464-2076).

SuperCities (11330 Blondo St., Omaha, NE 68164; phone: 800-333-1234 or 402-498-8234).

Travel Tours International (250 W. 49th St., Suite 600, New York, NY 10019; phone: 800-767-8777 or 212-262-0700).

Uncommon Boston (437 Boylston St., 4th Floor, Boston, MA 02116; phone: 617-731-5854).

Yankee Holidays (435 Newbury St., Suite 210, Danvers, MA 01923-1065; phone: 800-225-2550 or 508-750-9688).

Insurance

The first person with whom you should discuss travel insurance is your own insurance broker. You may discover that the insurance you already carry protects you adequately while traveling and that you need little additional coverage. If you charge travel services, the credit card company also may provide some insurance coverage (and other safeguards).

Types of Travel Insurance

Baggage and personal effects insurance: Protects your bags and their contents in case of damage or theft anytime during your travels.

Personal accident and sickness insurance: Covers cases of illness, injury, or death in an accident while traveling.

Trip cancellation and interruption insurance: Guarantees a refund if you must cancel a trip; may reimburse you for the extra travel costs incurred for catching up with a tour or traveling home early.

Default and/or bankruptcy insurance: Provides coverage in the event of default and/or bankruptcy on the part of the tour operator, airline, or other travel supplier.

Flight insurance: Covers accidental injury or death while flying.

Automobile insurance: Provides collision, theft, property damage, and personal liability protection while driving your own or a rented car.

Combination policies: Include any or all of the above.

Disabled Travelers

Make travel arrangements well in advance. Specify to all services involved the nature of your disability to determine if there are accommodations and facilities that meet your needs.

Organizations

ACCENT on Living (PO Box 700, Bloomington, IL 61702; phone: 309-378-2961).

Access: The Foundation for Accessibility by the Disabled (PO Box 356, Malverne, NY 11565; phone: 516-887-5798).

American Foundation for the Blind (15 W. 16th St., New York, NY 10011; phone: 800-232-5463 or 212-620-2147).

Information Center for Individuals with Disabilities (Ft. Point Pl., 1st Floor, 27-43 Wormwood St., Boston, MA 02210; phone: 800-462-5015 in Massachusetts; 617-727-5540 or 617-727-5541 elsewhere in the US; TDD: 617-345-9743).

Mobility International USA (*MIUSA;* PO Box 3551, Eugene, OR 97403; phone: 503-343-1284, both voice and TDD; main office: 228 Borough High St., London SE1 1JX, England; phone: 44-71-403-5688).

National Rehabilitation Information Center (8455 Colesville Rd., Suite 935, Silver Spring, MD 20910; phone: 301-588-9284).

Paralyzed Veterans of America (*PVA;* PVA/ATTS Program, 801 18th St. NW, Washington, DC 20006; phone: 202-872-1300 in Washington, DC; 800-424-8200 elsewhere in the US).

Partners of the Americas (1424 K St. NW, Suite 700, Washington, DC 20005; phone: 800-322-7844 or 202-628-3300).

Royal Association for Disability and Rehabilitation (*RADAR;* 25 Mortimer St., London W1N 8AB, England; phone: 44-71-637-5400).

Society for the Advancement of Travel for the Handicapped (*SATH;* 347 Fifth Ave., Suite 610, New York, NY 10016; phone: 212-447-7284).

Travel Information Service (MossRehab Hospital, 1200 W. Tabor Rd., Philadelphia, PA 19141-3099; phone: 215-456-9600; TDD: 215-456-9602).

Publications

Access Travel: A Guide to the Accessibility of Airport Terminals (Consumer Information Center, Dept. 578Z, Pueblo, CO 81009; phone: 719-948-3334).

Air Transportation of Handicapped Persons (publication #AC-120-32; US Department of Transportation, Distribution Unit, Publications Section, M-443-2, 400 7th St. SW, Washington, DC 20590).

The Diabetic Traveler (PO Box 8223 RW, Stamford, CT 06905; phone: 203-327-5832).

Directory of Travel Agencies for the Disabled and *Travel for the Disabled,* both by Helen Hecker (Twin Peaks Press, PO Box 129, Vancouver, WA 98666; phone: 800-637-CALM or 206-694-2462).

Guide to Traveling with Arthritis (Upjohn Company, PO Box 989, Dearborn, MI 48121).

The Handicapped Driver's Mobility Guide (*American Automobile Association,* 1000 AAA Dr., Heathrow, FL 32746; phone: 407-444-7000).

Handicapped Travel Newsletter (PO Box 269, Athens, TX 75751; phone: 903-677-1260).

Handi-Travel: A Resource Book for Disabled and Elderly Travellers, by Cinnie Noble (*Canadian Rehabilitation Council for the Disabled,* 45 Sheppard Ave. E., Suite 801, Toronto, Ontario M2N 5W9, Canada; phone: 416-250-7490, both voice and TDD).

Incapacitated Passengers Air Travel Guide (*International Air Transport Association,* Publications Sales Department, 2000 Peel St., Montreal, Quebec H3A 2R4, Canada; phone: 514-844-6311).

Ticket to Safe Travel (*American Diabetes Association,* 1660 Duke St., Alexandria, VA 22314; phone: 800-232-3472 or 703-549-1500).

Travel for the Patient with Chronic Obstructive Pulmonary Disease (Dr. Harold Silver, 1601 18th St. NW, Washington, DC 20009; phone: 202-667-0134).

Travel Tips for Hearing-Impaired People (*American Academy of Otolaryngology,* 1 Prince St., Alexandria, VA 22314; phone: 703-836-4444).

Travel Tips for People with Arthritis (*Arthritis Foundation,* 1314 Spring St. NW, Atlanta, GA 30309; phone: 800-283-7800 or 404-872-7100).

Traveling Like Everybody Else: A Practical Guide for Disabled Travelers, by Jacqueline Freedman and Susan Gersten (Modan Publishing, PO Box 1202, Bellmore, NY 11710; phone: 516-679-1380).

The Wheelchair Traveler, by Douglass R. Annand (123 Ball Hill Rd., Milford, NH 03055; phone: 603-673-4539).

Package Tour Operators

Accessible Journeys (35 W. Sellers Ave., Ridley Park, PA 19078; phone: 215-521-0339).

Accessible Tours/Directions Unlimited (Lois Bonnani, 720 N. Bedford Rd., Bedford Hills, NY 10507; phone: 800-533-5343 or 914-241-1700).

Beehive Business and Leisure Travel (1130 W. Center St., N. Salt Lake, UT 84054; phone: 800-777-5727 or 801-292-4445).

Classic Travel Service (8 W. 40th St., New York, NY 10018; phone: 212-869-2560 in New York State; 800-247-0909 elsewhere in the US).

Evergreen Travel Service (4114 198th St. SW, Suite 13, Lynnwood, WA 98036-6742; phone: 800-435-2288 or 206-776-1184).

Flying Wheels Travel (143 W. Bridge St., PO Box 382, Owatonna, MN 55060; phone: 800-535-6790 or 507-451-5005).

Good Neighbor Travel Service (124 S. Main St., Viroqua, WI 54665; phone: 608-637-2128).

The Guided Tour (7900 Old York Rd., Suite 114B, Elkins Park, PA 19117-2339; phone: 800-783-5841 or 215-782-1370).

Hinsdale Travel (201 E. Ogden Ave., Hinsdale, IL 60521; phone: 708-325-1335 or 708-469-7349).

MedEscort International (ABE International Airport, PO Box 8766, Allentown, PA 18105; phone: 800-255-7182 or 215-791-3111).

Prestige World Travel (5710-X High Point Rd., Greensboro, NC 27407; phone: 800-476-7737 or 919-292-6690).

Sprout (893 Amsterdam Ave., New York, NY 10025; phone: 212-222-9575).

Weston Travel Agency (134 N. Cass Ave., PO Box 1050, Westmont, IL 60559; phone: 708-968-2513 in Illinois; 800-633-3725 elsewhere in the US).

Single Travelers

The travel industry is not very fair to people who vacation by themselves — they often end up paying more than those traveling in pairs. Services catering to singles match travel companions, offer travel arrangements with shared accommodations, and provide useful information and discounts. Also consult publications such as *Going Solo* (Doerfer Communications, PO Box 123, Apalachicola, FL 32329; phone: 904-653-8848) and *Traveling on Your Own,* by Eleanor Berman (Random House, Order Dept., 400 Hahn Rd., Westminster, MD 21157; phone: 800-733-3000).

Organizations and Companies

Gallivanting (515 E. 79th St., Suite 20F, New York, NY 10021; phone: 800-933-9699 or 212-988-0617).

Jane's International and Sophisticated Women Travelers (2603 Bath Ave., Brooklyn, NY 11214; phone: 718-266-2045).

Marion Smith Singles (611 Prescott Pl., N. Woodmere, NY 11581; phone: 516-791-4852, 516-791-4865, or 212-944-2112).

Partners-in-Travel (11660 Chenault St., Suite 119, Los Angeles, CA 90049; phone: 310-476-4869).

Singles in Motion (545 W. 236th St., Riverdale, NY 10463; phone: 718-884-4464).

Singleworld (401 Theodore Fremd Ave., Rye, NY 10580; phone: 800-223-6490 or 914-967-3334).

Solo Flights (63 High Noon Rd., Weston, CT 06883; phone: 203-226-9993).

Suddenly Singles Tours (161 Dreiser Loop, Bronx, NY 10475; phone: 718-379-8800 in New York City; 800-859-8396 elsewhere in the US).

Travel Companion Exchange (PO Box 833, Amityville, NY 11701; phone: 516-454-0880).

Travel Companions (Atrium Financial Center, 1515 N. Federal Hwy., Suite 300, Boca Raton, FL 33432; phone: 800-383-7211 or 407-393-6448).

Travel in Two's (239 N. Broadway, Suite 3, N. Tarrytown, NY 10591; phone: 914-631-8301 in New York State; 800-692-5252 elsewhere in the US).

Older Travelers

Special discounts and more free time are just two factors that have given older travelers a chance to see the world at affordable prices. Many travel suppliers offer senior discounts — sometimes only to members of certain senior citizen organizations, which provide other benefits. Prepare your itinerary with one eye on your own physical condition and the other on a map, and remember that it's easy to overdo when traveling.

Publications

The Mature Traveler (GEM Publishing Group, PO Box 50820, Reno, NV 89513-0820; phone: 702-786-7419).

The Senior Citizen's Guide to Budget Travel in the US and Canada, by Paige Palmer (Pilot Books, 103 Cooper St., Babylon, NY 11702; phone: 516-422-2225).

Take a Camel to Lunch and Other Adventures for Mature Travelers, by Nancy O'Connell (Bristol Publishing Enterprises, PO Box 1737, San Leandro, CA 94577; phone: 510-895-4461 in California; 800-346-4889 elsewhere in the US).

Travel Tips for Older Americans (Publication #044-000-02270-2; Superintendent of Documents, US Government Printing Office, PO Box 371954, Pittsburgh, PA 15250-7954; phone: 202-783-3238).

Unbelievably Good Deals & Great Adventures That You Absolutely Can't Get Unless You're Over 50, by Joan Rattner Heilman (Contemporary Books, 180 N. Michigan Ave., Chicago, IL 60601; phone: 312-782-9181).

Organizations

American Association of Retired Persons (AARP; 601 E St. NW, Washington, DC 20049; phone: 202-434-2277).

Golden Companions (PO Box 754, Pullman, WA 99163-0754; phone: 208-858-2183).

Mature Outlook (Customer Service Center, 6001 N. Clark St., Chicago, IL 60660; phone: 800-336-6330).

National Council of Senior Citizens (1331 F St. NW, Washington, DC 20004; phone: 202-347-8800).

Package Tour Operators

Elderhostel (PO Box 1959, Wakefield, MA 01880-5959; phone: 617-426-7788).

Evergreen Travel Service (4114 198th St. SW, Suite 13, Lynnwood, WA 98036-6742; phone: 800-435-2288 or 206-776-1184).

Gadabout Tours (700 E. Tahquitz Canyon Way, Palm Springs, CA 92262; phone: 800-952-5068 or 619-325-5556).

Grand Circle Travel (347 Congress St., Boston, MA 02210; phone: 800-221-2610 or 617-350-7500).

Grandtravel (6900 Wisconsin Ave., Suite 706, Chevy Chase, MD 20815; phone: 800-247-7651 or 301-986-0790).

Interhostel (UNH Division of Continuing Education, 6 Garrison Ave., Durham, NH 03824; phone: 800-733-9753 or 603-862-1147).

OmniTours (104 Wilmont Rd., Deerfield, IL 60015; phone: 800-962-0060 or 708-374-0088).

Saga International Holidays (222 Berkeley St., Boston, MA 02116; phone: 800-343-0273 or 617-262-2262).

Money Matters

TRAVELER'S CHECKS AND CREDIT CARDS

It's wise to carry traveler's checks while on the road, since they are replaceable if stolen or lost. You can buy traveler's checks at banks and some are available by mail or phone. Although most major credit cards enjoy wide domestic and international acceptance, not every hotel, restaurant, or shop in Boston accepts all (or in some cases any) credit cards. Keep a separate list of all traveler's checks (noting those that you have cashed) and the names and numbers of your credit cards. Both traveler's check and credit card companies have international numbers to call for information or in the event of loss or theft.

CASH MACHINES

Automatic teller machines (ATMs) are increasingly common worldwide. Most banks participate in one of the international ATM networks; card-holders can withdraw cash from any machine in the same network using either a "bank" card or, in some cases, a credit card. At the time of this writing, most ATMs belong to the *CIRRUS* (phone: 800-4-CIRRUS) or *PLUS* (phone: 800-THE-PLUS) network. For further information, ask at your bank branch.

SENDING MONEY

Should the need arise, it is possible to have money sent to you via the services provided by *American Express* (*MoneyGram;* phone: 800-926-9400 or 800-666-3997 for information; 800-866-8800 for money transfers) or *Western Union Financial Services* (phone: 800-325-4176).

Time Zone

Boston is in the eastern standard time zone. Daylight saving time is observed from the first Sunday in April until the last Sunday in October.

Business Hours

Boston maintains business hours that are fairly standard throughout the country: 9 AM to 5 PM, Mondays through Fridays. Banks generally are open weekdays from 9 AM to 3 PM. Retail stores and department stores usually are open from 9:30 or 10 AM to 5:30 or 6 PM, Mondays through Saturdays. Some of the larger stores are open until 9 PM Wednesdays through Saturdays in warm weather, with Thursday being the most common late-closing night in winter. Many retail establishments also remain open on Sundays until 5 PM.

Mail

The main post office in Boston at 25 Dorchester Ave. (phone: 617-654-5083) is open 24 hours a day, with at least a self-service section for weighing packages and buying stamps. Downtown, John W. McCormack Station is located at Post Office SW and Devonshire St. (phone: 617-654-5083).

For other branches, call the main offices or check the yellow pages. Stamps also are available at most hotel desks and from public vending machines. For rapid, overnight delivery to other cities, use *Express Mail* (available at post offices), *Federal Express* (phone: 800-238-5355), or *DHL Worldwide Express* (phone: 800-225-5345).

You can have mail sent to you care of your hotel (marked "Guest Mail, Hold for Arrival") or to a post office ("c/o General Delivery, Hold for 30 Days"). *American Express* offices also will hold mail for customers ("c/o Client Letter Service"); information on this service is provided in their pamphlet *Travelers' Companion*. Members of the *American Automobile Association* (*AAA;* 1000 AAA Dr., Heathrow, FL 32746-5063; phone: 407-444-8544) also can have mail (marked "Hold for Arrival") held at *AAA* branches throughout the US.

Telephone

The Boston area code is 617; the adjoining suburbs are in the 508 area code. To make a long-distance call, dial 1 + the area code + the local number. The nationwide number for information is 555-1212; if you need a number in another area code, dial 1 + the area code + 555-1212. (If you don't know the area code, dial 0 for an operator.)

Although you can use a telephone company calling card number on any phone, pay phones that take major credit cards (*American Express, MasterCard, Visa,* and so on) are increasingly common. Also available are combined telephone calling cards/bank credit cards, such as *AT&T Universal* (phone: 800-662-7759), *Executive Telecard International* (phone: 800-950-3800), and *Sprint* (phone: 800-877-4646). *MCI VisaPhone* (phone: 800-866-0099) can add phone card privileges to your existing *Visa* card.

Long-distance telephone services that help you avoid the surcharges that hotels routinely add to phone bills are provided by *American Telephone and Telegraph* (*AT&T Communications,* International Information Service, 635 Grant St., Pittsburgh, PA 15219; phone: 800-874-4000), *MCI* (323 3rd St. SE, Cedar Rapids, IA 52401; phone: 800-444-3333), *Metromedia Communications Corp.* (1 International Center, 100 NE Loop 410, San Antonio, TX 78216; phone: 800-275-0200), and *Sprint* (offices throughout the US; phone: 800-877-4000). Some hotels still may charge a fee for line usage.

Also useful are the *AT&T 800 Travel Directory* (available at *AT&T Phone Centers* or by calling 800-426-8686), the *Toll-Free Travel & Vacation*

Information Directory (Pilot Books, 103 Cooper St., Babylon, NY 11702; phone: 516-422-2225), and *The Phone Booklet* (*Scott American Corporation,* PO Box 88, W. Redding, CT 06896; phone: 203-938-2955).

Medical Aid

In an emergency: Dial 911 for assistance, "0" for an operator, or go directly to the emergency room of the nearest hospital.

Hospitals

Boston City Hospital (818 Harrison Ave.; phone: 617-534-5000).

Massachusetts General Hospital (Fruit St., off Cambridge St.; phone: 617-726-2000).

Pharmacies

CVS (Porter Sq., Cambridge; phone: 617-876-5519). Open 24 hours daily.

Phillips (155 Charles St.; phone: 617-523-4372 or 617-523-1028). Open 24 hours daily; prescriptions available until midnight.

Additional Resources

International Association of Medical Assistance to Travelers (*IAMAT;* 417 Center St., Lewiston, NY 14092; phone: 716-754-4883).

International Health Care Service (440 E. 69th St., New York, NY 10021; phone: 212-746-1601).

International SOS Assistance (PO Box 11568, Philadelphia, PA 19116; phone: 800-523-8930 or 215-244-1500).

Medic Alert Foundation (2323 Colorado Ave., Turlock, CA 95380; phone: 800-ID-ALERT or 209-668-3333).

TravMed (PO Box 10623, Baltimore, MD 21285-0623; phone: 800-732-5309 or 410-296-5225).

Legal Aid

If you don't have, or cannot reach, your own attorney, most cities offer legal referral services maintained by county bar associations. These services ensure that anyone in need of legal representation gets it and can match you with a local attorney. In Boston, contact *Greater Boston Legal Services* (phone: 617-357-5757). If you must appear in court, you are entitled to court-appointed representation if you can't obtain a lawyer or can't afford one.

For Further Information

The **Massachusetts Office of Travel and Tourism** is at 100 Cambridge St., 13th Floor, Boston, MA 02202 (phone: 800-447-MASS or 617-727-3201). For local tourist information, see *Sources and Resources* in THE CITY.

The City

Boston

No matter how you approach Boston, it's hard not to be struck by the lovely siting of this city, which juts into the island-studded harbor and graces the banks of the Charles River with riverside parks and a distinctive skyline. Here are the narrow cobblestones where Boston's colonists walked, the Common where their cattle grazed, the churches where they prayed, and the tiny burial grounds that shelter their bones. Here, too, are the bold buildings of government, the fortresses of finance, the colorful chaos of the open market, and the free-wheeling spirit of the waterfront.

Anyone walking briskly could traverse this eventful terrain in an hour, but instead you should take the time to explore Boston at leisure, keeping an eye out for the little things — the odd quirks of architecture, the bright spots of whimsy and caprice. Spend a couple of hours in the North End, wandering along twisting streets barely wider than the ancient cowpaths they follow, or in Back Bay, strolling down the broad avenues lined with stately townhouses. Look for the famous brass nameplates and gas lamps of Beacon Hill, the intricate wrought-iron balconies along Commonwealth Avenue, the bronze litter set into the pavement near *Haymarket,* and the grasshopper atop *Faneuil Hall* — the site of many Revolutionary protest meetings. It was here that the impassioned protest "Taxation without representation is tyranny" was voiced; where Samuel Adams roused the citizenry and organized the Boston Tea Party; and where Paul Revere began his midnight ride when the British approached.

The 19th century saw the rise of commerce in Boston, and a simultaneous flowering of arts and letters — represented by such figures as Emerson, Hawthorne, Longfellow, and Thoreau. The boom of population and wealth, combined with the increasing noxiousness of the Back Bay wetlands, prompted the City Fathers to fill this area in to provide land for the city's expansion. Today, that barren landscape has been transformed by a century's growth of elms, magnolias, and fruit trees, and the early Back Bay homes are prized as exceptional examples of Victorian architecture in America.

After surviving half a century of neglect and deterioration, Boston experienced a renaissance, beginning in the 1960s with the creation of Government Center and the restoration of the city's historic neighborhoods. With the past revived for posterity, city planners turned their sights to the needs — or fancies — of a new generation of residents and visitors. During the 1970s, *Faneuil Hall Marketplace* became the prototype for a new concept of urban retail development when Benjamin Thompson and the Rouse Company successfully transformed the old, largely abandoned market buildings into a lively and congenial gathering place that thrives in a carnival atmosphere of jugglers, magicians, musicians, and street vendors outside, and eateries plain and fancy, trinket shops, and unusual boutiques inside. More recently, *Copley Place* and Cambridge's *Charles Square* have added vitality to the city.

Yet a civilized urbanity remains, a sense of ease combined with an abundance of opportunity. Do you like art? Boston's museums are among the finest in the world, and its galleries — on Newbury Street, along Fort Point Channel, and the up-and-coming South Street and South End — are worth a day in themselves. Music? The *Boston Symphony* is only the beginning. Baroque chamber music concerts often are sold out, jazz fans can sit through three sizzling sets in intimate cafés, and the biggest names in folk, country, and rock come back faithfully to sing in the clubs that gave them their start. There's also the ever-popular *Boston Pops,* a symphony orchestra with a crowd-pleasing repertoire of popular and classical music.

The *Boston Ballet* is world-renowned, and a variety of contemporary dance companies present frequent, innovative programs. Many Broadway shows get their start here, and local theater groups stage everything from Shakespeare to experimental plays. Besides the many commercial movie houses showing first- and second-run films, local colleges and cultural centers are always sponsoring film festivals where you can catch obscure movies from Eastern Europe or your favorite Chaplin, D. W. Griffith, or Bogart classics.

These same colleges and cultural centers provide virtually unlimited opportunities for education and self-improvement, from the large academic communities of Harvard, MIT, and Boston University to the dozens of smaller institutions. The list of lectures open to the public on any given day is overwhelming.

For many people, Boston is, above all, a sports town. It's easy for *Red Sox* fans to indulge themselves at *Fenway Park* — one of the last of the great old urban ballparks. Basketball and hockey fans flock to the *Boston Garden,* where the *Celtics* and *Bruins* have been not infrequent world champions. Football followers have to drive to Foxboro to watch the *New England Patriots* at *Sullivan Stadium,* but the distance doesn't seem to deter them — though the team's dismal performance last year may have. (Visitors should bear in mind that loyalties are intense in Boston. If you must cheer for the opposition, do so softly.)

Politics often seems like another favorite sport in Boston. Mayor James Michael Curley will live forever in the novel *The Last Hurrah,* and the grandson of another mayor, "Honey Fitz" Fitzgerald, became the 35th President of the US, John F. Kennedy. Such names as Elliot Richardson and Henry Cabot Lodge loom large in our national consciousness, as does that of Thomas P. "Tip" O'Neill, a North Cambridge boy and former Speaker of the House. But some Boston pols run for more than election — longtime Mayor Ray Flynn annually completes the grueling *Boston Marathon.*

Boston has long been known as "the home of the bean and the cod," but though scrod (as cooked cod filets are called here) is found on many menus, it isn't easy to find authentic baked beans. Local fishermen, however, pride themselves in providing Boston's tables with the finest fresh fish and shellfish — especially lobsters and clams. Two ethnic neighborhoods long known for their restaurants and groceries are Chinatown and the Italian North End. But today you can satisfy a desire for almost any kind of cooking in Boston, be it Thai, Japanese, Portuguese, Indian, Mexican, or Greek, to name a few, and there has been an exciting proliferation of restaurants dedicated to creative nouvelle cuisine using the freshest seasonal produce. Bostonians bargain for their own at *Haymarket,* the traditional farmers' market near *Faneuil Hall Marketplace.* If you're in town on a Friday afternoon or a Saturday, don't miss this chance to experience spirited haggling and lots of local color.

For more peaceful (and possibly healthful) recreation, you are never more than a few blocks from a green oasis suitable for strolling, jogging, picnicking, or simply people watching. Thanks to the genius and foresight of Frederick Law Olmsted, Boston enjoys several miles of continuous parkland known as the Emerald Necklace. Perhaps the prettiest jewel of them all is the Public Garden, with its ever-changing displays of luxuriant blooms and its graceful Swan Boats cruising the quiet pond. Next to the Public Garden is Boston Common, the nation's oldest public park. One of the best places for jogging is the path along the Charles River Esplanade, which provides plenty of aquatic as well as terrestrial scenery. In summer, it is the site of performances in the *Hatch Shell,* among them the famous *July Fourth* extravaganza of the *Boston Pops Orchestra.*

Boston has made the journey from its staid, Puritanical beginning to its vibrant, cosmopolitan present, treasuring its past but eager to experience the new.

Boston At-a-Glance

SEEING THE CITY

There are two unparalleled posts from which to view Boston: the John Hancock Tower's 60th-floor Observatory, and the 50th-floor Prudential Skywalk. The newly renovated Hancock Tower (Copley Sq.; phone: 247-1977; take the *Green Line* on the subway system to Copley Square or the *Orange Line* to the Back Bay station) offers a spectacular panorama that even includes the mountains of southern New Hampshire (weather permitting), telescopes, recorded commentaries, a topographical model of Boston in 1775 (this is a must — we promise you'll be surprised), and a 7-minute film of a helicopter flight over the city. Open daily. Admission charge. Like the Hancock, the Prudential Skywalk at the Prudential Center (800 Boylston St.; phone: 236-3318; *Green Line* to the Copley or Prudential stop) offers an excellent 360° view, but the Pru also has a restaurant and bar, the *Top of the Hub,* on the 52nd floor. Skywalk and restaurant are open daily. Admission charge.

SPECIAL PLACES

Boston is best seen on foot; the city is compact, and driving, even for residents, is often hair-raising.

DOWNTOWN

The confusing crisscross of narrow streets that gives Boston its charm is no more evident than in the city's cradle, the downtown area, which now consists of *Faneuil Hall,* Government Center, and the financial, retail, and waterfront districts. (For more about this area, see *Walk 6: Downtown* in DIRECTIONS.)

BOSTON COMMON This pastoral green, established in 1634, is the nation's oldest park. The earliest Bostonians brought their cows and horses here to graze. Today, you'll find their descendants engaging in free-form pastimes that range from music making to baseball and skateboarding. We suggest starting your tour of the city here. (It's not advisable to walk alone at night, since the Common is often inadequately patrolled.) You can park at *Motor Mart* on Stuart Street or at the *57 Park Plaza* hotel. The lovely Public Garden is adjacent to the Common, across Charles Street. For information about activities on the Common, call 536-4100. (Also see *Walk 4: Boston Common* in DIRECTIONS.)

FREEDOM TRAIL The city has made it both easy and fun to track down the important sites from its colonial and Revolutionary past. Just follow the red brick (or red paint) line set into the sidewalk; it takes about 2 hours to walk its length without stops or side trips. To begin, take the *Green* or *Red Line* to Park Street and walk down Tremont Street to the visitors' information center on the Common, which has maps available. Or you can take a double-decker bus tour (see *Getting Around*).

PARK STREET CONGREGATIONAL CHURCH AND OLD GRANARY BURYING GROUND Built in 1809, the church witnessed William Lloyd Garrison's famous first anti-slavery address in 1829, and heard the first singing of "My country, 'tis of thee" 3 years later. Open Tuesdays through Saturdays, July and August; otherwise by appointment (1 Park St.; phone: 523-3383). In the 1660 cemetery next door are the graves of such Revolutionary notables as John Hancock, Samuel Adams, Paul Revere, and the victims of the Boston Massacre, as well as the parents of Benjamin Franklin. Look for the grave of Mary Goose, popularly believed to be Mother Goose. Open daily. (Also see *Historic Churches* in DIVERSIONS.)

DOWNTOWN CROSSING A great meeting place. Winter meets Summer Street, the *Red Line* meets the *Orange Line,* and the display windows of the two giants of Boston retailing, *Filene's* and *Jordan Marsh,* face each other across a brick, pedestrians-only street. Downtown Crossing is also a favorite rendezvous for shoppers, who team up to march on this consumer haven. On Saturdays, when the shoppers, vendors, and street performers are out in force, this intersection resembles Mecca during *Ramadan,* which may be why a good proportion of the world's fringe religions are represented here, looking for new members or donations. Business is brisk for the vending carts, which sell everything from T-shirts to llama-skin luggage.

KING'S CHAPEL AND BURYING GROUND Founded as the Massachusetts Bay Colony's first Anglican Church in 1688, King's Chapel was the place of worship for British officers and the royal governor. Since the colonists had fled England to escape the Anglican Church, the church's founding was taken as an insult. The ornate Governor's Pew, the church's centerpiece, was removed from the church in 1826, only to be restored a century later after it was clear that the colony had rid itself of British elitism. The church hosts free classical concerts on Tuesday afternoons. Closed Mondays. Tremont St. at School St. (phone: 227-2155). (Also see *Historic Churches* in DIVERSIONS.)

OLD SOUTH MEETING HOUSE Though this well-preserved church was built in 1729 to serve Boston's Puritan congregation, its associations and greatest hour were secular. When dissent began to rumble in the colonies before the Revolution, it was here that patriots flocked to debate the issues of the day. In December 1773, Samuel Adams seemed to echo the collective anger of the colony when, after failing to persuade the royal governor to send back to England three ships that were filled with dutiable tea and moored in the harbor, he announced, "Taxation without representation is tyranny." The crowd's rejoinder was "Boston Harbor a teapot tonight." It was from here that the incensed mob, some disguised as Indians, set out toward the harbor to write a crucial chapter in the birth of this nation. In addition, Ben Franklin, who was born across the street, was baptized here when he was only hours old. An award-winning permanent audio exhibit that re-creates the Tea Party and other exciting moments from Boston's past is a must. Also on display are rare colonial artifacts and a scale model of early Boston. Open daily. Admission charge (310 Washington St.; phone: 482-6439). Across and just up the street is the *Old Corner Bookstore* (now called the *Globe Corner Bookstore* because of its former affiliation with the *Boston Globe*), built in 1718 and long the hub of Boston's literary scene. The eminent Boston publishers of yore, Ticknor and Fields, had their offices here, attracting the likes of Emerson, Thoreau, Longfellow, Holmes, and Lowell. It is now a working bookstore with abundant travel titles as well as books about New England and by New England authors (1 School St.; phone: 523-6658).

OLD STATE HOUSE The 18th-century seat of government, which sits in the middle of State Street, surrounded by modern towers of law and finance, served both the English colony and the American state of Massachusetts until Bulfinch's State House was built. As the council chambers of the royal governors sent from England, it was the site of numerous protests before the American Revolution. In front of its east side was the site of the Boston Massacre. Open daily. Admission charge (206 Washington St.; phone: 720-3290). Next door is a National Park Service visitors' center (15 State St.; phone: 242-5642), which provides useful information about Boston and sites in outlying areas. There are free guided tours of the nearby portions of the Freedom Trail, April through December.

CITY HALL The focal point of the Government Center plaza, Boston's looming concrete City Hall (1968), designed by Kallman, McKinnell & Knowles, is considered a landmark of modern architecture, although the local populace loves to revile it. City Hall sits in the middle of an 8-acre plaza that is often the scene of civic celebrations and politicking. Congress St. (phone: 725-4000).

FANEUIL HALL MARKETPLACE Opening in 1826, this was the site of the city's meat and produce markets (11 original tenants still do business here). Redesigned and reopened between 1976 and 1978, the market has become a much-copied prototype of urban renewal. Over a million people per month — natives and tourists alike — partake of its multiplicity of stalls, restaurants, and shops. An information booth in the South Market area stands inside the South Canopy in winter and outside in summer. The market takes its official name from adjacent *Faneuil* (pronounced *Fan-yool*) *Hall,* a historic meeting house. It is also known as *Quincy Market,* which is the name of the main market building. Open daily (phone: 523-3886). (Also see *Walk 6: Downtown* in DIRECTIONS.)

WATERFRONT

There's much to do and see along Boston's waterfront. Walk along Waterfront Park, with its invigorating views of the harbor, and browse in the many new shops set in the renovated wharf buildings. Long Wharf, the pier behind the *New England Aquarium,* is the departure point for a number of seagoing excursions — the ferry that crosses Cape Cod Bay to Provincetown in the summer and boats for harbor cruises, whale watches, and fishing excursions. For information, contact *Bay State Cruise Company* (phone: 723-7800), which provides service from *Memorial Day* through *Columbus Day* (and sometimes on warm weekends during the winter) out of two locations, Long Wharf and Commonwealth Pier. Boats take passengers on day trips to Georges Island (site of Fort Warren, used as a Civil War prison) and the Inner Harbor; Nantasket Beach and the Outer Harbor; and Provincetown, at the tip of Cape Cod. *Boston Harbor Cruises* (phone: 227-4320) runs whale watches and sends boats out among the harbor islands seasonally from April through mid-October. It also runs the Navy Yard water shuttle to Charlestown year-round. For $1, this is a great way to get from the aquarium to the Charlestown Navy Yard, where you can see "Old Ironsides" (the USS *Constitution*), its adjoining museum, the Bunker Hill Pavilion, or Bunker Hill itself (see *Other Special Places*). *Massport* (phone: 800-235-6426) runs a water shuttle from Rowes Wharf to Logan Airport (a 7-minute ride), year-round, except Saturdays and holidays. Just over the Congress Street Bridge, past the *Boston Tea Party Ship and Museum,* and into the commercial district of South Boston — some call it Wallpaper Row — are the wildly popular *Computer Museum* and *Children's Museum.* They are located on the park-like Museum Wharf, easy to find since it is the home of the enormous red-and-white H. P. Hood Milk Bottle, a vintage 1930s highway lunch stand that is 40 feet high. (Also see *Walk 6: Downtown* in DIRECTIONS.)

NEW ENGLAND AQUARIUM One of the world's top collections of marine life, it served as the model for the *National Aquarium* in Baltimore. Taking center stage is the 180,000-gallon Giant Ocean Tank, the home of 1,000 aquatic specimens and a 4-story coral reef. Divers regularly feed the multitude of turtles, fish, and sharks, so they don't dine on each other. Exhibits re-creating a tide pool, northern waters, and tropical marine environments surround the saltwater tank. Penguins cavort in their own habitat called the Penguin Tray, and seals and dolphins perform aboard the floating pavilion *Discovery,* next door to the main building. A variety of films is shown in the auditorium, and there's an interesting gift shop. *Blue Line,* Aquarium stop. Open daily. No admission charge for children under 3; Thursdays after 3 PM, no admission charge. Central Wharf, Waterfront (phone: 973-5200).

BOSTON TEA PARTY SHIP AND MUSEUM Board the *Brig Beaver II,* a full-size working replica of one of the three original ships at the Boston Tea Party. If you feel like it, you can even throw a little tea into Boston Harbor. The adjacent museum houses documents relevant to the period as well as films and related exhibits. *Red Line,* South Station stop. Open daily from March 1 through mid-December. Admission charge. Congress St. Bridge at Fort Point Channel (phone: 338-1773).

CHILDREN'S MUSEUM Formerly an old woolens warehouse, this kid-pleasing place has a number of hands-on exhibits, including Grandmother's Attic, a petting zoo, and an assembly line that teaches children how a factory operates. Open Tuesdays through Sundays; closed Mondays except during school holiday weeks and between July 1 and *Labor Day.* Admission charge. 300 Congress St., Museum Wharf (phone: 426-8855).

COMPUTER MUSEUM Beginning with the computerized contraption at the entrance that bounces sound waves off your head to determine your height and then announces its findings to all within earshot, this museum harbors several floors of dazzling gadgetry, interactive exhibits, and educational programs that trace the history and the future of what is probably the 20th century's greatest contribution to technology. A veritable circus of computerized equipment performs physical and mental feats: coloring a map of the US at your verbal command, charting a route through Boston, or providing your piano playing (no matter how bad) with the appropriate orchestral accompaniment. There's even an exhibit that alters the contours of your face on screen. A walk-through computer allows a visitor to sit on the keyboard (don't try this at home) and then examine a computer's components from the inside bit by bit (or is that byte by byte?). Created by the founder of the Digital Equipment Corporation, the *Computer Museum* is the first and only one of its kind in the US — a shrine to the profound importance of today's computer technology. Open daily from 10 AM to 5 PM in July and August; closed Mondays the rest of the year. Admission charge. Half price on Saturdays before noon. A short walk from the South Station stop on the *MBTA Red Line* (within sight of the *Boston Tea Party Ship*). 300 Congress St., Museum Wharf (phone: 426-2800 or 423-6758).

BEACON HILL

Walk along Mt. Vernon Street to see the stately old townhouses that were (and still are) the pride of the first families of Boston. Look for the famous brass knockers, the charming carriage houses, and the intimate backyard gardens. A few blocks down is Louisburg Square, a rectangle of terribly proper houses facing a tiny park; this was once home to Louisa May Alcott and Jenny Lind, among others. The cobblestone Acorn Street, parallel to Mt. Vernon and Chestnut Streets, is the most photographed street in town. (Also see *Walk 5: Beacon Hill* in DIRECTIONS.)

BLACK HERITAGE TRAIL A 1.6-mile walking tour that explores the history of Boston's black community throughout the 18th and 19th centuries. The tour, led by National Park Service rangers, passes 14 sites of historic importance on Beacon Hill, including the African Meeting House, the oldest black church in the country, and the homes of well-known abolitionists. (The tour also may be self-guided; pick up the brochure from the National Park Service Visitor Center at 15 State St. or 46 Joy St.) The guided tours begin at the Robert Gould Shaw Memorial in front of the State House at the corner of Beacon and Park Streets. The memorial honors the first US black regiment, which served under Shaw during the Civil War. Free tours begin at 10 AM, noon, and 2 PM daily from *Memorial Day* through *Labor Day*. (Registration is not required, but it's advisable to call ahead.) Tours are by appointment at other times of the year (phone: 742-5415).

STATE HOUSE Facing the Beacon Street entrance to the Common, the gold-domed State House designed by Charles Bulfinch dates from 1795. The gold leaf was added to the dome in 1866. Enter through the side door of the right wing (the main door is hardly ever used). Pick up informational pamphlets or join a guided tour in Doric Hall, which features busts, statues, memorials, and paintings of famous Americans. Also in the State House are Memorial Hall (or the Hall of Flags), the Chamber of the House of Representatives, the Senate Chamber, the Senate Reception Room, and a library (phone: 727-2590). Closed weekends. No admission charge. Beacon St. (phone: 727-3676).

BOSTON ATHENAEUM Home of one of the oldest libraries in the country, founded in 1807, this 5-story National Historic Landmark building (which dates from 1847–49; the top 2 floors, 1913–15) is a temple to civility. From its hushed tones, marble, mahogany, ornate table lamps, and endless sea of volumes, the *Athenaeum* has the feel of a study in a colonial mansion, a sumptuous yet studious place to which to retreat after dinner for a good smoke, a glass of brandy, and a volume of classical wisdom. Fortunately, for the sake of literary preservation, you can't smoke or drink here. From 1872 to 1876 the *Athenaeum* functioned as an art gallery, exhibiting American and European painting and sculpture on the building's top floor; this was the foundation of the collection that would later become the *Museum of Fine Arts.* The *Athenaeum* still has a permanent collection of American and European works. In addition, it displays the works of local artists and artisans in the second-floor gallery and contains more than 600,000 titles, including some of the world's most prized collections: the King's Chapel Library, sent in 1698 by England's William III; works from the John Quincy Adams Library; and part of George Washington's personal library. Guided tours of the library are given Tuesday and Thursday afternoons at 3 PM; reservations are necessary; no admission charge. At other times, the library is open only to members, scholars, and qualified researchers. 10½ Beacon St. (phone: 227-0270).

MT. VERNON STREET Henry James once called it the "only respectable street in America." This Beacon Hill street, which runs from behind the State House to Charles Street and beyond, is lined with homes that have rich historical associations — and owners. The most history-intensive part is between Louisburg Square and Joy Street, where you will find the *Nichols House Museum,* the only Beacon Hill home open to the public. Open Mondays, Wednesdays, and Saturdays from 1 to 5 PM in summer; hours vary during other seasons. Admission charge. 55 Mt. Vernon St. (phone: 227-6993).

CHARLES STREET This is Beacon Hill's one true commercial street, stretching from Beacon Street to Cambridge Street. The street began as a seawall; before the Back Bay was filled in, Charles Street marked Beacon Hill's western shoreline, where tides rose nearly 15 feet. Along with lower Chestnut Street, Charles Street today forms Beacon Hill's "Antiques Row" and is home to a number of restaurants, shops, and pubs. The street's most interesting building, the Charles Street Meeting House, was built in 1807 as a Baptist church. It has since been converted into retail space. George Grant, the first black graduate of Harvard and the inventor of the wooden golf tee, lived at 108 Charles Street. (Also see *Antiques: Boston's Best Hunting Grounds* in DIVERSIONS.)

NORTH END

The Paul Revere House and Old North Church are both snugly tucked away among the narrow red brick streets of the North End, a colorful, Italian-American community with a lively street life and some excellent little restaurants (see *Eating Out*). To experience *la dolce vita,* stop at the *Caffè Dello Sport* (307 Hanover St.; phone: 523-5063) for cannoli, cappuccino, and good people watching. (Also see *Walk 7: North End* in DIRECTIONS.)

PAUL REVERE HOUSE In addition to being home to the legendary Revolutionary War hero, this place has the distinction of being the oldest wooden house in Boston. Revere moved here in 1770 with his wife, mother, and five children. He had eleven more children with his second wife, which is why his house was the only one on the block that didn't have to quarter British soldiers. The exhibits inside the house, which include Revere's saddlebags, revolver, portraits, and the account of the ride in his own words, are sure to clear up some misconceptions about the man and his famous ride. Many visitors are surprised to learn that Revere was kind of chubby. And you probably thought he yelled "The British are coming" as he rode through the sleepy townships. Open daily (closed Mondays January through March). Admission charge. 19 North Sq. (phone: 523-2338 or 523-1676).

OLD NORTH CHURCH Affectionately known as Old North, the official name of this structure, built in 1723, is Christ Church. On the night of April 18, 1775, sexton Robert Newman hung two lanterns outside to warn Bostonians that the British were coming by sea. His action and Paul Revere's famous ride were later immortalized by Henry Wadsworth Longfellow in a poem that you probably read in school. (The line you will want to remember is: "One if by land, two if by sea.") The church's original clock still ticks in the back, and services are still held every Sunday. Open daily. 193 Salem St. (phone: 523-6676). (Also see *Historic Churches* in DIVERSIONS.)

BLACKSTONE BLOCK On the other side of the expressway, near City Hall, this was the city's first commercial district, named after Boston's first settler, William Blaxton (pronounced Blackstone). Though most of the original 17th-century dwellings are gone, several remain from the 18th century, including the *Union Oyster House* restaurant (41 Union St.; phone: 227-2750), and the Ebenezer Hancock House (10 Marshall St.), home of John's brother, a paymaster of the Continental Army. Ebenezer stored 2 million silver crowns — sent by France to help pay the Revolutionary troops — in his cellar. The Boston Stone, a paint mixing stone brought from England by a painter in the 1600s, is set in the foundation of a shop on Marshall Street. Like a similar stone in London, it was used as a marker for judging distances from Boston. In back of the block is Blackstone Street, a malodorous little thoroughfare that should be avoided except on Fridays and Saturdays, when it is the site of *Haymarket,* the city's colorful outdoor produce market.

BACK BAY

Arlington is the first of an alphabetically ordered series of streets created when the Back Bay was filled in during the mid-1800s. Broad streets and avenues were laid out in an orderly fashion, and along them wealthy Bostonians built palatial homes, churches, and public institutions. This area is a joy to walk and gives a better feeling of Victorian Boston than any other part of the city. (Also see *Walk 3: Back Bay* in DIRECTIONS.)

PUBLIC GARDEN A gem among city parks and a Boston treasure since 1861, the garden, which is adjacent to Boston Common, has fountains, formal gardens, and trees labeled for identification. A special treat is a ride on the Swan Boats, past the geese and ducks on the lagoon. Rides are offered daily, mid-April through *Labor Day,* except on windy or rainy days. Admission charge; group rates available. In the winter, hardy locals tour the lagoon on ice skates (phone: 522-1966).

COMMONWEALTH AVENUE Intended to replicate the broad boulevards of 19th-century Paris, with their stately, mansard-roofed homes, Commonwealth Avenue ("Comm Ave" to the locals) has fulfilled its early promise. Stroll down the shady mall, with its statues of famous Bostonians. In April, the magnolias are a special treat. On the corner of Clarendon Street stands the First Baptist Church, a splendid Romanesque structure designed by H. H. Richardson and completed in 1872. Open Tuesdays through Fridays, 11 AM to 2 PM, or by prior arrangement. No admission charge. 110 Commonwealth Ave. (phone: 267-3148).

ESPLANADE This is a strip of parkland that runs between Storrow Drive and the Charles River in the vicinity of Back Bay. Formerly just a 2-mile walkway, it was expanded into a park with money donated by Mrs. James Storrow, widow of a wealthy Boston banker. Bostonians from all walks of life — not to mention runners, bikers, roller skaters, and sunbathers — are deeply indebted to her. It is a plush, clean, and relatively safe stretch of parkland that is a convenient place for the Back Bay cardiovascular crowd. There are several footbridges that lead to the Esplanade from the Back Bay, over Storrow Drive, where Bostonians display their maniacal driving habits. (Also see *Quintessential Boston* in DIVERSIONS.)

COPLEY SQUARE Seagoing vessels used to drop anchor in Copley Square; now it harbors Richardson's magnificent 19th-century Trinity Church. There are free organ recitals every Friday at noon. Open daily. No admission charge (phone: 536-0944). A perfect reflection of the church can be seen in the modern blue glass façade of the John Hancock Tower, which stands across St. James Avenue. The tower's 60th-floor observatory offers spectacular views of the city and beyond (phone: 247-1977). The Boston Public Library, founded in 1852, is the oldest municipally supported library in the country. The main Copley Square building, completed in 1895, was designed by the famous New York firm of McKim, Mead & White and is considered one of the first outstanding examples of the Renaissance Beaux Arts style in the US. (The 1972 addition was designed by Philip Johnson.) Step inside the Copley Square entrance for a quiet moment in the lovely central courtyard. Closed Sundays (phone: 536-5400). Across Dartmouth Street from the *Copley Plaza* hotel is *Copley Place* (phone: 375-4400), a complex of hotels, fashionable shops (*Neiman Marcus, Tiffany, Godiva Chocolatiers,* and the like), restaurants, an 11-screen movie theater (phone: 266-1300), and an indoor waterfall.

NEWBURY STREET This is where fashionable Bostonians shop. There are many art galleries and boutiques, as well as a variety of restaurants and several outdoor cafés.

NEW ENGLAND HISTORIC GENEALOGICAL SOCIETY Since Bostonians are, by nature, extremely curious about their lineage, it is fitting that one of the country's most exhaustive collections of family history is located here. The collection includes 17th-century wills, deeds, diaries, and journals. People from all over the country who suspect their ancestors at one time lived in New England come to Boston's Genealogical Society for resources and assistance in determining their roots. Open Tuesdays through Saturdays. Admission is free just to look around. There is a small fee for using the facilities. 101 Newbury St. (phone: 536-5740).

INSTITUTE OF CONTEMPORARY ART Exciting contemporary art in several media, including an interesting film series, set in the halls of a 19th-century police station. *Green Line, Hynes Convention Center/ICA* stop. Open Wednesdays from 5 to 9 PM, Thursdays from noon to 9 PM, and Fridays through Sundays from noon to 5 PM. Admission charge. 955 Boylston St. (phone: 266-5151 or 266-5152).

KENMORE SQUARE Formerly a fashionable area, this square is notorious for its traffic jams and college students (*Fenway Park* and Boston University are nearby). The cherished Boston landmark, the Citgo sign, has evaded demolition several times and it looks as if it is here to stay. Though it was turned off during the days of energy conservation in the late 1970s, it has been splashing Kenmore Square with its blue, white, and red lights ever since.

THE FENS PARK Another lasting reminder of the genius of park designer Frederick Law Olmsted, who crafted a serene area of parkland out of what formerly were mud flats while preserving some of the area's original environment. There are footbridges, statuary, reed-bound pools, rows of magnolias, a rose garden, community gardens, and a running path, all surrounded by the Fenway area, where some of the city's finest medical, educational, and cultural institutions are located. The *Museum of Fine Arts* and the *Isabella Stewart Gardner Museum* are located on the Fens, as is Simmons College and Emmanuel College and branches of Northeastern University. The New England Conservatory of Music and Harvard Medical School (located in the world-renowned Longwood Medical Area) are nearby. (Also see *Walk 1: The Fens* in DIRECTIONS.)

MUSEUM OF FINE ARTS This is one of the world's great art museums, with comprehensive exhibits from every major period and in every conceivable medium. Noteworthy are the collection of Impressionist paintings (with more Monets than anywhere outside Paris); the decorative arts and sculpture from the colonial period to the present; an outstanding assemblage of Egyptian art; the greatest collection of Asiatic art under one roof; an exhaustive gathering of American art, including numerous works by Homer, Copley, Sargent, and Hopper; and an impressive classical collection with artifacts from the 6th, 5th, and 4th centuries BC, and the early Roman Imperial period. The wares of silversmiths on display at the *MFA* will prove that the patriot Paul Revere had many valuable talents on top of riding fast on a horse and disturbing the peace. The main building was built in 1909; the airy West Wing, designed by renowned architect I. M. Pei, was added in 1981. It houses additional exhibition space, as well as a cafeteria, restaurant, café, and museum shop; special shows are often mounted here. Outside is the Tenshin Garden, which features New England flora and Japanese landscape design. Directly in back of the *MFA* building are the Fens, a 12-acre marshy park with rose gardens, footbridges, and artists attempting to re-create it all from the banks of a tranquil pond. Open Tuesdays through Sundays from 10 AM to 5 PM, Wednesdays to 10 PM (the West Wing is open late on Thursdays and Fridays); closed Mondays. Admission charge except Wednesdays from 4 to 6 PM. 465 Huntington Ave. (phone: 267-9300).

ISABELLA STEWART GARDNER MUSEUM This marble Venetian palazzo houses one of the world's magnificent private art collections. Isabella Stewart came from New York to Boston in 1860 to marry John Lowell Gardner, a wealthy Brahmin industrialist. While she was a friend of some of the most famous folks of the era — art critic Bernard Berenson advised her on her collection, and artist John Singer Sargent painted her portrait — her flashy dress and spirited manner quickly made her suspect in the eyes of most Proper Bostonians. The art Gardner collected during her worldwide travels is housed in a 15th-century–style Italianate mansion, which she had built between 1899 and 1903, with capitals, columns, fireplaces, fountains, staircases, and other architectural elements imported from Europe. By the terms of her will, the mansion is open to the public with the proviso that the arrangement of paintings, furniture, tapestries, stained glass, antiques, and other objects remain as it was during her lifetime. As a result, objects that seem to have as much sentimental as aesthetic value are exhibited next to several Rembrandts, Titian's *Rape of Europa,* a number of Tintorettos, Manets, Botticellis, Whistlers, and one Corot. (Because the art is arranged haphazardly and the museum signs and labels are not particularly detailed, it's a good idea to purchase the museum guide, sold at the main entrance.) When your feet are tired, you can take lunch or tea at a pleasant café on the premises. Closed Mondays. No admission charge for children under 12. Take the *E* train (*Green Line*) to Museum/Ruggles St. stop. 280 The Fenway (phone: 566-1401 or 734-1359 for concert information).

SOUTH END

Though it contains fewer recognizable tourist attractions, this neighborhood is interesting for its beautiful architecture and its ethnic diversity. (Also see *Walk 2: South End* in DIRECTIONS.)

CHRISTIAN SCIENCE CENTER The world headquarters of the religion founded in the 19th century by the American religious reformer Mary Baker Eddy, this complex houses several interesting attractions. Mrs. Eddy's original granite First Church of Christ, Scientist, built in 1894, is visible but is enveloped by an overpowering Renaissance basilica erected in 1906. The rectangular reflecting pool, tucked in between two modern buildings designed by I. M. Pei, is good for a quiet walk and a view of the Boston skyline. Most interesting is the Mapparium, a 30-foot stained glass globe built in 1935 (and reflecting the world as it was in 1935, with only 70 countries) through which you walk on a glass bridge that is also an echo chamber. The Mapparium is located in the Christian Science Publishing Society Building, the editorial home of the *Christian Science Monitor,* a newspaper with a truly global focus. Massachusetts and Huntington Avenues. Mapparium is open 9 AM to 4 PM Mondays through Saturdays; tours of the complex are available (phone: 450-3790). Across Massachusetts Avenue is *Symphony Hall,* home of the *Boston Symphony Orchestra* and *Boston Pops Orchestra* (phone: 266-1492).

SOUTHWEST CORRIDOR A pleasant pedestrian walk stretching from the Back Bay station on the *Orange Line* (just behind *Neiman Marcus*) to Massachusetts Avenue and beyond. The Southwest Corridor affords a leisurely sampling of South End architecture and ethnic diversity, from a well-manicured and maintained footpath with a view to Boston's skyline.

UNION PARK Many Bostonians' favorite spot in the Hub. Union Park is a residential block of Victorian townhouses that were among the first built during the mid-19th-century development of the South End, a reclaimed wetland. There are fountains, foliage, and a strip of greenery dividing the two rows of houses that give this pocket of civility a quiet, lazy feel. It is studded with magnolias during the summer months.

OTHER SPECIAL PLACES

CHINATOWN This neighborhood has one of the largest Chinese-American populations in the country. Tucked among the Combat Zone (a 2-block area of pornography shops, nude dancers, triple-X movie theaters, and low-rent housing), the leather district, and the Southeast Expressway, Chinatown is a pocket of unabashedly preserved Chinese culture. There are frequent festivals in celebration of Chinese holidays, including a big bash for *Chinese New Year* (in January or February, depending on the Chinese calendar) complete with a snaking dragon and lion dance for good luck, lots of firecrackers, and plenty of food. This is an interesting place for strolling, although most visitors are attracted by Chinatown's many restaurants, which garner most of the city's late-night business. Try *Ho Yuen Ting* (13A Hudson St.; phone: 426-2316) or *Chau Chow* (52 Beach St.; phone: 426-6266) for excellent Cantonese food served with minimal fuss and minimalist decor. The latter stays open until 4 AM on weekends. The best approach to the neighborhood is through the Chinese arch at the head of Beach Street, where it meets Atlantic Avenue.

JOHN F. KENNEDY LIBRARY Designed by architect I. M. Pei, this presidential library sits on the edge of a point of land projecting into Dorchester Bay, with a magnificent view of the Boston skyline and out to sea. There's an exhibit of documents, photographs, and memorabilia that, even if you voted for Nixon, may conjure up a bit of nostalgia. JFK's famed rocking chair (the one in which he sat ruminating on a course of action during the Cuban Missile Crisis) is here, as is the desk at which he presided over nearly 3 years of this nation's administration. There are usually several films screened throughout the day, including a half-hour film on the Kennedy administration. The museum also has a section devoted to Robert F. Kennedy. The library houses the documents of the Kennedy administration — and, by special arrangement, the papers of Ernest Hemingway, which occupy an entire floor. Open daily from 9 AM to 5 PM except *Thanksgiving, Christmas,* and *New Year's Day.* Admission charge for adults; children under 16 free. The library is located off Morrissey Boulevard next to the University of Massachusetts campus, in Dorchester. By car, take the Southeast Expressway south to the JFK Library/UMass exit. The route to the library is well marked. Or take the *MBTA Red Line* (Ashmont train to the JFK/UMass stop; a shuttle bus will take you the rest of the way). Off Morrissey Blvd., Dorchester (phone: 929-4567).

The building next door houses the *Commonwealth Museum,* which has audiovisual presentations on the history of the people, places, and politics of Massachusetts. The state archives are also stored here; several are always on a rotating display. Closed Sundays. No admission charge (phone: 727-9268).

MUSEUM OF SCIENCE AND THE CHARLES HAYDEN PLANETARIUM Sitting astride the Charles River Dam and overlooking its boat locks is a cluster of modern buildings that makes up one of Boston's greatest educational tools. The *Museum of Science* includes over 400 interactive exhibits covering every aspect of science from medicine, biology, chemistry, astronomy, and geology to physics, technology, space exploration, and meteorology. Old favorites are the "Transparent Woman," whose internal organs light up as their functions are explained, the lightning exhibition where lightning — and a resulting clap of thunder — are created before your very eyes, and the *Charles Hayden Planetarium.* The planetarium puts audiences in touch with the stars and the cosmos through a $2-million Zeiss planetarium projector and a multi-image program on cosmic discoveries. Laser light shows with computer animation and brilliant laser graphics also are presented here. One of the museum's most exciting attractions is the *Omni Theater,* featuring a 70-foot domed screen that envelops the viewer in the ultimate film experience. The museum has a wonderful gift shop and a couple of cafeterias. Take the *MBTA Green Line* to Science Park. Closed Mondays. Admission charge for the museum, and additional charge for the *Omni Theater.* Advance reservations for the *Omni Theater* are advised. Science Park (phone: 742-6088).

CHARLESTOWN The Puritans first settled here in 1629 in their quest for a "city upon a hill." Breed's Hill was thought to be just fine until a scarcity of safe drinking water forced them to cultivate the marshy peninsula to the south (that is, Boston). The Battle of Bunker Hill was fought here on Breed's Hill, where the Bunker Hill Monument stands. Confused? Inquire within (phone: 242-5641). Monument Hill and Winthrop Square are laced with excellent examples of 18th- and 19th-century architecture. City Square is where Paul Revere began his famed midnight ride. Nearby is the Charlestown Navy Yard and the USS *Constitution.*

USS *CONSTITUTION* View famous "Old Ironsides," the oldest commissioned ship in the US Navy and the proud winner of 40 victories at sea. The adjacent shoreside museum (phone: 426-1812) displays related memorabilia and a slide show. City Square bus stop. Museum open daily. Admission charge. Charlestown Navy Yard, Charlestown (phone: 242-5670).

BUNKER HILL PAVILION Witness a vivid multimedia reenactment of the Battle of Bunker Hill on 14 screens, with 7 sound channels. Open daily, with shows every half hour from April through December. Admission charge. Adjacent to USS *Constitution* (phone: 241-7575).

ARNOLD ARBORETUM Contained in these 265 acres of beautifully landscaped woodland and park are over 14,000 trees, shrubs, and vines, most of them labeled by their assiduous Harvard caretakers. The visitors' center shop has a large selection of books on botany and horticulture. Open daily, sunrise to sunset. No admission charge. Six miles southwest of downtown Boston; the main gate and visitors' center are 100 yards south of the rotary junction of Routes 1 and 203. Take the *E* train (*Green Line*), the Arborway bus No. 39 from Copley Square stop, or the *Orange Line,* Forest Hills stop. The Arborway, Jamaica Plain (phone: 524-1717 or 524-1718). (Also see *Quintessential Boston* in DIVERSIONS.)

FRANKLIN PARK ZOO The highlight of this facility is an exciting rain forest exhibit, which allows jungle animals to prowl in their natural habitats. In the middle of the huge, climate-controlled, hangar-like structure is the gorilla area, where six mountain gorillas frolic over the rocky terrain and where birds fly free (sort of) under the soaring roof. Other animals — dwarf forest buffalos, crocodiles, a dwarf hippo, storks, and even scorpions — roam in a separate space; the zoo also boasts four waterfalls and the largest collection of tropical plants in New England. Other sections include Bird's World, Hooves and Horns, and a Children's Zoo. Open daily from 9 AM to 3:30 PM. No admission charge on Tuesdays after noon. Take Route 1 (VFW Parkway) to Route 203 East. Or take Bus No. 16 from the Wallaston stop on the *Orange Line.* Rte. 203, Franklin Park, Dorchester (phone: 442-0991 or 442-2002).

FREDERICK LAW OLMSTED NATIONAL HISTORIC SITE Olmsted, the premier 19th-century landscape designer, is honored through archives that include plans, drawings, and photographs. Best known as the designer of New York City's Central Park, Olmsted also designed Boston's 8-mile "Emerald Necklace" of greenspaces, which ties the city to the suburbs. There are tours of the house once occupied by Olmsted and his two sons and of the grounds, which illustrate the principles of Olmsted's designs. Open Fridays through Sundays from 10 AM to 4:30 PM. No admission charge. 99 Warren St., Brookline (phone: 566-1689).

CAMBRIDGE

HARVARD SQUARE Just across the Charles River from Boston, Cambridge has always had an ambience and identity all its own. Catering equally to the academic and professional communities, the square is a lively combination of the trendy, traditional, and "upscale." It has the greatest concentration of bookstores in the country (many are open until late into the evening), movie options that range from vintage films like *Casablanca* to the latest from Hollywood and abroad, and the ever-present street musicians. When hunger pangs strike, everything from muffins to nouvelle cuisine awaits — with an authentic Italian ice to top it off. Take the *Red Line* headed toward Alewife (the last stop), and get off at the Harvard Square stop.

HARVARD YARD This tree-filled enclave is the focal point of the oldest (1636) and most prestigious university in the country (the Law School is nearby, the Business School just across the river, the Medical School a bus ride away in Boston). Notice especially Massachusetts Hall (1720; Harvard's oldest building), Bulfinch's University Hall, and in the adjoining quadrangle, Widener Library and H. H. Richardson's Sever Hall. Campus tours are given year-round; check at the information office in Holyoke Center (phone: 495-1573).

WEEKS MEMORIAL BRIDGE This graceful footbridge was built to link Harvard's Cambridge campus with the school's Graduate School of Business Administration, on the Boston side. It offers a splendid view of the white, crimson, and gold Harvard steeples and the Harvard crew team's practices on the Charles River.

HARVARD UNIVERSITY ART MUSEUMS Harvard's impressive collection of paintings, drawings, prints, sculpture, and silver is housed in three fine museums. The *Arthur Sackler Museum*'s collection of ancient Roman, Egyptian, and Islamic antiquities, as well as traveling exhibitions, are displayed in a 1985 post-modern building (485 Broadway) designed by James Stirling. Nearby is the neo-Georgian building of the *Fogg Museum* (32 Quincy St.), which features European and American art from the Middle Ages to the present. Connected to the *Fogg* is the home of the *Busch-Reisinger Museum,* the only museum in the US that specializes in the art of Germanic-speaking countries. All three are open Tuesdays through Sundays from 10 AM to 5 PM. Admission charge (phone: 495-9400).

HARVARD UNIVERSITY MUSEUMS On a short block parallel to Oxford Street is this complex housing the *Comparative Zoology, Peabody, Mineralogical and Geological,* and *Botanical* museums. The *Peabody* houses extensive anthropological and archaeological collections, with an emphasis on South American Indians. There are also exhibitions on Africa and evolution, as well as a fine gift shop. The *Botanical* houses a famous collection of glass flowers handmade for Harvard between 1887 and 1936 by Leopold and Rudolph Blaschka, a German father and son. Renowned for their scientific accuracy as well as their beauty, the flowers are worth a special trip. Reservations must be made for either group (phone: 495-2341) or individual (phone: 495-3045) tours for any of the museums. Open daily. Admission charge except on Saturdays from 9 to 11 AM. 26 Oxford St. (phone: 495-2341).

RADCLIFFE YARD One of the Seven Sister colleges, Radcliffe has evolved from its historical role as "Harvard's Annex" to its current position, with its undergraduates fully integrated into the life of the university. Radcliffe offers special alternative programs for women at the graduate level and those interested in career changes. Its Schlesinger Library has one of the country's top collections on the history of women in America, as well as an important culinary collection. Open weekdays. No admission charge. 3 James St. (phone: 495-8647).

OLD BURYING GROUND This historic cemetery, also known as God's Acre, is on Garden Street, just past Christ Church. The graves date back to 1635, and a number of Revolutionary War heroes and Harvard presidents are buried here. On the Garden Street fence, there's a mileage marker dating to 1754.

BRATTLE STREET An elegant Cambridge street that was known in the 1770s as "Tory Row," since seven mansions owned by supporters of King George were located here. Today, a couple still stand. William Brattle, a Loyalist who fled Boston in 1774, lived at 42 Brattle, an 18th-century gambrel-roofed Colonial home that later became the home of Margaret Fuller, an early feminist. The building is now the headquarters of the Cambridge Center for Adult Education, which offers evening courses on everything from Italian cooking to word processing (phone: 547-6789). The yellow clapboard Pratt House at No. 56 is where Dexter Pratt, Longfellow's "Village Blacksmith," lived and plied his trade. It now houses the *Blacksmith House Café and Bakery* (phone: 354-3036). Though the "spreading chestnut tree" that Longfellow referred to is long gone, a plaque on the corner of Brattle and Story Streets preserves its memory. Longfellow lived just down the street at 105 Brattle from 1837 until his death in 1882. That house, built in 1759, served as the headquarters for General Washington during the British siege of Boston. Concerts are held here in summer. Open daily; guided tours are available. Admission charge. 105 Brattle St. (phone: 876-4491).

MASSACHUSETTS INSTITUTE OF TECHNOLOGY The foremost scientific and technological school in the country, MIT opened its doors in Boston in 1865 and moved across the river to its present Cambridge campus in 1916. In addition to its world-famous laboratories and graduate schools in engineering and science, its professional schools include the Sloan School of Management, the Joint Center for Urban Studies (with Harvard), and the School of Architecture. Architect I. M. Pei is an alumnus; next to his Green Building for the earth sciences stands Calder's stabile *The Big Sail*, one of a superb collection of outdoor sculptures on the campus. Also worth noting are Eero Saarinen's chapel and his *Kresge Auditorium*, just across from the main entrance on Massachusetts Avenue. The main *MIT Museum* (265 Massachusetts Ave.; phone: 253-4429 or 253-4444) contains permanent collections and changing exhibits of contemporary art and technology. Closed Mondays; admission charge. The *Compton Gallery* (77 Massachusetts Ave.; phone: 258-9118) features changing technical exhibitions. Open weekdays; no admission charge. The *Wiesner Building* (20 Ames St.; phone: 253-4680) is another I. M. Pei landmark, worth a visit for its arresting interior and the often provocative changing exhibitions. The *List Visual Arts Center* is located in this building. Open daily; no admission charge (phone: 253-4680). MIT campus tours are given year-round on weekdays at 10 AM and 2 PM. *Red Line,* Kendall Square/MIT stop, or No. 1 Dudley bus, headed toward Harvard Sq. 77 Massachusetts Ave. (phone: 253-4795).

MT. AUBURN CEMETERY The first garden cemetery in the United States, this rural retreat in the midst of Cambridge is bliss to the senses. Founded in 1831, Mt. Auburn's 170 beautifully landscaped acres include hills, ponds (4), magnificent trees (over 3,500 of them, including 575 varieties), and an observation tower. Visitors are encouraged to walk or drive around, and bird watchers find it especially appealing. Among the many famous people buried here are Mary Baker Eddy, Henry Wadsworth Longfellow, Julia Ward Howe, Oliver Wendell Holmes, and Winslow Homer. An hour's stroll might be the pinnacle of a sightseeing day. Open daylight hours, year-round; tower open in fair weather, from early spring to late fall. Stop for a map at the north entrance. 580 Mt. Auburn St. (phone: 547-7105).

Sources and Resources

TOURIST INFORMATION

For tourist information, maps, and brochures, visit one of the visitors' information centers — at City Hall, Boston Common, or the Hancock Tower. The Boston Convention and Tourist Bureau (Prudential Center; phone: 536-4100) has multilingual maps and brochures and is open weekdays. The Massachusetts Office of Travel and Tourism (100 Cambridge St.; phone: 727-3201) also can provide maps, calendars of events, health updates, travel advisories, and other tourist information. Another good source is the National Park Service Visitor Center, located across from the Old State House. There is an 8-minute film on the historic sites of Boston, and park rangers will answer any question and offer advice. Maps, brochures, books, and cards also are available. Various walking tours led by park rangers originate here (15 State St.; phone: 242-5642).

The *Visitor's Channel* of the Panorama Television Network, Channel 12, is offered on local hotel television sets. This 24-hour station provides weather updates every 15 minutes as well as travel advisories, traffic information, and half-hour bulletins on special attractions within Boston and day trips outside the city.

A comprehensive guidebook is *In and Out of Boston (With or Without Children),* by Bernice Chesler (Globe Pequot Press; $15.95). Also good is *Historic Walks in Old Boston,* by John Harris (Globe Pequot Press; $12.95).

LOCAL COVERAGE *Boston Globe,* morning daily; *Boston Herald,* morning daily; *Christian Science Monitor,* weekday mornings; *Boston Phoenix,* weekly; *The Tab,* weekly; *Boston* magazine, monthly; *Bostonia* magazine, quarterly.

TELEVISION STATIONS WBZ Channel 4–NBC; WCVB Channel 5–ABC; WHDH Channel 7–CBS; WGBH Channel 2–PBS; WXNE Channel 25–Fox; WSBK Channel 38; WLVI Channel 56.

RADIO STATIONS AM: WRKO 680 (talk); WHDH 850 (adult contemporary); WBZ 1030 (pop); WEEI 590 (sports). FM: WBUR 90.9 (classical/National Public Radio); WROR 93.5 (pop); WJIB 98 (pop); WFNX 101.7 (contemporary/new wave); WBCN 104.1 (rock/pop).

FOOD A good source is the *1994 Zagat Boston Restaurant Survey* (Zagat Survey, NY; $9.95), or *Robert Nadeau's Guide to Boston Restaurants* by Mark Zanger (World Food Press; $3.95). Also see the restaurant listings of the *Boston Globe* "Calendar" section (supplement to the Thursday paper).

TELEPHONE

The area code for Boston is 617. All numbers listed here are in the 617 area code unless otherwise indicated. *Note:* Some areas surrounding Boston are served by the 508 area code.

SALES TAX

The city sales tax is 5%; there also is a 9.7% hotel tax.

GETTING AROUND

BUS, TROLLEY, AND TRAIN The *Massachusetts Bay Transit Authority (MBTA)* operates a network of trolleys and subways (referred to by locals as "the *T*") with four major lines, the *Red, Blue, Green,* and *Orange.* The *MBTA* also runs the city's bus system. Compared to the mass transit systems in most major American cities, Boston is still a bargain: 60¢ for buses and 85¢ for the *T.* Exact change is required for the buses. Three-day visitor's passes are $9, and 7-day passes are $18. They allow you to ride free on all *MBTA* conveyances — trolleys, subways, trains, and buses. The pass also entitles the holder to $50 worth of discounts on entertainment, restaurants, and other attractions around the city. *MBTA* service is fairly frequent during the day, less frequent at night, and nonexistent after about 12:30 AM. *MBTA* stations are marked with large, white circular signs bearing a giant "T." For schedules, directions, timetables, and maps, call the Travel Information Center at 722-3200 or 800-392-6100 between 6 AM and 11:30 PM on weekdays and until 9 PM on weekends. They will answer any questions and help you plot the best travel routes. The *T* is the cheapest and often the fastest way to travel between downtown and the airport. Take the *Blue Line* to the airport stop. From there, a free *MBTA* shuttle bus will take you to your terminal. Warning: Don't try this at rush hour with several suitcases.

There are various trolley sightseeing tours of Boston that have gained a reputation for colorful — albeit not always accurate — information. The major ones are *Old Town Trolley Tours* (phone: 269-7010), fully narrated tours of more than 100 historic Boston sites, and the *Boston Trolley* (phone: TRO-LLEY), which has a number of boarding and reboarding stops at major Boston hotels. You also can see the city from 500 feet in the air, with *Business Helicopter* (phone: 423-0004), which departs daily from the Boston Heliport, minutes from South Station.

The commuter trains are an excellent way of getting to Boston's suburbs. From South Station (a gorgeous and sprawling train station inside an ornate 19th-century façade that deserves a look on its own merit), there are *MBTA* commuter trains to points south and west of Boston, for example, Framingham, Needham, Stoughton, and Providence, Rhode Island. South Station is also Boston's link with *Amtrak,* which makes frequent runs to Providence, Rhode Island, Connecticut, and New York City (phone: 482-3660). North Station (just behind the *Boston Garden*) is the point of departure for commuter trains north and west, including Concord, Gardner, Lowell, Ipswich, and other points on the North Shore (phone: 722-3200).

CAR RENTAL For information on renting a car, see GETTING READY TO GO.

TAXI Boston has several taxi fleets, and you can hail them on the street, pick them up at taxi stands downtown, or call for them: *Boston Cab* (phone: 536-5010); *Independent Taxi Operators Assn.* (phone: 426-8700); *Town Taxi* (phone: 536-5000); *Checker Taxi* (phone: 536-7000); *Yellow Cab* (Cambridge; phone: 547-3000); *Ambassador/Brattle Taxi* (Cambridge; phone: 492-1100).

> **NOTE** Electronic video machines placed on various street corners assist wandering visitors trying to get their bearings or searching for a particular spot in the area. A combination keyboard and video screen shows the address and telephone number. Or you can ask for a selection of shops and restaurants in the area, and the machine will present a detailed list. Other computer terminals located at Logan Airport provide information on cultural and tourist events throughout New England.

LOCAL SERVICES

For additional information about local services not listed here, call the Boston Chamber of Commerce (phone: 227-4500).

AUDIOVISUAL EQUIPMENT *Massachusetts Audio Visual Equipment Co.* (phone: 646-5410).

BABY-SITTING For Boston proper, call *Child Care Choices of Boston* between 10 AM and 1 PM (178 Tremont St.; phone: 357-6020, ext. 17). For surrounding communities, call *Child Care Resource Center* (552 Massachusetts Ave., Cambridge; phone: 547-9861) or *Parents in a Pinch* (45 Bartlett Crescent, Brookline; phone: 739-5437).

BUSINESS SERVICES *Bette James & Associates* (1430 Massachusetts Ave., Cambridge; phone: 661-2622); *OfficePlus* rents office space and provides access to a wide range of office services (8 *Faneuil Hall Marketplace;* phone: 367-8335).

DRY CLEANER/TAILOR *Sarni Original Dry Cleaners* has a dozen locations. Try the one at 122 Milk St. (phone 338-9133).

LIMOUSINE *Carey of Boston* (phone: 623-8700); *Classic Limo* (phone: 266-3980); *Waites Transportation, Inc.* (phone: 567-5867 or 567-0420).

MECHANIC Ray Magliozzi (one of the amusing hosts of National Public Radio's "Car Talk"), at the *Good News Garage,* will repair anything. But fame has its price, namely $40 an hour (75 Hamilton St., Cambridge, between Central Sq. and MIT; phone: 354-5383).

MEDICAL EMERGENCY For information on area hospitals and pharmacies, see GETTING READY TO GO.

MESSENGER SERVICES *Beacon Hill Courier Service* (phone: 742-1358); *Boston Cab Association* (phone: 536-5010); *Central Delivery Service,* 24-hour service (phone: 395-3213); *Town Taxi* (phone: 536-5000).

PHOTOCOPIES *Copy Cop* has many locations, including 815 Boylston St. (phone: 267-9267) and 85 Franklin St. (phone: 451-0233).

PROFESSIONAL PHOTOGRAPHER *Atlantic Photo Service* (669 Boylston St.; phone: 267-7480); *Fay Foto Service* (45 Electric Ave.; phone: 267-2000).

SECRETARY *A-Plus Secretarial Office,* 4 Brattle St., Cambridge (phone: 491-2200).

TELECONFERENCE FACILITIES The *Charles; Colonnade; Hyatt Regency, Cambridge;* the *Marriott* hotels in Cambridge, at *Copley Place* and on Long Wharf; the *Meridien*; *Omni Parker House*; and the *Royal Sonesta* (see *Best in Town*).

TRANSLATOR *Berlitz* (437 Boylston St.; phone: 266-6858); *Boston Language Institute* (636 Beacon St.; phone: 262-3500).

TRAVELER'S CHECKS *American Express* has several offices providing traveler's checks and travel agency services (1 Court St.; phone: 723-8400; 44 Brattle St., Cambridge; phone: 661-0005; and 55 Boylston St., Chestnut Hill, Newton; phone: 964-0622). Another traveler's check company with offices in the city is *Thomas Cook Currency Services* (160 Franklin St.; phone:

426-0016; 800 Boylston St.; phone: 247-3121; and 39 JFK St., Cambridge; phone: 868-6605).

TYPEWRITER RENTAL *Cambridge Typewriter Co.,* 2-day minimum. 102 Massachusetts Ave., Arlington (phone: 643-7010).

WESTERN UNION/TELEX Many locations around the city (phone: 800-325-6000).

OTHER *HQ, Headquarters Company,* word processing, telex, facsimile, conference rooms (phone: 451-2589); *Meeting House Offices,* office space, word processing, photocopying, postage meter (121 Mt. Vernon St.; phone: 367-7171).

SPECIAL EVENTS

The *Chinese New Year* is celebrated annually on every street in Chinatown in January or February, depending on the Chinese calendar. The 1-day event, from noon to 6 PM, features a dragon and lion dance, firecrackers, and lots of food. Don't miss the *International Cultural Festival* at the *Ritz-Carlton* hotel from the first week in January through the third week in March, featuring culinary celebrations and demonstrations and political and cultural lectures. Each week a different country is highlighted (phone: 536-5700). *St. Patrick's Day* and *Evacuation Day* (when the British fled Boston) are both celebrated in South Boston on March 17. *Patriot's Day,* featuring a number of parades, reenactments of revolutionary skirmishes, and other events, is observed in and around Boston (Concord, Lexington, and so on) on the third Monday in April and the weekend before. The *Boston Marathon,* the oldest and most celebrated marathon in the US, is also held that Monday. The front-runners usually cross the finish line in Copley Square around 2 PM. The *Big Apple Circus* comes to town from early April through mid-May, giving two performances daily. Sponsored by the *Children's Museum* (phone: 426-8855). *Lilac Sunday,* the annual viewing of over 300 varieties of lilacs at the Arnold Arboretum, is held on the third Sunday in May (phone: 524-1717). The *Cambridge International Fair,* a celebration of summer and the arts with theater, dance, music, food, and so on, in Central Square, is held in early June (phone: 349-4380). June is the month of colorful neighborhood street fairs, with the *Back Bay Street Fair* and the *Bay Village Fair* on the first Saturday, and the *St. Botolph Street Fair* in the South End on the third Saturday. The *Boston Globe Jazz Festival,* a week-long series of jazz performances and free midday concerts, is held each year in mid-June. Kicking off with a performance of local jazz artists in the plaza of the *Charles* hotel in Cambridge, the week of great jam sessions concludes in the grand finale at the *Hatch Shell* on the Esplanade, typically attended by a crowd of over 25,000 spectators (phone: 929-2651). This year, the *FIFA World Cup* soccer matches will be played at Foxboro's *Sullivan Stadium* (phone: 508-543-

1776) on June 21, 23, 25, and 30; and July 5 and 9 (also see *Sports and Fitness*). Boston is filled with color and pageantry during the annual *Fourth of July* celebrations: The waterfront comes alive with *Harborfest,* a series of events on land and water; the Declaration of Independence is read from the balcony of the Old State House at 10 AM on *July 4*; the annual turnaround of USS *Constitution,* "Old Ironsides," commences at 10:30 AM; and the *Boston Pops* hold their beloved annual holiday concert at the *Hatch Shell* in the evening, culminating with their rendition of the *1812 Overture* underneath a dazzling display of fireworks (phone: 800-858-0200). North End *Italian Festas,* a series of saint's day celebrations, always begin and end with religious services and processions, and feature a lot of food, games, dancing, and general festivity in between. They are held on nearly every weekend throughout July and August. The oldest American professional tennis championship, the 9-day *US Pro Tennis Championships at Longwood,* begins the third week of July. Many tennis greats participate (phone: 731-4500). Rowers from around the world — Belgium, France, the US, England, Mexico — and a wealth of American college teams compete in the annual *Head of the Charles Regatta* — which starts on the Charles near the Boston University Bridge and goes upstream to Harvard and beyond — the last Sunday in October. In even-numbered years, the *Harvard-Yale Football Game* is held in Cambridge (phone: 495-2207). Boston's best *Christmas* tradition, the presentation of the Handel & Haydn Society's *Messiah,* is on 5 evenings in early December (phone: 266-3605). The *Tea Party Reenactment,* where uniformed participants throw chests of tea off the *Tea Party Ship,* is on the Sunday closest to December 16 (Congress St. Bridge; phone: 338-1773). The *First Night Celebration,* a series of musical, culinary, theater, and film events that draws more than 500,000 people to Boston's Back Bay and downtown, is held on *New Year's Eve* (phone: 524-1399).

MUSEUMS

In addition to those described in *Special Places,* other fine museums worth visiting include the following:

BOSTON CENTER FOR THE ARTS Multi-use arts complex in a city block of historic buildings. Open Wednesdays through Sundays from noon to 4 PM. No admission charge. 539 Tremont St. (phone: 426-5000 or 426-7700).

CARPENTER CENTER FOR THE VISUAL ARTS Le Corbusier's only building in the US; at Harvard University. Rotating exhibitions are presented, as well as four or five film series running simultaneously during the school year. The center is open from 9 AM to 11 PM weekdays, 9 AM to 6 PM Saturdays, and noon to 10 PM Sundays; the Sert Gallery on the third floor is open Tuesdays through Sundays from 1 to 6 PM. No admission charge. 24 Quincy St., Cambridge (phone: 495-3251).

FIRST HARRISON GRAY OTIS HOUSE The house was designed in the late 18th century by Charles Bulfinch for Otis, a lawyer, congressman, and Boston mayor. It is now the headquarters of the Society for the Preservation of New England Antiquities. Guided tours are available Tuesdays through Fridays from noon to 4 PM and Saturdays from 10 AM to 4 PM. Admission charge. 141 Cambridge St. (phone: 227-3956).

GIBSON HOUSE A Victorian-era home. Open Saturdays and Sundays from 1 to 3 PM. Admission charge. 137 Beacon St. (phone: 267-6338).

MUSEUM OF AFRO-AMERICAN HISTORY Located in the African Meeting House, the oldest black church in the country. Open weekdays from 10 AM to 4 PM. No admission charge. 46 Joy St. (phone: 742-1854).

MUSEUM OF THE ANCIENT AND HONORABLE ARTILLERY COMPANY OF MASSA-CHUSETTS Chartered in 1638 to protect the early settlers, the Ancient and Honorable is America's oldest military outfit. On display are firearms, artifacts, flags, cannons, uniforms, and other memorabilia. Open Mondays through Fridays from 10 AM to 4 PM. No admission charge. *Faneuil Hall,* 3rd floor (phone: 227-1638).

MUSEUM OF THE CONCORD ANTIQUARIAN SOCIETY Fifteen period rooms with contents dating from the 17th to the 19th centuries. Open Tuesdays through Saturdays from 10 AM to 5 PM; Sundays 1 to 5 PM from April through December; during the winter months, Mondays through Saturdays, 11 AM to 4 PM and Sundays, 1 to 4 PM. Admission charge. 200 Lexington Rd., Concord (phone: 508-369-9609).

MUSEUM OF OUR NATIONAL HERITAGE A museum and library of American history. Open Mondays through Saturdays from 10 AM to 5 PM; Sundays, noon to 5 PM. No admission charge. 33 Marrett Rd., Lexington (phone: 861-6559).

RALPH WALDO EMERSON MEMORIAL HOUSE The former home of the essayist, philosopher, and poet. Open mid-April through October. Open Thursdays through Saturdays, 10 AM to 4:30 PM; Sundays from 2 to 4:30 PM. Admission charge. 28 Cambridge Tpke., Concord (phone: 508-369-2236).

SPORTS MUSEUM Features memorabilia, artifacts, photographs, equipment, temporary exhibits, and interactive video presentations about New England's rich sports history. Open Mondays through Saturdays from 10 AM to 9:30 PM; Sundays from noon to 6 PM. Admission charge. In the *Cambridgeside Galleria,* Memorial Dr., Cambridge (phone: 787-7678).

MAJOR COLLEGES AND UNIVERSITIES

Boston is the country's consummate college town, with tens of thousands of students, professors, and visitors from all over the world pouring onto the campuses every academic year. There are literally dozens of educational institutions, including many aristocratic New England prep schools. Check the bulletin boards and college newspapers for listings of campus events. Harvard University (see *Special Places*) is the most prestigious in the country. MIT (see *Special Places*) produces scientists in all fields, many of whom continue in government research and consulting positions. In Boston itself, Boston University, with its many colleges and graduate schools, sprawls along Commonwealth Avenue, west of Kenmore Square (phone: 353-2000). Boston College, located to the west in Chestnut Hill, is a large Jesuit university with a variety of undergraduate and graduate programs and a loyal following of sports fans (phone: 552-8000). Other schools in the area: Brandeis University (415 South St., Waltham; phone: 736-2000); Emerson College (100 Beacon St.; phone: 578-8500); Emmanuel College (400 The Fenway; phone: 277-9540); Endicott College (376 Hale St., Beverly; phone: 508-927-0585); Lesley College (29 Everett St., Cambridge; phone: 868-9600); Simmons College (300 The Fenway; phone: 738-2000); Suffolk University (8 Ashburton Pl.; phone: 573-8000); Tufts University (Medford-Somerville; phone: 628-5000); University of Massachusetts/Boston (Park Sq. and Columbia Point; phone: 287-5000); Wellesley College (Wellesley; phone: 235-0320); Wheaton College (Norton; phone: 508-285-7722); Wheelock College (150 The Riverway; phone: 734-5200).

SHOPPING

Boston is a browser's paradise, with plenty of elegant and one-of-a-kind stores in a small area. Newbury Street is the place to go if your tastes run to art galleries, designer clothing, fine jewelry, expensive antiques, and outdoor cafés. But even if your preferences are more eclectic than elegant, don't rule out this pretty, European-looking venue. Newbury Street begins, sedately enough, where Arlington Street borders the Public Garden, where the *Ritz* and the *Giorgio Armani* store hold sway. But continue its length to Massachusetts Avenue and the boutiques and the clientele gradually change: At this end are the mammoth *Tower Records* and the outrageous *Allston Beat*. Just 1 block away from the *Ritz*, at the end of Boylston Street, is the *Heritage on the Garden* complex, which has high-end, international stores, such as *Escada*, *Hermès*, and *Waterford-Wedgwood*. Here's where you also find *Biba*, one of Boston's trendiest restaurants, and *The Spa* at the *Heritage*, the perfect antidote to a hard day of shopping.

Just 2 blocks south of Newbury Street is *Copley Place*, a glitzy shopping mall near Copley Square. *Neiman Marcus* and *Tiffany* are at either end of the mall, and in between are plenty of top-quality boutiques.

For atmosphere, walk the length of Charles Street, just across the Public Garden from the *Ritz*. The winding, gaslit street contains antiques shops, art and print galleries, and several intimate cafés.

Boston — particularly Newbury and Charles Streets — is a paradise for antiques aficionados. Some of our favorite shops are listed below; for more information, see *Antiques: Boston's Best Hunting Grounds* in DIVER-SIONS.

And finally, the Downtown Crossing area has the city's two best-known department stores — *Jordan Marsh* and *Filene's* — surrounded by blocks of so-so shops. Below is a list of some of the city's best emporia.

ALLSTON BEAT Blue jeans, leather, and metal, much loved by teens and collegians. 348 Newbury St. (phone: 421-9555).

AUTRE FOIS The focus here is on French country furniture, although there is also furniture from Italy and England, plus a variety of decorative accessories. 125 Newbury St. (phone: 424-8823).

AVENUE VICTOR HUGO Offers a wide range of used books and magazines. 339 Newbury St. (phone: 266-7746).

BETSEY JOHNSON The wild 1960s-inspired fashions of this New York designer enliven this street. 201 Newbury St. (phone: 236-7072).

BODY SCULPTURE An unpretentious-looking little place that sells some of the city's most creative jewelry — gorgeous, handcrafted stuff. Be sure to ask to see everything, since some of the most interesting designs are in drawers. 127 Newbury St. (phone: 262-2200).

BRATTLE BOOK SHOP This Dickensian-style bookstore, located near the Boston Common, is an antiquarian book lover's Elysian Fields. More than 350,000 used, out-of-print, and rare books populate the 3-story building, with original manuscripts and authors' autographs for sale. Open Mondays through Saturdays from 9 AM to 5:30 PM. 9 West St. (phone: 542-0210 or 800-447-9595).

BROOKS BROTHERS *The* place for proper and durable men's attire. 46 Newbury St. (phone: 267-2600).

LE CHAPEAU A delightful little store that carries hats, caps, boaters, beanies, and other assorted headgear. *Copley Place* (phone: 236-0232).

CHOCOLATE BY DESIGN This company will shape chocolate for you in almost any way you can imagine. Or just wander in to see the offbeat designs. 134 Newbury St. (phone: 424-1115).

COLE-HAAN Classic men's and women's shoes and leather goods are showcased in a new store that feels more like a Victorian home. 109 Newbury St. (phone: 536-7826).

CUOIO SHOES Pronounced *kwao,* this little shop has some of the most unusual and elegant women's shoes around. 115 Newbury St. (phone: 859-0636).

DELUCA'S MARKET When almost every food emporium is now either part of a chain or homogenized to anonymity, here's a friendly, family-run food market devoted to high quality and personal service. 11 Charles St.

(phone: 523-4343). Also in the Back Bay at 239 Newbury St. (phone: 262-5990).

ESCADA Elegant, colorful clothing by German designer Margaretha Ley. 308 Boylston St., *Heritage on the Garden* (phone: 437-1200).

ESSENCE The master perfumer here custom-makes scents to match your skin's special needs and your olfactory preferences. He also mixes up great imitations of well-known fragrances. 223 Newbury St. (phone: 859-8009).

FAO SCHWARZ This huge children's funhouse is almost as large as the New York City flagship. The centerpiece is the singing, 2-story clock, with moving figurines, a singing giraffe, and a bear tea party on top. If you're lost, ask Spanky, the talking bear, for help. 440 Boylston St. (phone: 262-5900).

FILENE'S A fine department store with a full line of clothing, accessories, and housewares. It is located above the famous *Filene's Basement,* but the two stores now have different owners. Downtown Crossing, 426 Washington St. (phone: 357-2100).

FILENE'S BASEMENT For the best bargains in town. Where else can one find markdowns from every state in the union and nearly every country in the world? Take the *Red* or *Orange* lines to Downtown Crossing. 426 Washington St. (phone: 542-2011).

FIRESTONE AND PARSONS An elegant jewelry store in the *Ritz,* with perhaps the city's finest estate gems. Newbury and Arlington Sts. (phone: 266-1858).

GEORGE GRAVERT This orderly and uncluttered establishment specializes in 18th- and 19-century continental antiques. There's a good selection of French country furniture, decorative accessories, and even some 19th-century garden statuary. 122 Charles St. (phone: 227-1593).

GIORGIO ARMANI An understated emporium that is the proper venue for this Italian designer's understated and elegant clothing for men and women. 22 Newbury St. (phone: 267-3200).

GODIVA CHOCOLATIERS This store for chocolate fanciers sells wonderful confections that look like tiny — and edible — works of art. *Copley Place* (phone: 437-8950).

THE GODS Buddhas, pharaohs, flying dragons, icons, madonnas, all manner of religious relics, either sacred or pagan, are packed into this fascinating little shop. 253 Newbury St. (phone: 859-3034).

HARVARD BOOKSTORE CAFÉ Fine books combined with a classic café and restaurant, which is open-air in the warm months. 190 Newbury St. (phone: 536-0095).

HERMÈS Elegant and expensive French apparel and accessories for Boston's Brahmins. 22 Arlington St., at *Heritage on the Garden* (phone: 482-8707).

JOAN & DAVID The well-known shoe designers have a boutique stocked with their beautiful, unique shoes and a small line of their clothing. *Copley Place* (phone: 536-0600).

JORDAN MARSH New England's largest department store, this 132-year-old landmark carries clothing, including most of the top designer labels, accessories, and housewares. There's a bargain basement, but it is not as highly esteemed as *Filene's Basement,* located across the street. 450 Washington St. (phone: 357-3000).

JOSEPH ABBOUD A native Bostonian went to New York, went national with his line of classic, earthy menswear, and returned to build a lovely, 3-story boutique. 37 Newbury St. (phone: 266-4200).

KAKAS FURRIERS An elegant fur and leather store near the Public Garden where older fashionable Bostonians like to shop. 93 Newbury St. (phone: 536-1858).

LOUIS, BOSTON Trendy, elegant menswear designed to make a statement. Also in the graceful old building is a floor of women's clothing, *Café Louis,* a continental bistro, and a hair salon called *The Cutting Room.* 234 Berkeley St., Back Bay (phone: 262-6100).

MARIKA'S ANTIQUES Loaded with tapestries, paintings, vases, and furniture from the US, Europe, and the Orient. Jewelry is a specialty. 130 Charles St. (phone: 523-4520).

MUSEUM REPLICA GALLERY You might think you'd entered an art gallery until you notice that a Renoir is on sale for $500. These genuine-looking copies of some of the world's great paintings are created by using a unique form of photography. 212 Newbury St. (phone: 859-7654).

MUSEUM OF SCIENCE GIFT SHOP For children who have everything: toys, gifts, and artifacts. Science Park (phone: 723-2500).

NEIMAN MARCUS The glitzy Dallas specialty store is one of the anchors at *Copley Place* (phone: 536-3660).

NEWBURY COMICS All kinds of comic books, from classic to counterculture. 332 Newbury St. (phone: 236-4930) and seven other locations.

OILILY Rainbows look dull next to the brightly colored children's clothing in this Dutch company's Boston store. 31 Newbury St. (phone: 247-9299).

OUT OF TOWN NEWS A periodical lover's dream, staffed by folks who know when and where every journal under the sun is published: from a Des Moines Sunday paper to a magazine from Cairo. Harvard Sq. (phone: 354-7777).

PRISCILLA: THE BRIDE'S SHOP This exclusive bridal shop has been making gowns for society brides for decades. 137 Newbury St. (phone: 267-9070).

ROSE GARDEN Head to this florist for the city's best roses at the best prices. A dozen cost from $10 to $25, depending on season and stem length. 110 Newbury St. (phone: 859-9800).

ROSIE'S BAKERY AND DESSERT SHOP A brightly lit storefront bakery in Cambridge's Inman Square, it's known for its prize-winning brownie, an indescribably rich concoction delicately named a "Chocolate Orgasm," and the best poppyseed cake you'll find anywhere. A great place to order cakes for special occasions, too, should you find yourself in Boston with something to celebrate. 243 Hampshire St., Cambridge (phone: 491-9488).

SHARPER IMAGE An amusement park of adult "toys" — talking scales, massaging chairs, tiny pool tables, duck-shape telephones — and all manner of gadgets and contraptions. *Copley Place,* near the crosswalk over Huntington Ave. (phone: 262-7010).

SHREVE, CRUMP & LOW One of Boston's oldest and finest jewelry stores. There's also crystal, clocks, silver, and a fine collection of American and English antiques from the 18th and 19th centuries. 330 Boylston St. (phone: 267-9100).

SOCIETY OF ARTS AND CRAFTS Talented craftspeople have always gravitated to New England, and for the past 95 years, the *Society* has been carrying their unique works of furniture, jewelry, housewares, and clothing. 175 Newbury St. (phone: 266-1810) and 101 Arch St. (phone: 345-0033).

STRUTTERS Fans of vintage clothing and accessories should check out the high-quality goods here. 257 Newbury St. (phone: 247-7744).

SWEET ENCHANTMENTS Kids love walking over the bridge and through the fake forest in this unique candy store, especially since each tree knot is filled with a sweet surprise. 229 Newbury St. (phone: 236-2282).

TIFFANY & CO. The prestigious house for jewelry and more. *Copley Place* (phone: 353-0222).

TOSCANINI'S Ice cream heaven. Rumor has it that Bostonians eat more ice cream per capita than the residents of any other city. In a blizzard or in balmy weather, it's packed. The ice cream is made on the premises and features exotic foreign flavors such as Italian *nocciòla* (hazelnut) and *gianduia* (chocolate cream), and Indian cardamom-pistachio, mango, and saffron. 899 Main St., Central Sq., Cambridge (phone: 491-5877), and also in the MIT Student Center (phone: 494-1640).

TOWER RECORDS CDs, tapes, LPs, housed in a dazzling 3-story space at 360 Newbury St., on the corner of Massachusetts Ave. (phone: 247-5900). A second *Tower* store is near Harvard at 95 Mt. Auburn St. (phone: 876-3377).

VICTORIAN BOUQUET LTD. Especially noteworthy for its spectacular flower arrangements and cordial, thoughtful staff. 53A Charles St. (phone: 367-6648).

VOSE GALLERIES Specializes in 18th-, 19th-, and early 20th-century American paintings. 238 Newbury St. (phone: 536-6176).

WATERFORD-WEDGWOOD A full line of the classic brands of Irish crystal and English china in a classy store. 288 Boylston St. (phone: 482-8886).

WATERSTONE'S BOOKSELLERS Housed in an ornate old theater building, with about 150,000 titles, this is one of the largest in the city. 181 Newbury St. (phone: 859-7300).

WENHAM CROSS Country-style antiques, featuring hand-painted furniture, wooden toys, and hooked rugs. 232 Newbury St. (phone: 236-0409).

WOMEN'S EDUCATIONAL AND INDUSTRIAL UNION Since 1877, the *WEIU* has been providing training and support for working women. Despite its age, the gift shop has a modern collection of housewares, children's clothes and toys, and knickknacks. There is an extensive needlework and crafts section, too. 356 Boylston St. (phone: 536-5651).

WORDS WORTH BOOKSTORE A bookworm and gift-giver's paradise packed with every hard- and softcover book you can imagine, all discounted 10%-30%. 30 Brattle St., Cambridge, near Harvard Sq. (phone: 354-5201).

SPORTS AND FITNESS

No doubt about it, Boston is one of the all-time great professional sports towns.

BASEBALL The *Red Sox* play at *Fenway Park*, 4 Yawkey Way. *Green Line*, Kenmore stop (phone: 267-8661).

BASKETBALL The *Celtics* play at *Boston Garden*, 150 Causeway St. *Green* and *Orange* lines, North Station stop (phone: 523-3030 or 523-6050).

BICYCLING Although a flimsy, two-wheeled vehicle is not the safest mode of city transportation, Bostonians have long loved cycling and refuse to give it up. The city, in response, has built bicycle paths that are safe and extremely popular. A good place to rent a mountain or touring bicycle is the *Community Bike Shop* (490 Tremont St.; phone: 542-8623), which offers 12-speed Nishiki and Jakara bikes for $15 a day or $5 an hour. (You'll need identification.) Bicycle tours in and beyond the city are conducted by *American Youth Hostels* (phone: 731-5430), the *Charles River Wheelmen* (phone: 625-0610), and the *Appalachian Mountain Club* (phone: 523-0636), among others. The following are two of the better routes for seeing Boston by bike. Paths are marked with the international symbol of a cyclist. You can pick up a map of local trails from local bike shops or from the

Department of Public Works (Transportation Building, 10 Park Plaza; phone: 973-8000).

BEST BIKE ROUTES

Greenbelt Bikeway This path originates at Boston Common and traces the entire length of Boston's celebrated Emerald Necklace, an 8-mile chain of parkland stretching from the Common to Franklin Park. Along the way, cyclists pass magnolia-lined Commonwealth Avenue mall; Kenmore Square; the Fens Park; the Arnold Arboretum with its 14,000 species of trees and shrubs, lilacs, rhododendrons, and magnolias; and finally, Franklin Park, where the *Franklin Park Zoo* is located (see *Other Special Places*). The trip, along with a stop for a picnic at the Arnold Arboretum, is a great way to spend a warm spring day.

Dr. Paul Dudley White Bikeway Named after the late President Eisenhower's personal physician, a heart surgeon and loyal biking enthusiast, this path begins along the Charles River Esplanade and stretches through sections of Boston, Cambridge, Newton, and Watertown Square. In Watertown, the path crosses the Charles River (it's actually more like a creek at this point), and heads back to Boston on the river's other side. The 18-mile round trip offers rich and varied scenery and only a modicum of interference from auto traffic (you walk your bike across a couple of intersections). There are several footbridges that span Storrow Drive, the most handy being the Fiedler Footbridge at the intersection of Arlington and Beacon Streets, near the Public Garden. This allows the cyclist to get from Back Bay to the Esplanade, while avoiding a harrowing encounter with six lanes of traffic.

BILLIARDS Some know it or its variations as pool or even snooker. Whatever the nomenclature, it is making a glorious comeback in Boston. The city's best-known place for billiards is *Jillian's Billiard Club* (145 Ipswich St.; phone: 437-0300), a staid pool hall near *Fenway Park* that is furnished like an English gentleman's library. Some think the *Boston Billiard Club* (126 Brookline Ave.; phone: 536-7665) is even classier. Both offer cocktail service, snacks, billiards, pool, snooker, darts, and backgammon.

FISHING *Boston Harbor Fishing* for fishing charters, clambakes, or evening cruises (619 E. Broadway, South Boston; phone: 268-2244); *Yankee Fishing Fleet* for charters April through November (75 Essex Ave., Gloucester; phone: 508-283-0313 or 800-942-5464); *Boston Sail* for deep-sea fishing excursions (Long Wharf; phone: 742-3316); or *Captain's Fishing Parties and Boat Livery,* half- and full-day charters (Plum Island Pier, Newburyport; phone: 508-465-7733). (Also see *Gone Fishing* in DIVERSIONS.)

FITNESS CENTERS *Fitcorp Fitness and Physical Therapy Center* has a track and workout equipment available (133 Federal St.; phone: 542-1010); there's also the *Boston Health and Swim Club* (1079 Commonwealth Ave., Brighton; phone: 254-1711; and 695 Atlantic Ave.; phone: 439-9600) and *Le Pli* (5 Bennett St., Charles Sq., Cambridge; phone: 547-4081). Many Boston hotels have fitness centers for guests. The *Boston Athletic Club* (653 Summer St.; phone: 269-4300) offers daily memberships if you show a local hotel room key.

FOOTBALL The *New England Patriots* play at *Sullivan Stadium*, Rte. 1, Foxboro (phone: 800-543-1776).

GOLF There's a city course in Hyde Park, where the Parks and Recreation Department offers golf instruction. Contact *George Wright Pro Shop* (420 West St., Hyde Park; phone: 361-8313 or 361-9679); you also can play or take lessons at the *Fresh Pond Golf Club* (691 Huron Ave., Cambridge; phone: 354-9130). (Also see *Great Golf Outside the City* in DIVERSIONS.)

HOCKEY The *Bruins* play at *Boston Garden*, 150 Causeway St. *Green* and *Orange* lines, North Station stop (phone: 227-3200).

JOGGING Run along the banks of the Charles River on Memorial (in Cambridge) or Storrow Drive (in Boston), or both. Many bridges over the river make loops of varying lengths possible.

RACING Greyhounds race at *Wonderland Park*, Revere (on the *Blue Line;* phone: 284-1300).

SAILING Befitting its history as a port city, Boston offers several options for visitors interested in skippering their own skiffs on the Charles, or serving as crew members on larger vessels in the harbor and beyond. Instruction is always available for those not sure of their skills. The following are several of Boston's best sailing experiences.

TAKING TO THE WATERS

Boston by Sail For the more seasoned skipper, *Boston by Sail* has 23-foot Sonars and 27-foot O'Day sailboats for tooling about the harbor at $20 to $30 an hour. You may take these out alone if you are a licensed sailor; otherwise a skilled captain will accompany you. Larger boats, from a 47-foot vessel to a 95-foot schooner that can ferry over 49 people around comfortably, are available for larger parties, tour groups, or business functions. The proprietors remain flexible: They offer tailor-made sunset and moonlight cruises, voyages up the Charles River, and trips to the Harbor Islands and ports of call on the North Shore. Located on Lewis Wharf near the *Marriott* hotel and the *New England Aquarium*. 66 Long Wharf (phone: 742-3313).

Boston Sailing Center Specializing in sailboat charters, this outfit will chart any one of a number of courses for tourists. For history buffs, there's the water tour of Boston's historic sites, including a close inspection of the

USS *Constitution;* for speed demons, they'll unfurl the spinnaker for some swift sailing far from shore; for families, there are picnic cruises to the Harbor Islands; for couples, sunset and moonlight cruises. Other "theme" sailing excursions are also available. The basic rate for the 23-foot Sonar is $50 per hour (minimum of 2 hours); trips on the 29-foot craft are $70 per hour. There is a wealth of other vessels in their fleet. The *Boston Sailing Center* is a sailboat broker and, therefore, has access to hundreds of sailboats and yachts that are moored on Boston Harbor. Lewis Wharf (phone: 227-4198).

Community Boating Thanks to *Community Boating Inc.,* visiting and local sailors alike can find themselves skimming along the Charles River at the helm of a 15-foot Mercury or 13-foot Laser sailboat. The city's most popular sailing organization, *Community Boating* aims to promote sailing as an activity that should be enjoyed by all — not just the rich. Though known for its season passes, 2- or 7-day *Community Boating* memberships are available ($40/$70) for out-of-towners. Brush up on your nomenclature and points of sail since, in order to get going, you may have to answer a question or two about the operation of your boat. Lessons are available. The boathouse is located on the Esplanade near the Fiedler Footbridge and the Charles Street *T* stop on the *Red Line.* 21 Embankment Rd., (phone: 523-1038).

NOTE Launched in 1973, the Harvey Gamage, a 95-foot schooner, is one of the most technologically advanced of all the windjammers. The two showers aboard are cold, but only a few windjammers have any at all. The ship is also unusual in welcoming children of any age among its 30 passengers. Special rates are available for senior citizens. Cruises take in the New England coast in summer, the Virgin Islands during the winter. Sailing instruction is provided. Booked by *Dirigo,* which also represents other vessels, such as the ketch *Angelique* (with a deck lounge equipped with a piano and a fireplace), the *Nathaniel Bowditch* (bring your own beer for a lobster and clam cookout), and tall ships. Information: *Dirigo Cruises,* 39 Waterside La., Clinton, CT 06413 (phone: 203-669-7068 or 800-845-5520).

SKIING There's cross-country skiing at Weston Ski Track on *Leo J. Martin* golf course (Park Rd., Weston; phone: 894-4903) and at *Lincoln Guide Service* (152 Lincoln Rd., Lincoln; phone: 259-9204). Lessons available at 10 AM, noon, and 2 PM on weekends. There are a number of small downhill skiing areas within a 2-hour drive of the city: *Blue Hills Ski Area* in Canton (phone: 828-5070); *Boston Hill* in North Andover (phone: 508-683-2734); *Wachusett Mountain Ski Area* in Princeton (phone: 508-464-2300); and *Nashoba Valley Ski Area* in Westford (phone: 692-3033).

TENNIS There are courts at the *Charles River Park Tennis Club* (35 Lomasney Way; phone: 742-8922). The Metropolitan District Commission (MDC) also operates a number of tennis courts throughout the city on a first-come, first-served basis (phone: 727-8865), with the following exception. The *Charlesbank Courts,* which include 2 unlit courts on the bank of the Charles River and 2 lighted courts on the southwestern section of Boston Common, are the only MDC courts that require a permit, which may be picked up a few days in advance; for more information, contact *MDC Lee Memorial Pool,* 20 Somerset St. (phone: 354-9523). *Hyde Park,* another cluster of MDC courts, has 6 tennis courts, 4 of which are lighted; for further details, contact the MDC. Unlit courts are open until dusk, lighted courts until 11 PM. For municipal courts, they are well maintained. (Also see *Top Tennis Outside the City* in DIVERSIONS.)

> **SOCCER SPECIAL** International soccer's premier event, the *FIFA World Cup,* will be hosted for the first time by the US this year. The 52 games of the quadrennial event, the world's largest single-sport competition, take place from June 17 through July 17 in nine venues, including *Sullivan Stadium* in Foxboro. The games in the Boston region are set for June 21, 23, 25, and 30, and July 5; a quarterfinal game is scheduled for July 9. Tickets are available in groups of five games; prices range from $140 to $355 per group. Tickets for individual games will be available in February. For further information, call *Sullivan Stadium* at 508-543-1776.

THEATER

Catch a Broadway show before it gets to Broadway. Trial runs often take place at the *Shubert Theater* (265 Tremont St.; phone: 426-4520), the *Colonial Theatre* (106 Boylston St.; phone: 426-9366), the *Wilbur Theater* (246 Tremont St.; phone: 423-4008), and the *Wang Center for the Performing Arts* (270 Tremont St.; phone: 423-3566). Or check out the *Charles Playhouse* (74 Warrenton St.; phone: 426-6912); this is a much smaller and often livelier place, hosting consistently interesting contemporary plays. The *New Theater* (755 Boylston St.; phone: 247-7388) features new works with provocative themes. The *Lyric Stage* (140 Clarendon St.; phone: 437-7172) performs first-time, experimental works — often satiric and political — with aplomb. The *American Repertory Theater* (64 Brattle St., Cambridge; phone: 547-8300), one of the East Coast's premier repertory companies, is based at Harvard's *Loeb Drama Center* and features an ever-changing bill of classic and new plays during the school year. In addition, there are dozens of smaller theater groups, including several affiliated with colleges, such as Boston University's *Huntington Theatre Company* (264 Huntington Ave., Back Bay; phone: 266-3913 or 266-0800). The *Boston Ballet Company* gives performances at the *Wang Center* (see above; call 695-6950 for ballet information). Tickets for theatrical and musical events can be purchased through the *Out of Town Ticket Agency* (in the center of Harvard Square, now on the mezzanine level of that subway station of the *Red Line;* phone: 492-1900); *TicketMaster* (phone: 720-3434); or *Bostix* (day of the play; *Faneuil Hall Marketplace;* phone: 723-5181). For information on performance schedules, check the local publications listed above. (Also see *Inside Boston's Theaters* in DIVERSIONS.)

CINEMA

Boston features an array of movie theaters that screen everything from first-run action/suspense movies to zillionth-run classics and foreign films. The *Boston Globe*'s Thursday "Calendar" section is an invaluable source for current attractions and reviews. Or for a complete listing of films that are showing in the area, times, and locations, call 333-FILM.

Several theaters specialize in showing eclectic, hard-to-find films; two of the best are *Nickelodeon Cinemas* (606 Commonwealth Ave.; phone: 424-1500), which features foreign films and other first-run movies that are not intended to be "box office hits"; and the beloved, old *Coolidge Corner Cinema* (290 Harvard St., Brookline; phone: 734-2500), which has been saved from the wrecking ball on several occasions and continues to feature its traditional fare of foreign, classic, and avant-garde treasures.

In Cambridge, the *Brattle* (40 Brattle St.; phone: 876-6837) features oldies and the avant-garde; and *Harvard Square* (10 Church St.; phone: 864-4580) often screens non-mainstream movies. The *Harvard Film Archive* at the university (24 Quincy St.; phone: 495-4700) also shows classics and foreign films. In a struggle to compete with multiplex cinemas, the grand old *Somerville Theater* (Davis Sq., Somerville; phone 625-5700) now hosts first-run foreign and repertory films, classic Disney animation festivals, and performances by local musicians.

MUSIC

Almost every evening, Bostonians can choose from among several classical and contemporary musical performances, ranging from the most delicate chamber music to the most ferocious alternative rock. The *Boston Symphony Orchestra,* usually under the baton of director Seiji Ozawa, performs at *Symphony Hall,* September through April (301 Massachusetts Ave.; phone: 266-1492; in summer, they're at the *Tanglewood Music Festival* in Lenox, Mass.) Selected members of the *Boston Symphony* make up the *Boston Pops Orchestra,* which performs less weighty orchestrations of popular music at *Symphony Hall* (301 Massachusetts Ave.; phone: 266-1492), April through July, and gives free outdoor concerts in the *Hatch Shell* on the Charles River Esplanade in June and July. Thanks to the pioneering work of two orchestras, Boston has been at the forefront of the early music revival. Both the *Handel and Haydn Society* (300 Massachusetts Ave.; phone: 266-3605) and *Boston Baroque* (PO Box 380190, Cambridge, MA 02238; phone: 641-1310) perform historically correct music on period instruments. The *Boston Lyric Opera* performs a full season of classical operas at the *Emerson Majestic Theater* (219 Tremont St.; phone: 248-8660). Several colleges and universities also offer classical concerts: Harvard's *Sanders Theater* (Kirkland and Quincy Sts., Cambridge; phone: 495-5595); MIT's *Kresge Auditorium*, in a peculiar building on the West Campus that has a curved roof resting on only three points (77 Massachusetts Ave., Cambridge; phone: 253-2826); and the *Boston University Concert Hall* (855 Commonwealth Ave.; phone: 353-3345). Soothing piano music can be found in the *Plaza* bar of the *Copley Plaza* hotel (138 St. James Ave.; phone: 267-5300) and energetic sing-alongs at *Diamond Jim's Piano Bar* at the *Lenox* hotel (710 Boylston St.; phone: 536-2200). For jazz, try the classy, 2-level *Nightstage* (823 Main St., Cambridge; phone: 497-8200); the bustling, intimate *Ryles* (Inman Sq., Cambridge; phone: 876-9330); the mixed scene at *Scullers Jazz Lounge* in the *Guest Quarters Suite* hotel (400 Soldiers Field Rd.; phone: 783-0090); and the super-elegant *Regattabar* (in the *Charles* hotel, Cambridge; phone: 864-1200), the premier jazz club in the area. Top-name blues and pop musicians play here, too.

The *Paradise* (967 Commonwealth Ave.; phone: 254-2053) is an intimate room that regularly books top-name rock musicians. The *Rathskeller,* a.k.a. "The Rat" (528 Commonwealth Ave.; phone: 536-2750), is a head-banging Boston institution (though many people would contend its patrons belong in institutions) that relishes its role as the scourge of Kenmore Square. You'll find an endless stream of such bands as *The Queers* or *Slaughter Shack* there, as well as nearby Boston University's "existential" crowd. For some of the finest Irish music this side of Dublin, go to the *Purple Shamrock* (1 Union St.; phone: 27-2060); the *Black Rose* (160 State St.; phone: 742-2286); or the *Green Briar* (Irish music on Monday nights; 304 Washington St., Brighton; phone: 789-4100), where the old Irish adage that "a silent mouth is music" is roundly forgotten. The *Tam O' Shanter* (1648 Beacon St., Brookline; phone: 277-0982), though it sounds Scottish, is actually an excellent venue for folk, blues, and the occasional jazz performance, as is the *Plough and Stars* (912 Massachusetts Ave., Cambridge; phone: 492-9653), where they pack them in cheek-to-jowl and serve some of the finest ales anywhere in this fair city. For folk music in a coffeehouse atmosphere, visit *Passim* (47 Palmer St., Cambridge; phone: 492-7679), and for bluegrass, drop in at *Harpers Ferry* (158 Brighton Ave.; phone: 254-9734). The *Western Front* (343 Western Ave., Cambridge; phone: 492-7772) is Boston's focal point for reggae music. Once past the cover charge, you'll think you're in Kingston, Jamaica.

NIGHTCLUBS AND NIGHTLIFE

A sophisticated and well-heeled crowd gathers nightly in the elegant *Plaza* bar (*Copley Plaza* hotel; phone: 267-5300) or at the *Palm Court* at

Cricket's (101 *Faneuil Hall Marketplace;* phone: 720-5570). Boston has several fabulous rooms with views where you can relax with a drink and watch the sun set over the city. The most elegant is the *Bay Tower Room* on the 33rd floor of the 60 State Street tower, near *Faneuil Hall.* Enjoy free hors d'oeuvres, live music on weekends, and a dizzying view of the city's waterfront through 3-story-high windows (phone: 723-1666). For a 360° view, visit the revolving restaurant on top of the *Hyatt Regency Cambridge* (575 Memorial Dr., Cambridge; phone: 492-1234) or the *Top of the Hub* restaurant on the 52nd floor of the Prudential tower (800 Boylston St.; phone: 536-1775), which has picture windows on all four sides. If dancing cheek to cheek is your passion, try *Roxy,* the sumptuous nightclub where the *White Heat Swing Orchestra* plays big-band hits on weekend nights (279 Tremont St.; phone: 227-7699). *The Last Hurrah,* downstairs at the *Omni Parker House,* also has live jazz bands on weekends, with no cover charge (60 School St.; phone: 227-8600). Thursday through Saturday nights, there's dancing to pop music at *Club Nicole,* a spot in the *Back Bay Hilton* reminiscent of the old *Stork Club* in New York (Dalton and Belvedere Sts.; phone: 236-1100). Among the trendiest clubs are *Avalon* (15 Lansdowne St.; phone: 262-2424); *Alley Cat* (1 Boylston Pl.; phone: 457-6200); *Venus de Milo* (11 Lansdowne St.; phone: 421-9595); *Zanzibar* (1 Boylston Pl., off Boylston St.; phone: 451-1955); and the *Harbor Club* (145 Northern Ave.; phone: 426-8600). A rather disheartening sight is the *Bull and Finch* pub of television's "Cheers" fame. Only the façade of this tourist trap (84 Beacon St.; phone: 227-9605) is used for the show; the bar's interior is filled with enough kitsch to send "Cheers" fans running out the door.

COMEDY CLUBS It doesn't take long to realize that everybody in Boston is a comedian/comedienne — or wants to be. Those who have decided to turn professional can be found at one of the area's many comedy clubs. Big-name comics can be found at *Catch A Rising Star* (30 JFK St., Cambridge; phone: 661-9887); *Stitches Comedy Club* (835 Beacon St.; phone: 424-6995); and *Nick's Comedy Club* (100 Warrenton St.; phone: 482-0930). Other laughable joints are *Duck Soup,* which in its new space in *Faneuil Hall Rotunda* is the city's largest comedy club (phone: 248-9700); *Dick Doherty's Comedy Club* at *Remington's Eating & Drinking Exchange* (124 Boylston St.; phone: 337-6920); and the *Comedy Connection* in the *Charles Playhouse* (76 Warrenton St.; phone: 426-6339). Call for a schedule of present and upcoming acts.

Best in Town

CHECKING IN

Boston has some fine, old, gracious hotels with the history and charm you'd expect to find in this dignified New England capital. But Boston experienced a hotel building boom in the 1980s, and there are now many modern places offering standard contemporary accoutrements. Expect to pay $150 or more for a double room at those places noted as expensive; between $100 and $150 for those in the moderate category; and under $100 in places listed as inexpensive. Many of these hotels offer special weekend packages for relatively low rates. Reservations always are required, so write or call well in advance. For B&B accommodations, contact *Bed & Breakfast Associates of Bay Colony* (PO Box 166, Babson Park, Boston, MA 02157; phone: 449-5302); *Greater Boston Hospitality* (Box 1142, Brookline, MA 02146; phone: 277-5430); *Bed and Breakfast Cambridge & Greater Boston* (Box 665, Cambridge, MA 02140; phone: 576-1492); *Host Homes of Boston* (Box 117, Boston MA 02168; phone: 244-1308); *New England Bed and Breakfast, Inc.* (1753 Massachusetts Ave., Cambridge, MA 02138; phone: 498-9819); *Bed & Breakfast Agency of Boston* (47 Commercial Wharf, Boston, MA 02110; phone: 720-3540); or write to the Massachusetts Division of Tourism (100 Cambridge St., 13th Floor, Boston, MA 02202) for its *Spirit of Massachusetts Bed & Breakfast Guide.* Most of Boston's major hotels have complete facilities for the business traveler. Those hotels listed below as having "business services" usually offer such conveniences as meeting rooms, photocopiers, computers, translation services, and express checkout, among others. Call the hotel for additional information. All telephone numbers are in the 617 area code unless otherwise indicated.

For an unforgettable experience in Boston, we begin with our favorites, followed by our recommendations of cost and quality choices of accommodations, listed by price category.

GRAND HOTELS

Boston Harbor This distinctive $193-million, 16-story property, one of Boston's best hostelries, offers the most dramatic entry to the Hub. After landing at Boston's Logan Airport, the visitor is whisked by water taxi across Boston Harbor to dock within an anchor's throw of the hotel at Rowes Wharf, with its enormous 8-story golden arch that opens onto Atlantic Avenue and Boston's downtown area. The shopping district, the North End, and the *Faneuil Hall Marketplace* are all within walking distance. The property's 230 spacious guestrooms (some with balconies) have views of either the city or the harbor. Foster's Rotunda, a copper-domed observatory atop the arch, boasts views that are absolutely mesmerizing. Amenities include a spa, saunas, and a 60-foot indoor pool. There's also the glass-enclosed *Harborview Lounge,* a casual, outdoor café (in summer), and the elegant, paneled *Rowes Wharf* bar and restaurant, whose specialty is seafood prepared in unusual ways. For the business traveler, there is a full-service business center. 70 Rowes Wharf (phone: 439-7000 or 800-752-7077; fax: 330-9450; telex: 920027).

Copley Plaza This historic bowfront property, part of Copley Square's triangle of turn-of-the-century elegance, is on everybody's short list of great Boston hotels. *Wyndham Hotels & Resorts* recently assumed management of the property following the completion of a $30-million refurbishment. Although it has 373 splendid guestrooms, its public areas are what make this a truly great hotel. Corporate Boston fills the seats of the *Plaza* bar, which has been compared to a British officer's club in India. Adjacent to the bar is the airy tea court, which is painted in the precise Victorian technique of photographic realism, creating the illusion that you're outdoors. There are two restaurants: the elegant *Plaza* dining room has a French menu (see *Eating Out*), and *Copley's* serves excellent American/New England fare in richly decorated Victorian-style rooms. The multilingual staff is refined and helpful. Business services. 138 St. James Ave., Copley Sq. (phone: 267-5300 or 800-223-7434; fax: 267-7668).

Four Seasons With a regiment of 566 employees, service is where this 8-year-old refurbished hotel shines. Which is not to say that the place is lacking in ambience. On the contrary: The 288 guestrooms, each with a bar and two to three phones, resemble a gracious Beacon Hill residence, with cherry furniture, floral prints, and marble vanities. This is one of only two Boston hotels that overlook the Public Garden; half the guestrooms enjoy leafy (or snow-swept) garden views. The hotel's formal restaurant, *Aujourd'hui,* features an American-continental menu — the creation of a talented young chef, Michael Kornick (see *Eating Out*). The more informal *Bristol Lounge* offers live entertainment most nights and a Viennese dessert buffet Friday and Saturday nights from 9 PM to midnight. The location is convenient as well as attractive: Most of the city's popular sites are within walking distance. The full-service health club includes a pool, sauna, and whirlpool baths. Children get their own bathrobes, board games, Nintendo, milk and cookies, and food for the Public Garden ducks. Business services. 200 Boylston St. (phone: 338-4400 or 800-332-3442; fax: 423-0154; telex: 853349).

Meridien The stylish French-owned hotel chain has created a small and delightful Gallic world in this splendid 1922 Renaissance Revival structure in downtown's Post Office Square. The 326 guestrooms, each with a mini-bar and a small sitting area with a writing desk, are decorated in 150 different styles, from traditional to fin de siècle to chic. The elegant *Julien* restaurant offers a classical Gallic-inspired menu (see *Eating Out*) — the creation of consulting chef Marc Heaberlin of the three-Michelin-star *L'Auberge de L'Ill* in Alsace. Also on the premises is *Café Fleuri,* a French bistro housed in a leafy 6-story atrium. The hotel hosts a delectable all-you-can-eat buffet of chocolate desserts on Saturday afternoons from 2:30 to 5:30 PM; Sunday brunch is wonderful here as well. *La Terrasse,* an informal outdoor café, serves breakfast, lunch, and cocktails. There's also a health club, an indoor pool, lobby shops, 24-hour room service, and a concierge.

Business services. 250 Franklin St., Post Office Sq. (phone: 451-1900 or 800-453-4300).

Omni Parker House When it opened in 1855, the *Parker House* became a Boston institution almost immediately. It was only within its elegant rooms that Charles Dickens would dwell during his heavily publicized Boston visits. Though it is now operating under the corporate name of *Omni Parker House,* a stay here still affords a close encounter with Boston's illustrious history. The 540 rooms are richly decorated with dark wood and tapestries, and the building, located on the historic Freedom Trail, is within walking distance of the King's Chapel, the Park Street Church, Beacon Hill, Boston Common, and the *Faneuil Hall Marketplace.* Boston cream pie and Parker House rolls were born at *Parker's,* the hotel's main restaurant (which still features both on its contemporary continental menu). The restaurant was once the meeting place of the *Saturday Club,* a 19th-century literary association whose membership rolls included such luminaries as Longfellow, Emerson, and Oliver Wendell Holmes. Business services. 60 School St. (phone: 227-8600 or 800-THE-OMNI; fax: 742-5729).

Ritz-Carlton This grande dame of Boston hotels has reigned since 1927. Strategically located near most of Newbury and Boylston Streets' smart shops, it sits — very properly — overlooking the Public Garden. The windows on the north side of the building offer views of the magnolia-lined Commonwealth Avenue mall. All 278 guestrooms are traditionally furnished and decorated with 17th- to 19th-century paintings. (The rooms in the hotel's older section are the fanciest.) Afternoon tea in the upstairs lounge is a Boston institution (see *Quintessential Boston* in DIVERSIONS). The upstairs formal dining room is large and lovely, serving excellent continental fare (see *Eating Out*), and the serene *Ritz* bar makes the best martini in town. Both the dining room and the bar look out over the Public Garden. Legions of staff members step on each other's toes to serve you. Business services. 15 Arlington St. (phone: 536-5700 or 800-241-3333; fax: 536-1335; telex: 940591).

EXPENSIVE

Back Bay Hilton The rooms in this 26-story hostelry, wisely located near the *Hynes Convention Center* and Prudential Center, are known for their peace and quiet. Each room is soundproofed; each floor contains only 16 rooms; and the bay windows actually open. *Fitcorp,* a health club with fitness machines and a swimming pool, is available to guests. *Club Nicole,* a look-alike of New York City's legendary *Stork Club,* plays popular dance music Thursday through Saturday nights. Children stay free in their parents' rooms. Some moderately priced rooms are available. Business services. Dalton and Belvedere Sts. (phone: 236-1100 or 800-874-0663; fax: 267-8893).

Bostonian Understated and small (152 rooms), this beautifully appointed hotel is across from the shopping and entertainment activities of *Faneuil Hall Marketplace* and just 2 blocks from the North End and the revitalized waterfront. Its glass-enclosed, rooftop *Seasons* restaurant — which serves fine continental fare — discreetly overlooks the colorful bustle below. Business services. North and Blackstone Sts. at *Faneuil Hall Marketplace* (phone: 523-3600 or 800-343-0922; fax: 523-2454; telex: 948159).

Charles Between the Charles River and Harvard Square, this handsome red brick building is the centerpiece of the *Charles Square* complex. The 296 rooms are well decorated, and those on the 10th floor have teleconferencing and telecommunications facilities. Relaxation can be sedentary in the pleasant *Bennett Street Café* or elegant *Rarities* restaurant (see *Eating Out*), or more active at the lavish *Le Pli* health spa, complete with an indoor pool. The *Regattabar* features live jazz by top names Tuesday through Saturday nights. Business services. One Bennett St., Cambridge (phone: 864-1200 or 800-882-1818; fax: 864-5715).

Colonnade This distinguished property offers 288 large rooms, a (seasonal) rooftop pool, the classy *Promenade Café,* and *Zachary's,* a bar that features jazz on weekend nights. The hotel is near the Prudential Center, Copley Square, and Newbury Street. Business services. 120 Huntington Ave. (phone: 424-7000 or 800-962-3030; fax: 424-1717; telex: 940565).

Guest Quarters Suite A distinctive property on the Charles River with 10 conventional guestrooms and 310 luxurious suites, and *Scullers Grille* restaurant. Complimentary breakfast is served on weekends. *Scullers Jazz Lounge,* one of the city's premier jazz venues, showcases both national and local talent. Health club facilities include a pool, whirlpool bath, sauna, and exercise machines. Business services. 400 Soldiers Field Rd., at the Cambridge/Allston exit of I-90, the Massachusetts Turnpike (phone: 783-0090 or 800-424-2900; fax: 783-0897).

Hyatt Regency, Cambridge Some 469 rooms surround an atrium with fountains, greenery, and glass-walled elevators. The revolving rooftop restaurant offers a spectacular view of Boston, especially at sunset. Health club facilities are complemented by an indoor pool, sauna, whirlpool bath, and steamroom. Business services. On the Charles River, near MIT and Harvard (not easily accessible by public transportation). 575 Memorial Dr., Cambridge (phone: 492-1234 or 800-233-1234; fax: 491-6906; telex: 921409).

Lafayette Although the ambitious *Lafayette Place* complex has sunk to dismal lows, the hotel within maintains classic European standards of elegance and service. The 497 beautifully appointed rooms are grouped around four atriums. As befits a member of the Swissôtel group, one dining room is called the *Café Suisse;* for dinner, the *Lobby Lounge* serves informal

American fare. A lap pool, sun terrace, and saunas are available. Business services. 1 Ave. de Lafayette (phone: 451-2600 or 800-621-9200; fax: 451-21989; telex: 853840).

Lenox Built in 1900 and modeled after New York City's *Waldorf-Astoria,* this property's 222 guestrooms have high ceilings and rocking chairs, and each is decorated in one of four styles — French provincial, two types of colonial, and Oriental (the corner rooms have fireplaces). The lobby is handsomely decorated in blue with gold trim and a fireplace — always blazing in the winter — that evokes the feel of a country inn. *Diamond Jim's Piano Bar* features sing-alongs starring musically talented waiters and waitresses. There also are 2 restaurants — the casual *Lenox Pub* and the more formal *Lenox Grill.* Business services. 710 Boylston St. (phone: 536-5300).

Logan Airport Hilton Just 10 minutes from downtown Boston, and the only hotel located at Logan Airport (luckily the rooms are soundproofed), it has all the necessary facilities, including a restaurant, a lounge, an outdoor pool, and a health club. There's free limousine service to your airline. Business services. 75 Service Rd., E. Boston (phone: 569-9300; fax: 569-3981).

Marriott, Cambridge The fifth Marriott in Greater Boston is in the heart of the Kendall Square construction boom near MIT. This understated yet posh 431-room property features a comfortable restaurant and lounge, an indoor pool, and a health club with a whirlpool bath and saunas. Business services. 2 Cambridge Center (phone: 494-6600 or 800-228-9290; fax: 494-6600).

Marriott, Copley Place This 1,147-room giant is a focal point of the *Copley Place* development. Among its premium facilities are 3 restaurants, 3 bars, and the largest ballroom and most expansive exhibition area in any Boston hotel. For relaxation, there's an indoor pool, health club, and gameroom. Business services. 110 Huntington Ave. (phone: 236-5800 or 800-228-9290; fax: 236-9378; telex: 6712126).

Marriott, Long Wharf A striking 5-story atrium is the centerpiece of this big, downtown property (412 rooms) at the foot of State Street. The *Harbor Terrace Sea Grille* requires a jacket and tie; the more casual *Rachel's Lounge* provides taped contemporary music for dancing nightly. A ballroom, indoor-outdoor pool, and health club offer diversions. Business services. 296 State St. (phone: 227-0800 or 800-228-9290; fax: 227-2867).

Park Plaza This venerable establishment is located just south of the Public Garden and is between Back Bay and the theater district. The lobby is large and bustling and the rooms are spacious. *Legal Sea Foods,* with good seafood (see *Eating Out*), and *Café Rouge,* with respectable American dishes, are here. Business services. One Park Plaza at Arlington St. (phone: 426-2000 or 800-225-2008; fax: 426-5545; telex: 940107).

Royal Sonesta This flagship of the Sonesta chain boasts 400 tastefully decorated rooms and 5 eye-catching suites, along with an outpost of *Davio's* (see *Eating Out*), one of the area's best northern Italian restaurants. There's also a fully outfitted health club with a pool. Business services. 5 Cambridge Pkwy. (near Kendall Sq.), Cambridge (phone: 491-3600 or 800-SONESTA; fax: 661-5956).

Sheraton Boston A huge, 1,252-room modern hotel in the Prudential Center, surrounded by fine places to shop. Its 3 restaurants, 2 cocktail lounges, and year-round pool and health club provide plenty of diversion. Business services. 39 Dalton St., Prudential Center (phone: 236-2000 or 800-325-3535; fax: 236-1702; telex: 940034).

Sheraton Commander A comfortable 176-room hotel directly on the Cambridge Common, within walking distance of Harvard University and Harvard Square, this is where many visiting scholars stay. The lobby is formal and elegant, with gold trim and a large chandelier. There's a fitness room and sun deck with lovely views of Cambridge. Business services. 16 Garden St., Cambridge (phone: 547-4800 or 800-325-3535; fax: 868-8322).

Westin, Copley Place This opulent 36-story, 804-room property is one of two hotels in burgeoning *Copley Place,* a $500-million development adjacent to Copley Square. Its *Turner Fisheries* restaurant serves award-winning clam chowder in a town renowned for its chowder. There's also a fully outfitted health club with a pool, saunas, and masseuse. Business services. 10 Huntington Ave. (phone: 262-9600 or 800-228-3000; fax: 451-2750).

MODERATE

Eliot Partially residential, this all-suite Back Bay establishment was built in 1925 as the nearby *Harvard Club*'s guest facilities. The elegant lobby and all the rooms shine in a classic European manner; each room boasts a marble bath, antique furnishings, and French doors between rooms. If you succeed in getting a guestroom away from bustling Commonwealth Avenue, it can be one of the best deals in town. Amenities include continental breakfast and mini-bars. Business services. There is a popular bar of the same name next door that is not part of the hotel. 370 Commonwealth Ave. (phone: 267-1607 or 800-44-ELIOT; fax: 536-9114).

57 Park Plaza Howard Johnson's They're pretty much the same everywhere. This one offers 353 rooms, free parking, a year-round pool, and a location convenient to downtown. Business services. 200 Stuart St. (phone: 482-1800 or 800-654-2000; fax: 451-2750).

Holiday Inn–Boston Government Center In Boston's old West End, convenient to Beacon Hill, the Freedom Trail, *Faneuil Hall Marketplace,* and the Massachusetts General Hospital medical complex, this 15-story, familiar replica of the national chain offers 301 guestrooms (including some on a deluxe Executive Level), an outdoor pool, 2 restaurants (notably, the *James Michael*), and a top-floor lounge. A movie theater is next door. All rooms are air conditioned and have cable TV. 5 Blossom St. (phone: 742-7630 or 800-HOLIDAY; fax: 742-4192).

Howard Johnson's Cambridge On the Charles River 10 minutes from downtown Boston, this modern, 205-room facility is a few minutes' drive from both Harvard and MIT and is popular with tour groups and parents visiting their student offspring. It's not easily accessible by public transportation. A few rooms have balconies, and all have good views. There's a pool and free parking. Business services. 777 Memorial Dr. (phone: 492-7777 or 800-654-2000; fax: 492-7777, ext. 1799).

Inn at Harvard This post-modern building juts into an intersection near Harvard Square, and its style echoes that of the Georgian and Federal brick dormitories that surround it. With 113 rooms and a central atrium, it has a homey, distinctly collegiate feel. Each room is hung with replicas of art from Harvard's museums. Although it was built by the university to host its many visitors, the inn is also open to the public. Updated New England–style food is served in the atrium for breakfast and dinner. Business services. 1201 Massachusetts Ave., Cambridge (phone: 491-2222; fax: 496-5020).

Newbury A brick and brownstone townhouse that has been converted into an urban bed and breakfast establishment. Its location — in the heart of Back Bay, on a street of boutiques, cafés, and galleries — is perfect for city-philes who prefer country living. The 15 rooms are decorated in a simple, 19th-century style. A continental breakfast is served in the parlor and on the streetside patio in the summertime. 261 Newbury St. (phone: 437-7666).

Tremont House Set in the heart of Boston's theater district, this 281-room property was built as the national headquarters of the *Elks Club* in 1925. The resplendent lobby features a marble staircase, a mammoth crystal chandelier, and lots of gold leaf. There are 2 nightclubs — the *Roxy* offers big band and 1940s music, and the *Juke Box* has a 1950s and 1960s theme — and an already famous eatery, the *Stage Deli*. The double rooms have queen-size beds. Business services. 275 Tremont St. (phone: 426-1400 or 800-228-5151; fax: 482-6730).

267 Commonwealth A stay in this 9-room urban inn in the middle of Boston's Back Bay can be a memorable experience. Built in an 1880 townhouse, it was restored several years back (by Bob Vila, former host of the "This Old House" series on public television). The suites, all of which include kitchens, are graced with working fireplaces and gorgeous woodwork. The helpful staff provides guests with a variety of personal services, from dry cleaning to tour arrangements. Even if you don't stay here, you may want to incorporate this place into your tour of the Victorian buildings of the Back Bay (see *Walk 3: Back Bay* in DIRECTIONS). No credit cards accepted. 267 Commonwealth Ave. (phone: 267-6776).

INEXPENSIVE

Chandler Inn Modest and comfortable, conveniently located between Copley and Park Squares, near *Copley Place,* it has 56 rooms and provides a complimentary continental breakfast in the lobby. 26 Chandler St. at Berkeley St. (phone: 482-3450 or 800-842-3450).

Howard Johnson's Fenway A perfect location for *Fenway Park,* the *Museum of Fine Arts, Isabella Stewart Gardner Museum,* and the Prudential Center. There is a restaurant, lounge, air conditioning, outdoor pool, valet service, bellhops, and a multilingual staff. 1271 Boylston St. (phone: 267-8300; fax: 267-8300, ext. 151).

Howard Johnson's Kenmore Square Ideally suited near Boston University, this one features a restaurant, 2 lounges, an indoor rooftop swimming pool, air conditioning, valet service, and free parking. Business services. 575 Commonwealth Ave. (phone: 267-3100; fax: 267-3100, ext. 40).

Midtown In Back Bay, across the street from the Christian Science Center and near the Prudential Center. This low-rise property, flanked by rather ritzier lodgings on either side, is a darling of many tour groups. All rooms feature cable TV and air conditioning. 220 Huntington Ave. (phone: 262-1000 or 800-343-1177; fax: 262-8739).

Ramada Inn/Airport Conveniently located just over a mile from Logan Airport. There is a pub, a restaurant, air conditioning, a glass-enclosed swimming pool, health facilities with sauna, and free shuttle to the airport. Business services. 225 McClellan Hwy. (phone: 569-5250 or 800-228-2323; fax: 569-5159).

EATING OUT

Boston doesn't have a reputation as a culinary capital, but the 1980s brought a wealth of sophisticated restaurants — both expensive and moderately priced — opened by talented young chefs, many of whom actively sought to develop a new New England–style cuisine. Bostonian's appetites and culinary standards rose to the occasion, and the city now supports a vital restaurant community. Visitors have their pick of many wonderful dining spots. Expect to pay $100 or more for two at one of the places we've noted as expensive; between $50 and $100, moderate; and $50 or under, inexpensive. Prices do not include drinks, wine, or tips. All telephone numbers are in the 617 area code unless otherwise indicated.

For an unforgettable dining experience, we begin with our culinary favorites, followed by our recommendations of cost and quality choices listed by price category.

INCREDIBLE EDIBLES

Biba Owner Lydia Shire inspires intense feelings among foodies. Most rave; some think she tries too hard. But all keep coming back to see what Lydia will do next. The surprises start with the six-part menu: Instead of the typical divisions of appetizer, entrée, and dessert, here you'll find meat, fish, legumina (salads and vegetables), starch, sweets, and offal (sweetbreads and other animal parts, such as tongue and kidneys, prepared in a variety of tasty ways). Other entrées are less esoteric, drawing on the spices and flavors of many cultures. The kitchen makes good use of its tandoori and wood-burning ovens, so you're sure to find Indian-spiced viands and tasty grilled specials. The street-level bar, with its light menu, has become the place to see and be seen. The striking photos of exotic lands that grace its walls were taken by Shire on her many travels. The decor throughout — bold geometric patterns in burnt reds and golds — is the handiwork of noted designer Adam Tihany. 272 Boylston St. (phone: 426-7878).

L'Espalier Time-tested European cooking techniques with fresh New England ingredients characterize the fare at this polished Back Bay restaurant. The three-course meals are prix fixe (and a bit expensive). Among devotees' favorites are the salad of Maine lobster with corn fritters, tempura soft-shelled crab, grilled Atlantic salmon, morels and minted peas, and maple cheesecake. During the weekdays, a sampler menu is available. Chef Frank McClelland now features simpler dishes and larger portions; but he has not tampered with the impressive 150-item wine list. Set in a restored 19th-century townhouse, this elegant eatery has three lovely dining rooms: The salon and the parlor, both on the first floor, are light and airy thanks to their large windows; the library, on the second floor, has a clubby atmosphere, enhanced by deep peach walls and lots of mahogany. Each of the dining rooms has a marble fireplace and dazzling displays of flowers. 30 Gloucester St. (phone: 262-3023).

Hamersley's Bistro A bustling little place in the chic South End, it offers all the atmosphere and inexpensive delights of a French country bistro. A favorite is the roast chicken (marinated in garlic, lemon, and parsley) and old-fashioned mashed potatoes. Also featured are veal chops, bouillabaisse, and, as an appetizer, grilled shiitake mushrooms with garlic on toast. The extensive wine list is prepared and explained by one of the best stewards in town, and you can order excellent wine by the glass. The main dining room has a window on the kitchen; the redhead in a red baseball cap working over the grill is none other than proprietor Gordon Hamersley. On Sunday nights, he hands the kitchen over to his sous-chef. Prices drop slightly and the experimental factor rises. But you're much more likely to taste a rising star than a mistake: The last sous-chef, Jody Adams, is now getting rave reviews as the head chef at *Michela's* restaurant (below). 578 Tremont St. (phone: 267-6068).

Jasper's Owner/chef Jasper White attracts local seafood aficionados by featuring Yankee classics with a twist including an elegant version of a New England boiled dinner with johnnycakes and caviar, pan-roasted lobster with chervil, and a mixed grill of marinated quail and duck sausage. But the menu changes often to take advantage of local produce and seafood, so you're likely to find other surprises. In deference to the economic climate, Jasper lowered his prices a few years back; now, two people can enjoy an excellent meal here for under $100 (including wine). *Jasper's* has three intimate dining areas, one with booths. The decor, with its exposed brick, red lacquer chairs, and blown-glass sculptures, shows the same artful blend of rusticity and elegance as the menu. 240 Commercial St. (phone: 523-1126).

Locke-Ober Café An authentic Boston institution. Tucked into an unassuming side street within sight of *Filene's Basement,* this restaurant has more mahogany, Victorian stained glass, and blue serge suits than you can shake a croquet mallet at. About the only thing that has changed since the restaurant opened in 1875 is that women are now allowed in the *Men's Grill.* This Brahmin stronghold has probably hosted more business deals and political arrangements than most of the office towers in the nearby financial district. The menu seems to be immune from change, still heavy on seafood dishes such as lobster bisque, baked oysters, and such traditional dishes as steak tartare and Indian pudding. The gray-haired staff, in black ties and long white aprons, is almost as venerable as the restaurant itself. On the wall behind the dark-mahogany L-shaped bar is a painting of a reclining nude who is draped in black when Harvard loses to Yale. 3 Winter Pl. (phone: 542-1340).

EXPENSIVE

Anago Bistro An understated, tranquil space (formerly *798 Main Street*) enlivened by bouquets of fresh flowers, it serves some of the city's best continental fare from a menu that changes constantly. Specialties include crab and scallop casserole, braised venison, maple barbecued chicken, and wild mushroom stew. Closed Sundays and Mondays. Reservations advised. Major credit cards accepted. 798 Main St., Kendall Sq., Cambridge (phone: 492-9500 or 876-8444).

Anthony's Pier 4 Sometimes overrun with tourists, this Boston institution has a dramatic location on the harbor, plus a commodious waterfront deck where you can have drinks and enjoy the view while you wait for your table. Good seafood, generous servings. Open daily. Reservations advised. Major credit cards accepted. 140 Northern Ave. (phone: 423-6363).

Aujourd'hui The lovely, second-story centerpiece of the *Four Seasons,* this hotel dining room has few peers for ambience, food, or wine. The American-cum-continental menu, which changes seasonally, features appetizing "alternative cuisine" specials that are both good and good for you. Excellent service. Open daily, 8 AM to 10 PM. Reservations advised. Major credit cards accepted. 200 Boylston St. (phone: 451-1392).

Bay Tower Room Featuring a breathtaking view of Boston Harbor from 33 stories up, this restfully elegant dining room is the perfect setting for special-occasion suppers and banquets. The American and continental specialties change seasonally. Piano music is featured during early evening hours, with a live combo taking over later on Fridays and Saturdays. Open Mondays through Saturdays, 5:30 to 10 or 11 PM; open on Sundays for special functions. Reservations necessary. Major credit cards accepted. 60 State St. (phone: 723-1666).

Le Bocage Some of the most consistently delectable French food available in New England is served in this elegant establishment, located in a suburb west of Boston. Both Gallic regional and classic entrées grace the menu, which changes to suit the season. A bright, efficient staff and a fine wine cellar add to the pleasurable dining. Closed Sundays. Reservations advised. Major credit cards accepted. 72 Bigelow Ave., Watertown (phone: 923-1210).

Café Budapest Decorated in the lavish Eastern European tradition, and renowned for fine continental and Hungarian cooking. This is a wonderful place to linger over superb strudel and some of the best coffee anywhere. Open daily. Reservations advised. Major credit cards accepted. 90 Exeter St. (phone: 266-1979).

Chez Nous Sophisticated French fare is served in a luxurious, yet intimate, setting. The service is truly accommodating and, in the tradition of quiet, elegant establishments, nearly invisible. Daily fresh fish, rack of lamb Provençal, beef tenderloin spiced with thyme and port, and roast duck garnished with green peppercorns and cognac are all menu standouts. Closed Sundays. Reservations advised. Major credit cards accepted. 147 Huron Ave., Cambridge (phone: 864-6670).

Davide Though on the edge of the North End, it's far from the typical neighborhood red-checked tablecloth and red sauce place. Specialties include rack of lamb *valdostana,* a lightly breaded veal chop stuffed with prosciutto and fontina cheese, and pasta, which is hand-rolled by Davide himself. Open daily for dinner and weekdays for lunch. Reservations advised. Major credit cards accepted. 326 Commercial Ave. (phone: 227-5745).

Davio's This northern Italian eatery has developed into a local chain. Regional and continental entrées are consistently well prepared, highlighted by veal chops, homemade pasta, and "upscale" pizza combinations. Good wines, good service, elegant surroundings. Open daily. Reservations advised. Major credit cards accepted. Three locations: 269 Newbury St. (phone: 262-4810); 204 Washington St. in Brookline Village (phone: 738-4810); and in the *Royal Sonesta,* 5 Cambridge Pkwy., Cambridge (phone: 661-4810).

Hampshire House Thoroughly evocative of 19th-century Boston is this former mansion-turned-tavern, restaurant — and tourist trap. The *Oak Room Lounge* is a paneled, clubby café-bar with moose heads on the wall and a fire blazing in the winter. It offers a simple continental menu and a range of lighter fare. In the eminently Victorian dining room overlooking the Public Garden, more elegant American offerings, such as New York strip steaks and chicken Divan, are served. The *Bull & Finch* pub, a boisterous meeting, eating, and drinking place that was the inspiration for the television series "Cheers," is still jam-packed with tourists despite an expansion from its basement locale into part of the first floor. Open daily. Reservations necessary. Major credit cards accepted. 84 Beacon St. (phone: 227-9600).

Harvest A colorful dining room, lively bar, café, and (weather permitting) a secluded outdoor patio, all tucked into a back corner of the former Design Research complex in Harvard Square. The dining room menu features nicely executed international dishes in its nouvelle cuisine repertoire as well as fine salads, wines, and desserts. The café serves bistro fare. Open daily. Reservations advised. Major credit cards accepted. 44 Brattle St., Cambridge (phone: 492-1115).

Julien The grandeur of the decor, with its high ceilings, gilded walls, and graceful Queen Anne chairs, creates a wonderful dining atmosphere. Situated in the old Members Court of the former Federal Reserve Bank Building (now the *Meridien* hotel), this dining spot produces Alsatian-inspired creations such as homemade terrine of foie gras, a ragout of sea scallops and sea urchins, and breast of squab with cabbage and truffles, under the attentive eye of consulting chef Marc Heaberlin, whose *L'Auberge de L'Ill* in Alsace has earned three Michelin stars. Open daily. Reservations advised. Major credit cards accepted. 250 Franklin St. (phone: 451-1900).

Maison Robert Among the finest French restaurants in the city, with first-rate food, drink, ambience, and service. Owner-chef Lucien Robert, one of the founding fathers of Boston's culinary revolution, has taught many of the city's chefs and continues to prepare unusual sauces for his fish, fowl, and meat dishes. Two dining areas, *Ben's Café* downstairs (on the patio in summer) and the elegant *Bonhomme Richard* upstairs, are open for lunch and dinner. Closed Sundays. Reservations necessary. Major credit cards accepted. 45 School St., in the Old City Hall (phone: 227-3370).

Marais The latest hot spot in Boston's theater district, it resembles an intimate Paris bistro from the 1920s, with dark wood furniture, yellow walls, and authentic posters from the period. The menu features a wide array of Mediterranean dishes. Open for dinner only. Closed Sundays. Reservations advised. Major credit cards accepted. 116 Boylston St. (phone: 482-7799).

Mr. Leung's Linen napery, artful flower arrangements, lavish service, and a subdued, elegant setting dispel the myth that Chinese restaurants have to mean Formica tables and noisy dining. The flavors of the dishes are as subtle as the decor. Specialties include Peking duck and lobster with ginger and scallions. Open daily for dinner and on weekdays for lunch. Reservations advised. Major credit cards accepted. 545 Boylston St. (phone: 236-4040).

Plaza The space and decor are the height of Victorian splendor, the menu is classic continental, and the service is exquisitely correct. A great place to go when you want to impress someone. Open for dinner Tuesdays through Saturdays. Reservations advised. Major credit cards accepted. *Copley Plaza Hotel,* 138 St. James St. (phone: 267-5300, ext. 1048).

Rarities This elegant hotel dining spot features a creative nouvelle American menu, impeccable service, and a quality wine list. The seasonal menus highlight fresh local products, prepared with an international touch; the chefs take inspiration from Asian and South American cooking styles. Open for dinner Mondays through Saturdays. Reservations advised. Major credit cards accepted. *Charles Hotel,* 1 Bennett St., Cambridge (phone: 864-1200, ext. 1214).

Ritz-Carlton Large, lovely, serenely elegant, and one of only two places in town where you can enjoy a view of the Public Garden while dining with old-fashioned formality. The cuisine is continental, very good, and served by an expert staff. Men must wear jackets and ties at dinner. Open daily. Reservations advised. Major credit cards accepted. *Ritz Carlton Hotel,* 15 Arlington St. (phone: 536-5700).

St. Cloud One of the first culinary outposts in the now-trendy South End and still one of the best. The menu changes monthly, but you'll always find dishes such as rack of lamb with grilled vegetables and roasted salmon served with artichoke risotto. They serve the city's best hamburgers, too: A recent incarnation was accompanied by avocado salsa and a Maine crab fritter. A light, café-style menu is also available. Open daily. Reservations advised. Major credit cards accepted. 557 Tremont St. (phone: 353-0202).

Upstairs at the Pudding Set in the old upstairs dining room of Harvard's famous *Hasty Pudding Club* (the walls are lined with original, hand-painted show bills from the club's productions of years past), this elegant place is truly Old Ivy, but the food is decidedly contemporary — and first-rate. Subtle northern Italian fare is featured. The veal scaloppine is excellent. Order from the à la carte menu, or choose the prix fixe tasting menu, which allows you to choose one dish from each of the four courses offered. The outdoor terrace, situated in the herb garden, offers a savory dining experience on warm summer nights. Harvard singing groups frequently perform at Sunday brunch. Open daily. Reservations advised. Major credit cards accepted. 10 Holyoke St., Cambridge (phone: 864-1933).

MODERATE

Another Season An intimate spot on Beacon Hill with murals evoking turn-of-the-century Paris, its menu changes monthly and features inventive continental cooking. Fresh seafood, a vegetarian entrée, and a marvelous array of desserts always are available. There's also an inexpensive prix fixe menu that has a weekly culinary theme. Dinner only; closed Sundays. Reservations advised. Major credit cards accepted. 97 Mt. Vernon St. (phone: 367-0880).

Blue Diner This is authentic American food in a refurbished downtown diner — despite its wine list, fancy neon lights, and designer label clientele. Though there are items on the menu that lean toward the nouvelle, there is enough hearty meat loaf, mashed potatoes, gravy, cranberry sauce, and coconut pie to make up for it. Since there aren't many tables, this is a cozy dining experience. Open daily, 24 hours, except Sunday and Monday late nights. No reservations. Major credit cards accepted. 178 Kneeland St. (phone: 338-4639).

The Blue Room The latest inspiration of local restaurateurs Chris Schlesinger (*Green Street Grill*) and Stan Frankenheimer. Despite the name, the room feels as warm and cozy as a red brick oven, thanks to the open kitchen, glowing grills, and exposed brick walls. The house specialties are grilled and roasted meat and seafood, such as rabbit mole, black-and-blue T-bone steaks, Persian spiced duck, and peanut-crusted tuna steaks. Their pupu platter — an assortment of exotic salads, pickles, and noodles — is a real treat. Open daily for dinner and on weekdays for lunch. Reservations necessary. Major credit cards accepted. 1 Kendall Sq. (phone: 494-9034).

Bnu This hip trattoria (pronounced *Buh*-noo) in the theater district serves nouvelle Italian dishes made from ingredients that are as fresh and simple as its ambience. Their classic dish is spaghetti with sausage, plum tomatoes, and herbs. The imaginative pizzettas (individual pizzas) are topped with everything from pesto to grilled chicken. Open daily for dinner; weekdays for lunch. Reservations advised. Discover, MasterCard, and Visa accepted. 123 Stuart St. (phone: 367-8405).

Cajun Yankee The granddaddy of the New England crawdaddy crowd, this down-home, creole place is perpetually packed. All the Cajun staples are here — blackened fish, jambalaya, sweet potato pie — in spicy, pungent abundance. Beverages are correspondingly "down south," thirst-quenching. Closed Sundays and Mondays. Reservations advised on weekends. Major credit cards accepted. 1193 Cambridge St., Inman Sq., Cambridge (phone: 576-1971).

Changsho The food served in the recently relocated home of this Cambridge institution is still the best Chinese cooking you'll find outside New York's Chinatown. The restaurant has moved from its tiny, crowded storefront into a strikingly elegant — and much larger — space a block away. Open daily. No reservations. Major credit cards accepted. 1712 Massachusetts Ave., Cambridge (phone: 547-6565).

Chart House In the oldest building on the waterfront, its interior is a strikingly handsome arrangement of lofty spaces, natural wood, exposed red brick, and comfortable captain's chairs. The menu lists abundant portions of steaks and seafood, with all the salad you can eat included in the reasonable prices. The award-winning clam chowder is superb. Open daily. Reservations advised on weekend nights. Major credit cards accepted. 60 Long Wharf (phone: 227-1576).

Cornucopia Off the beaten track, between the Common and *Lafayette Place,* is the historic home of the Peabody family. Here Nathaniel Hawthorne married Sophia, and Elizabeth opened the bookstore that became the meeting place for such literati as Emerson and Thoreau. Today, it has been renovated to accommodate a striking restaurant that features an eclectic blend of regional and ethnic dishes. The menu changes seasonally. Lunch, weekdays only; dinner, Tuesdays through Saturdays. Reservations advised. Major credit cards accepted. 15 West St. (phone: 338-4600).

Cottonwood A very popular café, with both food and decor done in a modern Southwestern style. Look for such imaginative dishes as Rocky Mountain lamb chops, served over cilantro with raspberry *chipotle* chili sauce. At the bar, snack on deep-fried jalapeños stuffed with cheese and shrimp. Sipping fresh fruit margaritas on the tiny terrace makes for a chic, summertime Cambridge evening. Open daily for lunch and dinner. Reservations advised. Major credit cards accepted. 1815 Massachusetts Ave., Cambridge (phone: 661-7440).

Dali Garlic braids hanging from the ceiling, white plaster walls daubed with kitschy swirls, and waiters in red jackets and black cummerbunds are not the only things that make this *tapas* bar not far from Harvard seem authentic: The kitchen turns out Spanish specialties seldom seen outside Iberia. From the marinated olives served with drinks to the changing list of *tapas* (hors d'oeuvres) and entrées such as *pescado al sal* (whole snapper baked in a salt crust) or *conejo escabechado* (rabbit braised in red wine with juniper berries), dining here is a delicious adventure. There's usually a wait for a table, but if you're not in a hurry, order a pitcher of sangria and have another dish of olives. Closed Sundays. No reservations. Major credit cards accepted. 415 Washington St., Somerville (phone: 661-3254).

Dover Sea Grille An understated, relaxed, beautifully appointed seafood restaurant and lounge in Brookline, just a clamshell's throw from both *Fenway Park* and the Harvard Medical School. Marvelous grilled entrées, especially salmon and swordfish, are specialties, as are bountiful salads and superb desserts. A lighter café menu is also served. "Early Catch" specials are available weeknights from 5:30 to 6:30 PM. Open daily. Reservations advised. Major credit cards accepted. 1223 Beacon St. (phone: 566-7000).

Durgin-Park Though famed for generous servings of roast beef, pot roast, prime ribs, oyster stew, Boston baked beans, and Indian pudding, the kitchen now is way below par. However, its long, communal tables are still crowded with convivial diners and brusque, no-nonsense waitresses. Open daily. No reservations or credit cards accepted. 340 *Faneuil Hall Marketplace* (phone: 227-2038).

East Coast Grill You might not expect great Southern barbecue around Beantown, but this coolly stylish Inman Square grill repeatedly wins national praise and prizes — and the crowds waiting to be seated testify to the attitude of the locals. In addition to authentic North Carolina shredded pork barbecue, Texas brisket barbecue, and Memphis-style dry-rub ribs, you can get a great spit-roasted chicken, imaginative duck and lamb dishes, and delectable grilled swordfish paired with something spicy — ginger-scallion relish or a mayonnaise of smoked *chipotle* chilies. And if the food isn't hot enough for you, the owners thoughtfully leave a bottle of their Inner Beauty Hot Sauce on every table. Open daily. No reservations (and there's usually a good wait). Major credit cards accepted. 1271 Cambridge St., Cambridge (phone: 491-6568).

Genji An intimate Japanese restaurant in the Back Bay that serves beautifully prepared traditional fare, including tantalizing tempura and sushi. A picturesque, private tearoom can be reserved for special occasions. The service is friendly and informative. Try the complete dinner, sumptuous and reasonably priced. Open daily for lunch and dinner. Reservations advised. Major credit cards accepted. 327 Newbury St. (phone: 267-5656).

Icarus For some reason, this respected restaurant is never crowded, making it a great place for a quiet, intimate meal. The room resembles a Brahmin's drawing room with dark wood, green walls, and oversize sculptures. The contemporary American food is always imaginative and well prepared. The menu, which is predominantly seafood, changes every 6 weeks. On

Sunday nights, the wine café offers *tapa*-size portions and wine by the glass. Open daily for dinner and on Sundays for brunch. Reservations advised. Major credit cards accepted. 3 Appleton St. (phone: 426-1790).

Jimmy's Harborside Located about a whale's tail from the Fish Pier, this is an incredibly popular seafood spot with a solid reputation. Every seat in the main dining room has an excellent view of Boston Harbor. The traditional seafood menu has been expanded to include some Italian dishes, veal, and tenderloin. The wine list is replete with fine American wines. Don't mistake *Jimmy's* for *Jimbo's,* a less engaging place across the street. Open daily. Reservations advised. Most major credit cards accepted. 242 Northern Ave. (phone: 423-1000).

Legal Sea Foods If you don't mind waiting in line, you'll find fresh and well-prepared seafood. Open daily. No reservations. Major credit cards accepted. Four locations: *Park Plaza Hotel,* corner of Columbus Ave. and Arlington St. (phone: 426-4444); in the *Chestnut Hill Shopping Mall,* 43 Boylston St. (phone: 277-7300); 5 Cambridge Center, Kendall Sq., Cambridge (phone: 864-3400); and *Copley Place* (phone: 266-7775).

Loading Zone Among the city's trendiest dining spots, it features delicious barbecued meat, served in a funky former warehouse. The tables are especially interesting — dioramas under glass, they were created by local artists especially for this place, and each one is different. These witty works of art are great conversation pieces, making this a good spot for a first date. Open daily. Reservations advised. Major credit cards accepted. 150 Kneeland St. (phone: 695-0087).

Michela's Housed in a huge, converted building in the Kendall Square area of Cambridge, this chic eatery draws the cognoscenti from all around Boston to sample American food with a distinct northern Italian accent. Choose either the dining room proper or the café (which doesn't take reservations). The menus are completely different but not the panache with which the food is prepared. Closed Sundays. Reservations advised for the dining room, especially on weekend nights. Major credit cards accepted. 1 Atheneum St., Cambridge (phone: 225-2121).

Milk Street Café Its original home sandwiched into a sparkling niche of the financial district (there's now a second location), this bustling vegetarian and fish cafeteria presents superb breakfasts and lunches. The muffins, smoked salmon platter, flavorful soup, and generous, artful quiche are perennial pleasers. Open weekdays until 3 PM. Reservations advised. No credit cards accepted. Two locations: 50 Milk St. (phone: 542-2433) and 101 Main St., Kendall Sq., Cambridge, near MIT (phone: 491-8286).

Mirabelle Beautifully adorned with murals and warms woods, this place is the pride of catering wizard Stephen Elmont. Chefs are adept at many culinary climes. Open daily for breakfast, lunch, and dinner. Reservations advised. Major credit cards accepted. 85 Newbury St. (phone: 859-4848).

Olives Superb Tuscany-influenced Italian food served in a soothing dove-colored dining room with comfortable banquettes. Try the grilled lobster with white bean *raviolone* and artichoke sauce or the *tortelli* of butternut squash with brown butter and sage. Open Tuesdays through Saturdays. Reservations advised for groups of 6 or more. MasterCard and Visa accepted. 67 Main St., Charlestown (phone: 242-1999).

Paolo This sophisticated place is piles of pasta above every other Hanover Street eatery, offering elegant northern Italian fare in intimate subterranean rooms. You can choose from unusually shaped homemade pasta — the lasagna is a delicate roulade — and delicious meat dishes, such as a veal chop with wild mushrooms in cognac. Ray Santisi and other local pianists make the most of the 1917 Steinway grand. Open for dinner Tuesdays through Sundays. Reservations advised. Major credit cards accepted. 216 Hanover St. (phone: 227-5550).

Rebecca's White walls decorated with hand-painted flowers, exposed brick, blond wood furniture, and works by local artists dominate the comfortable, modern decor. The menu, described as "new American," borrows from French, Greek, Indian, and Italian cuisines. Open daily. No reservations. Major credit cards accepted. 21 Charles St. (phone: 742-9747).

Rocco's The decor in this theater district dining place is as dramatic as the neighborhood's atmosphere, with stage-scale curtains, murals on the ceiling, and 2-story picture windows to the street. The menu offers an eclectic choice of Italian fare. Open for lunch and dinner; closed Sunday dinner. Reservations advised. Major credit cards accepted. 5 S. Charles St. (phone: 723-6800).

St. Botolph Actually a restored 19th-century brick townhouse, this 2-story eatery sports a contemporary interior with exposed brick walls and a continental menu with good, fresh seafood. Lunch served weekdays; dinner nightly; brunch on Sundays. Reservations advised. Major credit cards accepted. 99 St. Botolph St. (phone: 266-3030).

Skipjack's Seafood Emporium With a dazzling aquarium-like decor, this mariner's delight features an extensive array of innovative seafood dishes (they claim to serve the widest variety of seafood in New England). Snapper Veracruz, grilled cilantro shrimp, and blackened redfish are just three of the outstanding choices. For dieters, a spa menu is available, which offers 10 items of 400 calories or less. The wine list is extensive and carefully assembled. Special Sunday jazz brunch is a treat (from 11 AM to 3 PM). Open daily, 11 AM to 11 PM. Reservations advised. Major credit cards accepted. 500 Boylston St., Copley Sq., Back Bay (phone: 536-3500); 2 Brookline Pl., Brookline (phone: 232-8887).

Small Planet Formerly the *Back Bay Bistro,* this casual place just across Boylston Street from the majestic Trinity Church is one of Boston's best modestly priced eateries. The various awards displayed in the bay window tell the story. The duck, venison, and roasted hen dishes are all excellent. Perhaps the best single item is an interesting preparation of catfish in cornmeal with black beans. The wine list is extensive and the decor inviting. Open daily for dinner; no lunch on Sunday. Reservations advised for large parties. Major credit cards accepted. 565 Boylston St. (phone: 536-4477).

Stage Deli The Boston–New York "deli wars" have found a savory, satisfying harmony in this bright, bustling little eatery in the theater district. From corned beef and chopped liver to authentic egg creams and ultra-rich cheesecake, all the required deli delights are available at tables and for takeout. Open daily. No reservations. Major credit cards accepted. 275 Tremont St. (phone: 523-3354).

Toscano Authentic northern Italian food, served in an elegant room with brick walls and red tiles. The menu changes daily, but you'll always find excellent risotto, homemade pasta, and fresh truffles in season. Open for lunch and dinner; closed Sunday lunch. Reservations necessary. American Express accepted. 41 Charles St. (phone: 723-4090).

Ye Olde Union Oyster House It's the real thing: Boston's oldest restaurant. Daniel Webster himself used to guzzle oysters at the wonderful mahogany bar, where skilled shuckers still pry them open before your eyes. Full seafood lunches and dinners are served upstairs, amid well-worn colonial ambience. (One booth is dedicated to John F. Kennedy, once a frequent diner.) Don't miss the seafood chowder. Open daily. Reservations advised. Major credit cards accepted. 41 Union St. (phone: 227-2750).

INEXPENSIVE

Addis Red Sea Boston's best Ethiopian restaurant (it doesn't have a lot of competition). Patrons sit on tiny, handwoven benches, and (the fulfillment of everybody's secret dream) eat only with fingers without social demerit. You just scoop up piles of *watts* (stew) with *injera,* the spongy Ethiopian pancake. Portions are large, the music and ambience are quietly mesmerizing, and the Ethiopian red wine is a delight. Open daily for dinner; lunch on Saturdays and Sundays. Reservations advised. Major credit cards accepted. 544 Tremont St. (phone: 426-8727).

Bob the Chef Located in the South End, it is Boston's best soul food restaurant. If you're looking to get downright stuffed, this is the place. All the favorites are served here in generous portions: chitterlings (just say chitlin'), barbecued spareribs, black-eyed peas, collard greens, and grits with breakfast. The sweet potato pie is excellent. All meals come with biscuits and corn bread. Open daily. Reservations advised for large parties. No credit cards accepted. 604 Columbus Ave. (phone: 536-6204).

Casa Romero Though most people don't link Boston with Mexican food — and even become a little disturbed at the idea — there are indeed a couple of good Mexican eateries. The food here is authentic — marinated tenderloin of pork, *enchiladas verdes,* garlic soup, and *mole poblano.* The tile tables and wrought iron give this place enough of a Latin American feel to forget for a moment that when Bostonians think of south of the border, they're thinking Rhode Island. Open daily for dinner. Reservations advised. Major credit cards accepted. 30 Gloucester St. (phone: 536-4341).

Chau Chow Delicious and inexpensive Cantonese food, served in a plain, crowded little diner in Chinatown. Critics rave over the soup and seafood, particularly the salt-baked shrimp and oysters with black bean sauce. Open daily, 10 AM to 2 AM, and until 4 AM on weekends. No reservations. No credit cards accepted. 52 Beach St. (phone: 426-6266).

Elsie's Lunch This storefront shop, a block from Harvard Yard, has been serving food and drink to famished Harvard students for longer than anyone can remember. A great place to go when your feet are tired, or when you just want to fill up with a basic sandwich or salad. Open daily. No reservations or credit cards accepted. 71 Mt. Auburn St., Cambridge (phone: 354-8781 or 354-8362).

Goeman The best noodle/tempura shop you'll find outside Tokyo, this is Japan's version of fast food. Big hearty bowls of flavorful broth, *udon, soba,* or *ramen* noodles, and artfully arranged meat or vegetables. Order a classic combination or create your own by choosing ingredients from their list. Open daily for lunch and dinner. Reservations accepted for parties of six or more only. Major credit cards accepted. 267 Huntington Ave. (phone: 859-8669) and 1 Kendall Sq., Building 100, Cambridge (phone: 577-9595).

La Groceria Northern Italian cooking in an old house with several dining rooms, each with a distinct character (the intimate top floor is recommended). The pasta is homemade, as are the cheesecake and cannoli. The veal dishes and antipasto, hot and cold, are excellent. Extensive wine list. Open daily for dinner. Reservations advised for large parties. Major credit cards accepted. 853 Main St., Cambridge (phone: 547-9258 or 876-4162).

Jae's Café The food is Korean in inspiration and healthy in preparation. You can find *yukhai* (Korean raw beef), pan-fried dumplings stuffed with shrimp, and several light, mild curries. Every dish has lots of fresh vegetables and little oil. There's also a sushi bar downstairs. Open daily for lunch and dinner. Reservations advised. Major credit cards accepted. 520 Columbus Ave. (phone: 421-9405).

Jake and Earl's Dixie BBQ If you feel more like jumping in a taxi, grabbing some great takeout, and heading back to your hotel, aim for this place next door to the *East Coast Grill* (above). It's owned by the same duo, and it's equally passionate about authenticity-in-barbecue. In addition to doing all the smoking for its sibling next door, this spot offers its own list of spicy specialties. The half-jerk chicken is hot and juicy; the daily specials, such as a barbecued bologna sandwich, are always original and surprisingly good. And for $3.95, the pulled-pork sandwich (it comes with a moist hunk of corn bread, fresh coleslaw, rich, spicy beans, and a slice of watermelon) is a bargain hunter's delight. The Elvis memorabilia (from license plates to an assortment of plastic and plaster busts) will keep you entertained while you're waiting, which is never very long. Open daily. Reservations unnecessary. Major credit cards accepted. 1273 Cambridge St., Cambridge (phone: 491-7427).

Massimino's A lovely little spot that serves fresh, delicious Italian food at incredibly low prices. Specialties include hot seafood antipasto, saltimbocca, veal marsala, pork chops with vinegar peppers and potatoes, and homemade *tiramisù*. Open Mondays through Saturdays for lunch and dinner. No reservations. MasterCard and Visa accepted. 207 Endicott St. (phone: 523-5959).

No-Name Restaurant The name was not a conscious decision. Beginning as a ramshackle joint that counted only the local fishermen as its clientele, this has become a Boston institution serving the freshest seafood in the city (though the folks at *Jimmy's* might dispute this point) to tourists, businesspeople, and the ancient mariners who still frequent the place. With a view of the harbor, this nameless place is also frill-less: Expect Formica tables, paper napkins, and plastic cups. But that's its charm. Though the waitresses are a tad surly, they will fetch some of the finest fried seafood, boiled lobster, and broiled scallops on record. Open daily for lunch and dinner. No reservations. No credit cards accepted. 15½ Fish Pier, just off Northern Ave. (phone: 338-7539).

Rubin's Kosher Delicatessen One of only a few kosher restaurants in the Boston area, its chopped liver, potato *latkes* (pancakes), and lean pastrami (hot or cold) are the genuine articles. Open Sundays through Thursdays; closes Fridays at 2 PM. Reservations unnecessary. Major credit cards accepted. 500 Harvard St., Brookline (phone: 566-8761).

S&M New York Deli This large, bright, and bustling delicatessen is filled with the financial district crowd at lunchtime. The food is authentically New York-style, and the sandwiches (try the Reuben) rival the Big Apple's best. There are about 10 stools along a front counter and 20 tables in the back, or take your order out, and have a picnic on Boston Common, a short walk up Beacon Street. Closed Sundays. No reservations. No credit cards accepted. 12 Beacon St. (phone: 523-8776).

Venus Seafood in the Rough The city's only urban clam shack. Sit at a picnic table under a tent, look out over a none-too-scenic channel of water, and order fresh seafood — fried clams, grilled fish, and boiled lobsters — from a take-out window. Don't miss the homemade clam chowder (New England, natch) and coleslaw. It's rustic, but that doesn't stop legions of suited businesspeople from the nearby financial district from stopping in for a summertime lunch. Open mid-April through mid-October only. No reservations. No credit cards accepted. 88 Sleep St. (phone: 426-3388).

NORTH END RESTAURANTS

This Old World neighborhood boasts literally dozens of restaurants crowded into a few square blocks. The range of quality and price is considerable. In most places here, you won't go wrong if you stick to basic pasta, but in a few, you will go incredibly *right* with about everything. These places offer delicious renditions of pasta, seafood, and meat all at very reasonable prices. For cozy, homemade meals, try *Mother Anna's* (211 Hanover St.; phone: 523-8496). Open daily. Reservations only on weekdays. American Express accepted. For great seafood Italian-style, try the *Daily Catch,* which specializes in calamari (squid) dishes, cooked in an open kitchen (323 Hanover St.; phone: 523-8567). Open daily. Reservations advised. Major credit cards accepted. Similar in spirit but less well known is *Giacomo's* (355 Hanover St.; phone: 523-9026). Open daily. No reservations. American Express accepted. Many locals swear by the crunchy, crusty pizzas at *Circle Pizza* (361 Hanover St.; phone: 523-8787). Open daily. Reservations accepted for large groups only. No checks or credit cards accepted. Don't leave the North End without experiencing *la dolce vita* — that's short for how sweet life seems when you're sitting at a sidewalk café, sipping espresso, savoring a cannoli or gelati, watching the world go by. The best espresso and sweets are at *Caffè Dello Sport* (307 Hanover St.; phone: 523-5063) and *Caffè Roma* (241 Hanover St.; phone: 723-1760). Both have no reservations and cash-only policies.

Diversions

Exceptional Experiences for the Mind and Body

Quintessential Boston

Whether savoring a hot dog at a *Red Sox* game, gutting fish on a harbor pier, participating in a heated political discussion, or sipping tea, pinkie out, at the *Ritz,* lowbrows, highbrows, and all other brows justly (to some extent) lay claim to Boston's soul. Nurtured from the very first Puritans to the recent influx of Russian emigrés, Boston's soul has become as richly textured as it is egalitarian. It is fitting, then, that all the emissaries of the city's essence — every creed, color, and credit rating — meet once a week (on Fridays at 5 PM) in about 12 lanes of traffic in Kenmore Square. If there is anything at all quintessential about Boston, it is trying to merge in this mess, the Kenmore Krush. Other uniquely Bostonian experiences are described below.

BOSTON GARDEN AND FENWAY PARK Sports are as close to Boston's soul as colonial history or the Democratic Party. Just as strings of *Celtics* victories and the ever-present hope of yet another championship enliven the city's spirit as spring gives way to summer, a pall of apocalyptic gloom is cast over the horizon in autumn as the annual *Red Sox* jinx rears its ugly head yet again. In the fabled *Boston Garden* (properly pronounced "*gah*-den"), the green-and-white and black-and-gold championship banners are so crowded together that they hide this venerable coliseum's rusty rafters. The place is steeped in the glory of the *Celtics,* 16-time NBA champions. The *Celtic* Dynasty, created by such legends as Bill Russell, Bob Cousy, John Havlicek, and the recently retired Larry Bird, is alive and in the process of rebuilding. Here, too, is the place where Bobby Orr and other hockey greats created the legend of the big, bad *Bruins,* 5-time winners of the *Stanley Cup.*

The legend of the place looms so large that many first-time visitors to the *Garden* are surprised that it is so small and cramped. The musty smell, and the sheets of riveted metal that hold together its balconies (painted a fresh coat of yellow for the umpteenth time) lend the aged arena the aura of a mothballed battleship. The charming shabbiness that the city's sports purists adore, however, may soon be a memory. Though the *Celtics* won't be trading in their black sneakers for more chic models anytime soon, plans are being considered for a modern, new arena, which will likely be built next to the present structure.

Just as winter is best spent under the protective roof of the *Garden,* summer is the season when Boston's long-suffering — though cocky-to-the-bitter-end — *Red Sox* fans converge on Kenmore Square to delight in the city's other venerable sporting venue, *Fenway Park* (pronounced *"Fen-*w'y *Pak"*). Enjoy the smell of freshly mown grass while munching on a Fenway Frank (hot dog) and sipping a "beah" in this, one of the last great urban ballparks. Built in 1912, *Fenway* is home of the Green Monster (the 37-foot high left-field wall that has driven many a pitcher into early retirement) and many precious memories — for *Red Sox* fans, that is. The *Red Sox,* more often than not, beat up on their opponents at home, setting the stage for their annual plummet. (The team hasn't won a *World Series* since 1918, but have come oh, so agonizingly close, so many times.) Any summer visit to Boston should include a *Red Sox* game, even if you aren't a fan and they're winning, or if you are and they're on the skids. (See *Sports and Fitness* in THE CITY.)

When tickets are impossible to get — if the Boston teams are playing out of town, the *Celtics* or *Bruins* are in the playoffs, or Roger Clemens is on the mound for the *Red Sox* — it's almost as much fun to join the cheering crowds watching the game at one of Boston's many sports bars (almost any bar in Boston is a sports bar). Since contemporary Bostonians take their sports every bit as seriously as the Puritans took their religion, the sports bar has become the latter-day temple for local team boosters, of which there are legions. Probably the holiest of shrines, then, is the *Sports Depot* (353 Cambridge St., Allston; phone: 617-783-2300), which bills itself as "the ultimate in casual dining." It's actually the ultimate in casual viewing, with 38 color television sets trained to as many sporting events around the world as its two mammoth satellite dishes can track at any one time (there even are TV sets in the men's and women's rooms, so that not a single play is missed). Two other spots have unbeatable locations — the *Cask and Flagon* (corner of Lansdowne St. and Brookline Ave.; phone: 617-536-4840) is a foul ball away from *Fenway Park;* and the *Sports Café* (120 Causeway St.; phone: 617-723-6664), tucked into the *Boston Garden* complex, is a favorite of the pre- and post-*Celtics* game revelers.

CAMBRIDGE COFFEEHOUSE CONVERSATIONS In Cambridge, home of the country's oldest university, the connoisseur of the fading art of conversation may still hear witty references to Kierkegaard, Kandinsky, and Roger Clemens — all in the same breath. Cantabrigians love to converse, and never more than on Sundays in one of their wonderfully cramped coffeehouses. Armed with the Sunday papers, a good dose of Viennese coffee, a piece of linzertorte or a croissant, they settle down for hours of leisurely exchange. An alert eavesdropper in one of Cambridge's coffeehouses might overhear anything from the pedantic disputations of tweedy, professorial types to the moving confessions of a lovestruck coed. It's almost as much fun to listen as it is to hold one's own in the discourse. Snatch some reading material from *Out of Town News,* a kiosk with the unique address of Zero Harvard Square. This international temple to the written word is the axis around which all Cambridge revolves — newspapers and magazines from around the world, from *The London Times* to *Pravda,* can be purchased here. There are coffeehouses here to suit every temperament. More reserved residents cherish *Café Pamplona* (on Bow St.; no phone or restroom), a little dungeon with a black-and-white tile floor that is so small it seems you might bump your head on the rear wall when entering. The *Coffee Connection* (36 JFK St.; phone: 617-492-1881) is a favorite of the Harvard crowd, and *Passim* (47 Palmer St.; phone: 617-492-7679), a coffeehouse (and folk music venue in the evenings and on Sunday afternoons), attracts an earthy, musical clientele.

CONCERTS AT THE GARDNER Among the scores of places to take in a classical concert in Boston, the most outstanding is one built by a bon vivant New Yorker who liked to shock Proper Bostonians by wearing a headband at performances of the *Boston Symphony Orchestra* that read, "Oh, you *Red Sox.*" The *Isabella Stewart Gardner Museum* is not only the most charming place to see a concert, but among the most splendid spaces with four walls and a roof in all of Boston. Gardner, a daring member of New York society who married John Lowell Gardner, a wealthy Brahmin industrialist in 1860, built this marble Venetian palazzo with its magnificent courtyard to house the art that she had collected during her worldwide travels. As is stipulated in her will, all the objects in the museum are arranged in the same quirky and crowded way as they were when Mrs. Jack (as she was called) lived on the top floor. Every Sunday afternoon and Tuesday evening (except during the summer), the museum's Tapestry Room hosts performances by anyone from grand masters to young local artists. The large room, with its dark tile floor and subdued lighting, has the quiet serenity of an ancient chapel. Among a wealth of art, Mrs. Gardner's "knickknacks" fill the room: an iron pulpit from 16th-century Spain, a Gothic stone fireplace that dates from the early 1500s, and three oaken choir stalls from the late 16th century. The 16th-century Belgian tapestries shimmer in the indirect light that streams in from the mansion's astounding courtyard, while the great mahogany beams in the ceiling — the secret behind the room's excellent acoustics — reverberate with the sound of violin sonatas, piano concertos, or string quartets. In the center of the room, several handfuls of patrons sit comfortably in wooden chairs, and are transported. The stillness of the room and the richness of its treasures somehow make the experience of the music all the more complete. Though Mrs. Gardner preferred champagne and doughnuts, wine and hors d'oeuvres are served in the Spanish Cloister area after each performance. (Also see *Special Places* in THE CITY.)

A RIDE IN THE SWAN BOATS The graceful circling of the swan in the Public Garden's Lagoon is as sure a sign of summer in Boston as the disappearance of ski racks from the tops of automobiles. A 10-minute ride in the Swan Boats, which putter (pedaled by the strong legs of student athletes earning next year's tuition) under what is regarded as the world's smallest suspension bridge, is admittedly not the most adventurous experience. But it upholds a 115-year-old tradition that has been carried out since Bostonian Robert Paget adapted the idea from *Lohengrin,* his favorite opera, where the hero glides to the rescue of his beloved on a boat pulled by a swan. Since most children identify the swan pond with the happy ending of Robert McCloskey's story *Make Way for Ducklings!* (Mr. and Mrs. Mallard and their brood find a safe haven here), the boats are particularly enjoyable for them. (Look for the bronze statuettes of the Mallards along the path to the pond.) The fattened descendants of the Mallard clan skim about the lagoon, keeping a lazy but vigilant eye out for bread. All is calm until crumbs are cast, causing these otherwise docile creatures to bolt into action in a no-holds-barred feeding frenzy. Don't forget the bread crumbs, or your children may unjustly accuse you of cruelty to animals. After your ride, be sure to stroll about the painstakingly manicured flower beds, monuments, fountains, and exotic trees of the Public Garden. (Cold-weather visitors needn't be disappointed — even when the Swans are put to bed for the winter, the Public Garden retains its almost magical charm. Ice skaters swirl across the lagoon, and the icy trees give the snowy scene a fairyland feel.)

INTELLECTUAL BOSTON — THE LECTURE CIRCUIT The old adage states that in Washington success is measured by one's influence, in New York by one's wealth, and in Boston by one's knowledge. If this is true, then Boston's vast lecture circuit is where thoughtful Bostonians go to share in (and acquire) such success. The city's tradition of serious public lectures dates back to the Puritans, who conducted their "Thursday Lecture" for those assembled near *Faneuil Hall* for market day. Rogues and rapscallions were subjected to fire-and-brimstone excoriations before being hustled out of the meeting hall, the audience fast on their heels, for public punishments and executions. Although those festive times are long past, the tradition of the Thursday Lecture lives — fed by area residents' acute political awareness, varied cultural interests, and the intellectual ferment provided by more than a dozen local colleges and universities. In any given week there could be a choice of lectures by both local and visiting distinguished authors and academics, profs, poets, pols, pundits, and policymakers intent on presenting and defending their ideas on topics ranging from "Racism and Science" and "Roots of US Global Policy" to "Women Filmmakers from Quebec" and "Urban Gardeners."

But the actual presentation is only half the fun. Since most Bostonians are not content with just being talked at, be sure to wait around for the question-and-answer session that follows every talk. On the whole, local lecturegoers are an inquisitive bunch (some are opinionated to the point of being obnoxious), so the Q&A sessions often lead to a lively exchange of ideas, and occasionally decline into an ugly shouting match. Both can be interesting. The most respected of the city's ongoing lecture series are the Arco Forum at Harvard's Kennedy School of Government, the Ford Hall Forum lectures, and the midday Thursday lectures at the Old South Meeting House. Check the Thursday "Calendar" section of the *Boston Globe* or the weekly *Boston Phoenix* for complete listings.

ON AND ALONG THE CHARLES Despite its pollution problem, the Charles River, which flows along the northern edge of Boston and separates it from Cambridge, plays a big role in making Boston the livable city that it is. Bostonians relish playing both along and on the Charles. During the warm-weather months sailboats dot the river, their masts glistening in the sun and mainsails puffing with the steady breeze that sweeps in from the harbor. No image of Boston is complete that doesn't include these compact vessels lazily tacking back and forth, with the gold dome of the State House high atop Beacon Hill shimmering in the background. Thanks to *Community Boating, Inc.,* a sailing club that offers a 2-day membership to out-of-towners, visitors can join the other sailors navigating 15-foot Cape Cod Mercuries in the stretch of river between the Longfellow and Memorial bridges. Even if you can't distinguish a jib from a gibe, or think points of sail are *Jordan Marsh* and *Filene's Basement,* you can get your start as a sailor with the assistance of seasoned instructors. The savvy seaman — or seawoman — will time a Charles River voyage with the occasional summer evening concerts at the *Hatch Shell,* where the *Boston Pops Orchestra* performs its lighthearted repertoire of popular and classical favorites. Only the expert boatman, however, should be on the Charles on *July 4,* when the *Independence Day Boston Pops* concert and fireworks display lead to bumper-to-bumper boat traffic. Thousands of people also pack into the Esplanade for the traditional event, which features a sing-along of all-American favorites, a rousing rendition of the *1812 Overture,* and a truly spectacular fireworks show. Whether you spectate from land or sea, be advised that your craft must be moored by sundown — and there's usually a tussle for the choice spots of terra firma. You'll want to bring along picnic supplies.

For those who prefer to keep their feet firmly on the ground, the Esplanade, a cool strip of parkland along the banks of the Charles, is the perfect place to enjoy the river. The Esplanade is Boston's backyard — from this peaceful stretch of greenery the distant sounds of Boston can be heard in all directions — Cambridge to the right, Back Bay to the left, and Boston University straight ahead. It's a favorite spot of cross-country skiers and skaters in the winter; bikers, runners, Frisbee throwers, and sunners in the summer; and walkers, runners, and joggers year-round. If you're feeling especially spirited, take the path that borders the Charles River to Watertown, meandering first through a thin strip of thickets and past the duck-filled lagoon to the west. On the way you'll encounter a number of sprawling parks where there are ample benches, gardens, and green stretches to sit and watch the river flow by.

FILENE'S BASEMENT This subterranean sea of clothing, housewares, luggage, shoes, and accessories is the ultimate Boston shopping experience. The original *Filene's Basement* (Downtown Crossing, 426 Washington St.; phone: 617-542-2011; there is now a chain of *Filene's Basement* stores that offer the discounts, but not the ambience, of the flagship) is a favorite stop for visitors to the city, as well as for the locals who come here in droves. Considered by many Bostonians to be a one-stop clothing shop, a trip to the "World Famous *Filene's Basement*" (as the sign above the entrance reads) requires grit, assertiveness, endurance, and an indefatigable passion for getting good clothes on the cheap. The atmosphere here is frenetic, with shoppers pawing through huge racks and tables of merchandise. Don't be surprised if you see women trying on garments in the aisles — for years there was no ladies' dressing room here so public disrobing, within reason, is de rigueur. (There is now a small communal dressing room for women.) The fervor stems from the possibility of truly stupendous bargains. The diversity of the stock (designer items from such upscale shops as *Neiman Marcus* and *Saks,* more moderate name-brand merchandise, and some goods of questionable quality) makes timing and a little information crucial. The price tags, though they may resemble an upside-down score sheet for a game of gin rummy, are easy enough to understand: After an item is in the *Basement* 12 shopping days, the (already low) price goes down 25%; if it's still there after 18 days, the discount is 50%; after 24 days the price is reduced by 75%. When the item has been in the *Basement* a full 30 days, it is donated to charity. There are occasional $60 men's suit sales, $10 dress sales, and $200 wedding gown sales that are advertised in the *Boston Globe.* To some shoppers, *Filene's Basement* is a way of living life on the edge. They gamble that a coveted item will still be around for the next markdown (some shoppers even hide soon-to-be-reduced items — under an ugly coat on the other side of the store, say — in the hopes that they will remain there, undetected, until the next discount kicks in). With the frenetic turnover, however, there are frequent disappointments. Since the store is restocked on Sunday nights, Monday morning is the best time to strike.

TEA AT THE RITZ From the wing-back chairs and ornate gilded ceiling to the Earl Grey tea and delicate watercress sandwiches, afternoon tea at the *Ritz-Carlton* hotel is an experience simply dripping with Bostoniana. This cherished Boston tradition (okay, it's actually British) allows the itinerant highbrow to go a step beyond daydreaming outside the sanctified Beacon Hill and Back Bay residences of the upper crust. Stomp right into this

Brahmin stronghold (to avoid immediate ejection, gentlemen should don a jacket first), and experience the rarified lifestyle first hand. The grande dame of Boston hotels, the *Ritz-Carlton* sits elegantly on the southwest corner of Commonwealth and Arlington, its doorman keeping a vigilant watch for limousines. The daily ritual in the second-floor *Tea Lounge* has been a favorite of Boston society since the hotel opened in 1927. But don't be intimidated by the aura of tradition. Slide right into that gilded chair, exchange bons mots with your cultivated brethren, and daintily sip and nibble the afternoon away. If you're not sure as to protocol, just follow the lead of the punctilious ladies whose ceaseless poise leads one to conclude that they've spent the better parts of their lives here. There certainly are worse places to while away time. A prim musician gently strums soothing melodies on the harp while the doting, tuxedo-clad waiters and waitresses bring delicate, crustless sandwiches; scones with Devonshire cream and strawberry preserves; assorted pastries; and the obligatory teas and coffees. Lean back and enjoy the restful ambience and remember that here, "quite" would be a perfectly proper reply to an observation regarding your state of well-being. Tea is served daily from 3 to 5:30 PM. In true democratic tradition, everyone who pays the bill is welcome. (Also see "Grand Hotels" in *Checking In,* THE CITY.)

AN ARNOLD ARBORETUM PICNIC Bostonians are irrepressible in the zeal with which they reacquaint themselves with nature after the seemingly never-ending winter. Heavy togs are shed and people burst outdoors in a frenzy that few Sunbelters can understand. One of the places that draw city dwellers during the months of poor skiing is the Arnold Arboretum. Located in the city's Jamaica Plain neighborhood, this link in the Emerald Necklace (an 8-mile chain of parkland designed by famed landscape architect Frederick Law Olmsted) is a living laboratory of flowers and foliage. A network of paths weaves among the lilacs, azaleas, rhododendrons, magnolia trees, cherry blossoms, and about 14,000 other species of flowers, fruit trees, and shrubs. The Arboretum is an ideal place for a picnic — these 265 acres provide an ample selection of vine-veiled nooks in which to throw the perfect spread, including tablecloth, wicker basket, drumsticks, a loaf of bread, a glass of wine . . . Don't be surprised if a wedding party passes through — this is a favorite place of June brides and grooms. If you're really feeling chipper, you might consider working up an appetite by walking the 3½ miles of parkland from the Fens Park west to the Arboretum, passing over footbridges and around lakes, streams, and woodland, but rarely an intersection.

BOSTON'S FISH PIER Every morning as the sun inches out of the Atlantic to the east, fishing boats carrying salty crews creep back into Boston Harbor to market their catch. A spirited gang of restaurateurs, fish brokers, wholesalers, and assorted fish hucksters shuffle, slurp coffee, and banter like brothers as they await the anglers. But all is business on the Boston Fish Pier when the boats arrive, the ruddy fishermen — in their hip-high boots — scrambling to get heaping crates of cod, haddock, flounder, and monkfish onto refrigerated trucks without losing a moment's freshness. The buyers move in for a closer look, as do the scavenging gulls overhead, who squawk their approval. Everybody seems to know everybody. The brokers, after poking and prodding and inspecting the finny fare with a keen eye for its firmness, shine, and color, snatch it up by the boatload, forcing the shop and restaurant owners to buy their fish from these middle-men. The haggling continues until everybody seems satisfied — except the sea gulls. They never learn. While most of those who do the buying are in the restaurant or food business, you can try your own hand at bidding from the brokers if you make the 6:30 AM curtain call. If you prefer to have your fish prepared to perfection for a slight charge, the *No-Name* restaurant (15½ Fish Pier, just off Northern Ave.; phone: 617-338-7539), right on the renovated Fish Pier, packs fishermen, tourists, and locals in like sardines for, unquestionably, Boston's freshest seafood. *No-Name* is strictly no frills — no credit cards, no fancy sauces, no discernible decor — but the seafood, simply broiled or fried, is excellent (wine and beer are available). There's also no sign, so ask at the Fish Pier — or look for the line at the door.

Antiques: Boston's Best Hunting Grounds

One of the by-products of Boston's venerable history is its antiques, though the most proper of Proper Bostonians won't admit to actually shopping for them. (The quintessential Boston shopping story is the oft-told tale of the 19th-century Boston woman who was asked by a lady from New York where she buys her hats. The Boston matron replies, "My dear, in Boston we don't buy our hats. We already have them.") But those of us not fortunate enough to be direct descendants of Endicotts or Cabots or Lowells — much less to be written into their wills — must make do with what has made its way from Back Bay and Beacon Hill attics to the city's many antiques shops. With two great antiques avenues — Charles Street, at the base of Beacon Hill, is known by locals as "Antiques Row," and Newbury Street is the site of a number of upscale antiques proprietors — Boston is an ideal place for "antiquing." But be aware that there are some new dynamics at work. American antiques, which are so much in vogue of late (if you can say antiques are in vogue without being oxymoronic), have filtered into the suburbs. Boston shops, on the other hand, are strong on European antiques. And what actually constitutes an antique in Boston? Though Art Deco may seem nostalgic in California, here nothing made after the Civil War is considered really broken in. For some of the better antiques shops in the area see *Shopping* in THE CITY.

RULES OF THE ROAD FOR AN ODYSSEY OF THE OLD

Buy for sheer pleasure, not for investment. Forget about the carrot of supposed retail values that dealers habitually dangle in front of amateur clients. If you love something, it will probably grace your home long after the British sail once again into Boston Harbor.

Buy the finest example you can afford of any item, in as close to mint condition as possible. Chipped or broken "bargains" will haunt you later with their shabbiness. They also don't increase in value the way the mint stuff does.

Train your eye in museums and/or collections of things in the period that interests you. These are the best schools for the acquisitive senses, particularly as you begin to develop special passions.

Get advice from specialists when contemplating major acquisitions. Much antique and collectible furniture and many paintings have been restored several times. If you want to be absolutely certain that what you're buying is what you've been told it is, stick with the larger dealers. *Don't be afraid to haggle — a little.* Most dealers don't have fixed prices, so sharpen your negotiating skills and make an offer they can't refuse. A word of warning: While most larger dealers take credit cards, smaller shops do not.

When pricing an object, don't forget to figure the cost of shipping. Shipping home a large piece — furniture, sculpture, antique garden paraphernalia — can be considerable. Be sure to figure this into the cost of your purchase.

Inside Boston's Theaters

Boston is America's second city of theater. Though normally Bostonians aren't proud of playing any supporting role if New York is playing the lead, this casting suits them just fine because it means a steady stream of productions come here for final polishing and refinement on the way to Broadway. As a result, a section of Boston between downtown and the South End has evolved into a real theater district, with a number of grand old stages. Since Bostonians are such avid theatergoers, however, getting impromptu tickets to performances can be a scramble. Before you shell out a premium price for last-minute tickets in the nose-bleed section with a view obstructed by a Doric column, you should explore two options. First, concierges in many downtown hotels have mysterious methods for quickly securing theater tickets for their guests. Second, check with *Bostix,* the city's largest ticket agency. From its booth just to the south of *Faneuil Hall Marketplace, Bostix* sells tickets at half price for same-day performances. You'll want to arrive early to beat the line. *Bostix* is open Tuesdays through Sundays from 11 AM to 6 PM; it's closed major holidays. For a pre- or post-theater repast, stop in at the *Stage Deli* (275 Boylston St.; phone: 617-523-DELI), located in the heart of the theater district. It rates close to a real New York delicatessen, with kosher pickles trucked in from the Big

Apple and some of the best corned beef sandwiches and blintzes in town. The following is a list of Boston's most outstanding theaters.

COLONIAL Even if the performance stinks, just the opportunity to see the exquisitely restored interior of this Victorian theater, with its marble, mirrors, brass, and bas-reliefs, is worth the ticket price. It is a lavish theater, despite the fact that it's situated within an office building. Built in 1900, the *Colonial* was one of the 11 Boston theaters designed by Clarence Blackhall, a renowned architect and the first president of Boston's architectural club. The oldest Boston theater to survive, intact, under the same name, it has been the setting for many theatrical debuts, from Irving Berlin and the *Ziegfeld Follies* to Rodgers and Hammerstein. Such luminaries as Fred Astaire, George M. Cohan, and Noël Coward have graced its stage. Today, the *Colonial* often hosts major productions en route to Broadway. Information: *Colonial Theatre,* 106 Boylston St. (phone: 617-426-9366).

HUNTINGTON Under the auspices of Boston University, this has become Boston's largest resident professional theater company. The building, built in 1925, is nondescript on the outside, but has a handsome interior with lots of dark wood and brass. Its location — on Huntington Avenue near Northeastern University, bordering on the rough edges of the South End — is a bit awkward, but the company's five annual productions are worth a little inconvenience. Each season's line-up usually includes established classics and 20th-century plays; a typical mix might include the works of Harold Pinter, George Bernard Shaw, Henrik Ibsen, Tom Stoppard, and a Shakespearean work for good measure. Information: *Huntington Theatre,* 264 Huntington Ave. (phone: 617-266-0800 or 617-266-3913).

WANG CENTER This is one of the world's largest theaters, with seating for 4,400 patrons, and a stage that is 60-feet wide, 30-feet high, and 60-feet deep. Home to the *Boston Ballet,* the large stage is particularly suited for the elaborate annual production of "The Nutcracker Suite," a local *Yuletide* tradition. Its stage is also used for other major dance, opera, and theater events. Originally opened as a "movie palace" in 1925, the theater began hosting live performances in the 1940s. Originally called the *Metropolitan,* it was renamed the *Wang Center for the Performing Arts* in 1983 after large gifts from An Wang and the Wang computer corporation saved the theater from going under. A $10-million restoration has turned the dilapidated giant into the city's most sumptuous theater: Brightly colored murals adorn the walls; a huge chandelier hangs from the central dome; gilt trim sparkles everywhere; and seraphim and cherubim float around the great arch over a huge stage. Information: *Wang Center for the Performing Arts,* 270 Tremont St. (phone: 617-423-3566).

WILBUR Another Blackhall creation, this Boston favorite, built in 1914, has been restored to its original splendor. Like the *Colonial,* the *Wilbur* hosts many productions that are either on their way to Broadway or fresh from a stint in Manhattan. The *Wilbur* is considerably smaller then the *Colonial,* and makes for an intimate theatrical experience. The theater's portals are modeled after the Thomas Bailey Aldrich home on Beacon Hill. Information: *Wilbur Theater,* 246 Tremont St. (phone: 617-423-4008).

Historic Churches

One of the lasting vestiges of Boston's Puritan past (aside from the fact that you can't buy alcohol in stores on Sundays) is its rich array of churches. The city's most outstanding churches were built at a time when the place of worship was the focal point of the community and all its artistic and architectural energy was devoted to constructing soaring spires, painstakingly crafted woodwork, and grand altars, and to fostering a sense of permanence. The activities within these early churches, however, were not limited to the spiritual. A church figured prominently in the midnight ride of Paul Revere, and it was in a church that the Sons of Liberty worked themselves into a frenzy before withdrawing to the harbor for a spot of tea. All of the following are operating churches; services are open to the public.

KING'S CHAPEL This stately church, reminiscent of an English cathedral, was built as the Massachusetts Bay Colony's Anglican church for British officers and the royal governor (much to the dismay of the colony's Puritans, who had left their homeland to escape the Anglican church). Established in 1688, the original church was a modest wooden building. When the present structure of Quincy granite was erected in 1799, it was literally constructed around the original church. The church within the church was then dismantled and thrown out the windows of the new structure board by board. King's Chapel is a welcome sight amid the jungle of skyscrapers in the surrounding financial district. The chapel's bell is Paul Revere's largest and, according to him, the sweetest-sounding one he ever cast. The church's interior has been restored to its earlier Georgian elegance. Its centerpiece is the Governor's Pew, on the right upon entering, a gilded reminder of a bygone era. It was banished from the church in 1826, when memories of British hegemony were still fresh, but restored a century later when some historical distance was achieved from the British crown. In 1785, after the Revolution and the demise of the area's Anglican congregation, the building became the first Unitarian church in America. The best time to visit the chapel is around noon on Tuesdays, when free classical music concerts are presented in its quiet interior, an oasis from the frenzy of modern finance in the area. On Thursdays, the chapel turns literary with a noontime program of readings, called the King's English. Open 10 AM to 2 PM weekdays; 10 AM to 4 PM Saturdays; Sunday services at 11 AM.

Tuesday concerts and Thursday readings begin at 12:15 PM. Information: *King's Chapel,* 64 Beacon St. (phone: 617-227-2155).

OLD NORTH CHURCH Built in 1723, this is Boston's oldest church structure. But the "Old North," as it is affectionately called (its official name is Christ Church), is better known for its contribution to the American Revolution. It was from this steeple on the night of April 18, 1775, that church sexton Robert Newman, at the request of Paul Revere, hung two lanterns ("one if by land, two if by sea") to warn the good people of Charlestown of British troop movements. Actually, the most famous steeple in the American Revolution toppled over in a gale in 1804. Its replacement stood solid until it, too, was blown down in 1954. The existing steeple was put up at that time. Revere's ride and Newman's bravery — he was later jailed by the British for hanging the lanterns — was immortalized by poet Henry Wadsworth Longfellow with more than a little embellishment. Newman, the unsung hero of the incident, is also remembered with a plaque in the quiet garden on the church's north side.

To be inside Old North is, well, a religious experience. The ancient wooden floor creaks beneath your feet. The church bells, which bear this inscription: "We are the first ring of bells cast for the British Empire in North America," sound as sweet as they did when Paul Revere rang them as a boy. (It's easy to understand why he went on to cast bells for a living.) Members of the Revere family still worship here occasionally. As you advance down the center aisle, look for a niche near the altar that contains the nation's first memorial to George Washington. Also of note are brass chandeliers made in England in the 1700s, the oldest clock still running in a public building in America, and pews that were once rented by colonial families and still bear their brass nameplates. The pews are arranged like the box seats at *Fenway Park.* Each box was bought by a colonial family (40 British pounds sterling for the center aisle, 20 pounds for the side aisles), which retained the box for life without the option of selling it. After the owner died, the church would get to sell it again. All this is according to the church's guide, who, when he is not dozing, is a font of information. (Ask him to tell the tale of the burial of Major John Pitcairn.) Though several pews near the rear are labeled "Strangers," visitors attending the Episcopalian services held each Sunday may sit anywhere they like. Open daily from 9 AM to 5 PM; Sunday services at 9 AM, 11 AM, and 4 PM. Information: *Christ Church,* 193 Salem St. (phone: 617-523-6676).

PARK STREET CHURCH This early-19th-century Congregational church sits at perhaps the busiest corner in all of Boston. It is called Brimstone Corner because of the gunpowder that used to be kept in its basement during the War of 1812 (a major ingredient of gunpowder is sulfur, or brimstone), or because of the demonstrative speechifying that used to spew from its pulpit (depending on whose version you listen to). The Park Street Church was designed by Peter Banner and was completed in 1810. Abolitionist William

Lloyd Garrison delivered the first of his famous anti-slavery addresses here in 1829, one of the earliest such attacks on slavery. It was also here that the patriotic song "America" ("My country, 'tis of thee . . .") was first sung, on July 4, 1832. Baptist clergyman Samuel Smith, who wrote the lyrics, borrowed the tune from an old German hymn, which also happened to have been borrowed for the British national anthem. The church bells play such old-time favorites as "Ragged Old Cross" and "Rock of Ages" daily at 9 AM, noon, and 4:45 PM. These mini-concerts are well worth lingering around for. The Old Granary Burying Ground, which dates back to 1660, is next door. It's the final resting place of such Revolutionaries as John Hancock, Paul Revere, and Samuel Adams. The church is open Tuesdays through Saturdays from 9 AM to 3:30 PM during the summer, otherwise by appointment. Sunday services are at 9 and 10:45 AM. Information: *Park Street Church,* 1 Park St. (phone: 617-523-3383).

TRINITY CHURCH Visitors to this masterpiece by architect H. H. Richardson invariably describe it, in reverential tones, as "magnificent." Located in Copley Square in Boston's Back Bay, Trinity Church is certainly one of the most impressive churches in the city — probably in the US. Built in 1877, the exterior is deep red sandstone in the Italian Romanesque style (it reflects well in the mirror windows of the ultramodern Hancock Building across the street). The intricate stained glass windows scatter jewels of colored light throughout the church, which, upon entering, is startling in its sheer enormity. The wooden pews and balconies are sumptuously carved. To appreciate the immensity of this structure — the tower itself weighs 12½ million pounds — one must first understand the difficulties of building in this area. Since the Back Bay was created from filled-in wetlands, the church was built on 4,500 wood pilings, which must be kept constantly wet to avoid dry rot. The water level is checked periodically from a hatch in the church's basement. Richardson employed some of the greatest artistic talent of the day to adorn the church's interior walls and vaulted ceilings with paintings and murals. Open daily; Episcopalian Sunday services at 11 AM and Communion at 8 AM and 6 PM. Guided tours are available by appointment. Information: *Trinity Church,* Copley Sq. (phone: 617-536-0944).

Salem: More Than a Witch Hunt

About 18 miles north of Boston on Route 107 is the town of Salem. It was the capital of the Massachusetts Bay Colony from 1626 to 1630, and again, briefly, in 1774, when the British closed Boston Harbor after the Boston Tea Party. However, Salem earned a bitter name in American history as the scene of the witch trials, in which a group of women and children accused more than 100 villagers of witchcraft. The hysterical allegations resulted in the deaths of 25 of the accused. Several of the judges subsequently regretted their roles in the tragedy. Salem is also the site of Nathaniel Hawthorne's *House of the Seven Gables* (54 Turner St.; phone: 508-744-0991). Open daily. Admission charge. Hawthorne worked in the Salem Custom House and wrote his masterpiece, *The Scarlet Letter,* at 14 Mall Street. Like Boston, Salem has a history trail winding through its streets and port. Visit the Salem Maritime National Historic Site, run by the National Park Service, for information, maps, and a variety of seasonal tours. Open daily 8:30 AM to 5 PM (174 Derby St.; phone: 508-744-4323 or 508-745-1470).

While you're in the neighborhood, stop at the *Witch Museum* (19½ Washington Sq. N.; phone: 508-744-1692). Closed *Thanksgiving, Christmas,* and *New Year's Day.* Admission charge. The *Witch House,* site of some of the interrogations, radiates a claustrophobic, spooky feeling, especially at night. Open daily, mid-March through December 1. Admission charge (310½ Essex St.; phone: 508-744-0180). You can get in the mood for this tour by picking up a copy of Arthur Miller's play *The Crucible.*

The *Peabody Museum* (E. India Sq.; phone: 508-745-1876) has fascinating scrimshaw carvings and nautical regalia from the early days of shipping and from far-off ports. Closed *Thanksgiving, Christmas,* and *New Year's Day.* Admission charge. *Pier Transit Cruises* offers harbor tours that leave from Salem Willows Pier (phone: 508-744-6311 or 800-696-6311).

A few miles east of Salem, the sailboating town of Marblehead has myriad colonial houses, places to sit and look at the harbor, lots of boats, and shops selling New England seascapes and elegant, old-fashioned furnishings. Toward evening, you can watch fishermen unloading the day's catch.

Great Golf Outside the City

Golf is beloved in and around Boston for several reasons: the clubby atmosphere of the grand old game; the local love of a challenge; and, perhaps foremost, the escape it offers from the urban jungle. A round of golf provides the perfect opportunity to stride through the green spaces, draw deep breaths of clean air, and enjoy nature while testing your skills against its wily ways. There are a number of surprisingly well-manicured, challenging, and scenic public golf courses throughout the greater Boston area that can be reached in a short drive (with a car, not a club).

COLONIAL COUNTRY CLUB Located just outside the *Colonial Hilton* hotel in Wakefield, north of Boston, this is an excellent 18-hole course that is open to the public. A benign front nine will stroke a golfer's ego, and the feeling of elation will last until the dreaded hole 13, the front end of a trio of golf holes (a par 4, par 3, and par 5 respectively) that are so daunting they are known in these parts as "Amen Corner." They may help you find religion — or just your ball in the holy water. Since the back nine is located along the Saugus River, water figures prominently in the experience. Eleven of the course's 18 holes are encroached by marshland. Tee times for weekend play should be made on Thursday mornings. Information: *Colonial Country Club,* Exit 43 off Rte. 128, Wakefield, MA 01880 (phone: 617-245-9300).

GEORGE WRIGHT GOLF COURSE This hilly course, thick with pine and sassafras trees, was designed by Donald Ross, the great American golf course architect. It is of medium length (6,166 yards) and must be the only course in the country with a brick wall around it. (The hopelessly erratic golfer can thank the New Deal government, which erected the wall in 1937, one year before the course was built.) Though there is no water to speak of, there are plenty of other impediments on these links to test your mettle. Greens fees are reasonable. Weekend tee times should be made by 11 AM on Thursdays. There is a restaurant and bar. Information: *George Wright Golf Course,* 420 West St. (near Rte. 28), Hyde Park, MA 02136 (phone: 617-361-8313).

NEWTON COMMONWEALTH GOLF COURSE This old course, originally built in 1895, is known for its small targets, its fast greens, and its premium on hitting the ball straight. It was a country club until it filed for bankruptcy in the late 1970s, when it was converted into a public course. Very accessible by public transportation, it is located about a tee shot from the *MBTA* station at the end of the Boston College branch of the *Green Line.* There is not much water and not many trees, but it is tight and challenging. Make tee times a week in advance for weekend play. Information: *Newton Commonwealth Golf Course,* 212 Kerrick St., Chestnut Hill, MA 02158 (phone: 617-244-4763).

STOW ACRES Several years ago, this was rated by *Golf Digest* magazine as one of the top 50 public courses in the country. The verdant pine trees make a round on either of the two 18-hole courses here seem like a trek into an enchanted forest, a feeling enhanced by repeated rescue missions (for your ball) into its treacherous roughs. There are hills and dales, cleverly crafted ponds, fairway traps, nettlesome streams, and even a craggy old rock wall, a vestige of the farm that formerly occupied this land. All of these combine to create a course of uncommon beauty or unrelenting obstacles, depending on your skill and state of mind. There is a driving range, putting green, and a good crowd on the weekends. Open daily; make reservations at least 5 days in advance. Golfers are juggled about on the roster to create foursomes. About 15 miles northeast of Boston. Information: *Stow Acres Country Club,* 58 Randall Rd., Stow, MA 01775 (phone: 508-568-8690).

Top Tennis Outside the City

There are several private courts near the city that occasionally offer limited playing time to non-members. Still other courts offer membership, yet don't require it for the visiting player. If you belong to a club back home, you may have reciprocity with one of the more exclusive clubs. Two of our favorites are described below; check the telephone book for a complete list of private tennis clubs in the area. For information on Boston's public courts, see *Sports and Fitness* in THE CITY.

LONGWOOD CRICKET CLUB The name is a misnomer — it's not in Longwood, and tennis, not cricket, is the game played here. The club was named Longwood by the owner of this estate after Napoleon's exile home on St. Helena, and a cricket club that once played on the land added the rest. Name aside, as the home of the *US Pro Tennis Championships at Longwood*, the oldest American professional championship, this is the primary site of competitive tennis in Boston. The championship, which takes place in mid- to late July for approximately 9 days, draws some of the top names in tennis. Longwood literally introduced tennis on grass to the nation, having installed America's first grass court in 1878. The club boasts 12 clay and 36 grass courts; 3 hard courts have been resurfaced especially for the tournament. Only members and their guests may play here, but tickets to the *US Pro* matches are available (phone: 617-731-4500). Information: *Longwood Cricket Club,* 564 Hammond St., Brookline, MA 02167 (phone: 617-731-2900).

SPORTSMEN'S TENNIS CLUB This private, nonprofit tennis club features 7 indoor and 8 outdoor courts. Memberships are available here, but are not required. Information: *Sportsmen's Tennis Club,* Franklin Field Tennis Center, 950 Blue Hill Ave., Dorchester, MA 02124 (phone: 617-288-9092).

Gone Fishing

A trip to see the nearly 2,000 species of aquatic life at the *New England Aquarium* on Boston's Central Wharf may inspire visitors to partake in some angling. There are several bodies of fresh water in and around Boston that are stocked with everything from bass and crappie to trout and perch. Freshwater fishing in Boston requires a license from the Division of Fisheries and Wildlife (phone: 617-727-5215, ext. 3153). Nonresidents may purchase a special 7-day license for $16.50. In some cases an additional permit is needed from the city of Boston. Since ten questions about whether fish caught in Boston are safe to eat would yield ten different answers, it's best to be cautious — if fellow fishermen seem doubtful, don't do it. There is, however, ample saltwater fishing in the Atlantic, but since this is a metropolitan area with a notorious pollution problem, don't expect to just throw a line off any city pier and come up with anything other than sunken galoshes, spare tires, or a shopping cart. There are commercial fishing tours of the harbor, as well as boats and equipment that can be rented for deep-sea fishing. The following places are some of the favorite spots of local anglers and are open year-round.

CASTLE ISLAND A landfill project attached this island to South Boston in 1930. The pier, which juts out into the harbor from Day Boulevard in South Boston, is one of the best saltwater fishing spots in the city. The causeway is so long that the angler feels far removed from the surrounding industrial blight. This is a favorite among locals, who have reported landing good-sized striped bass, blue fish, and flounder from this area. No permit is required.

CHARLES RIVER The old muddy water of the Charles carries a surprising array of freshwater fish, including largemouth bass, catfish, crappie, and sunfish. Many local fishermen recommend the Chárles, though not very loudly since they consider it a well-kept secret. The fishing is better the farther upstream you go. The Watertown area is a particularly good place to sink a hook.

JAMAICA POND This 68-acre freshwater pond (and the surrounding park area and bicycle paths) is part of Frederick Law Olmsted's Emerald Necklace of parkland that stretches west for 8 miles from the Boston Common. Jamaica Pond is stocked primarily with trout and bass. There are a number of woodsy spots near the water's edge that will shelter you from the thunder of joggers huffing and puffing around the pond. Whether or not you catch anything, this is a serene place to try. Fishing here may require an additional license from the city of Boston. On Jamaica Way in Jamaica Plain. You can get a license from the Boston Park Rangers, Franklin Park, Dorchester (phone: 617-522-2639).

WALDEN POND This will require a pilgrimage from Boston à la Henry David Thoreau, who adopted this pond as his home for 2 years of solitary living during the mid-1800s. The pond is stocked heavily with brook and rainbow trout. Be sure you have enough fishing line — at 102 feet, this is one of the deepest ponds on the eastern seaboard. If you wish, you may take one of the many rarely trodden paths to escape the usual crush of people sunning themselves on the beach, laughing, playing games, and, as Thoreau said, generally leading lives of quiet desperation. Walden Pond is easily accessible by commuter rail. Take the Fitchburg or South Acton train from North Station to Concord. Information: *Walden Pond State Reservation,* 915 Walden St., Concord, MA 01742 (phone: 508-369-3254).

DEEP-SEA FISHING *Boston by Sail,* a company based at Long Wharf, offers the private rental of a 40-foot sport fishing boat that comes equipped with tackle, bait, and a skipper who harbors a wealth of information on where to land the real lunkers. The boat is ideal for up to six people, and rents for $80 per hour (3-hour minimum). The skipper will take you and your mates 5 miles out in search of flounder, cod, tuna, striped bass, and shark. But you can just putter around the harbor fishing for galoshes if you choose. The boat embarks from Long Wharf. Information: *Boston by Sail,* 66 Long Wharf, Boston, MA 02110 (phone: 617-742-3313).

A Shutterbug's Boston

If you can get it to hold still long enough, Boston is an exceptionally photogenic city. There is architectural variety: Old juxtaposed with new, ornate with ordinary, and a skyline bristling with the temples of modern commerce that's also graced with an 18th-century church spire — a humble reminder of when God was the only game in town. There is also natural variety: A column of magnolias embroiders a park footpath, ivy inches up a colonial red brick building, and a summer sunset sparks the river ablaze. There's human variety as well: Immigrants exchange the latest news from the Old Country in rapid-fire Sicilian, ruddy fishermen return with their catch, and stocky sports fans sit cheek by jowl dressed in their team's full regalia. The thriving city, the shimmering sea, the parks, the people, and traces of rich history make Boston a fertile stomping ground for shutterbugs. Even a beginner can achieve remarkable results with a surprisingly basic set of lenses and filters. Equipment is, in fact, only as valuable as the imagination that puts it into use.

LANDSCAPES, SEASCAPES, AND CITYSCAPES Boston's bustling byways and historic buildings are most often visiting photographers' favorite subjects. But the city's green spaces and waterways provide numerous photo possibilities as well. In addition to the State House, the Hancock Building, and Trinity Church, be sure to look for natural beauty: magnolia trees that line the Commonwealth Avenue mall, the well-manicured plots of flowers in the Public Garden, the marshy ponds of the Fens Park, and the sailboats that skim along the Charles River are just a few examples.

Although a standard 50mm to 55mm lens may work well in some landscape situations, most will benefit from a 20mm to 28mm wide-angle. The Common, with city skyscrapers looming in the distance, for example, is the type of panorama that fits beautifully into a wide-angle format, allowing not only the overview, but the opportunity to include people or other points of interest in the foreground. A flower, for instance, may be used to set off a view of the Public Garden; or people can provide a sense of perspective in a shot of Copley Square. To isolate specific elements of any scene, use your telephoto lens. Perhaps there's a particular carving in a historic church that would make a lovely shot, or it might be the interplay of light and shadow on a cobblestone Beacon Hill street. The successful use of a telephoto means developing your eye for detail.

PEOPLE As with taking pictures of people anywhere, there are going to be times in Boston when a camera is an intrusion. Consider your own reaction under similar circumstances, and you have an idea as to what would make others comfortable enough to be willing subjects. People are often sensitive to having a camera suddenly pointed at them, and a polite request, while getting you a share of refusals, will also provide a chance to shoot some wonderful portraits that capture the spirit of the city as surely as the scenery does. For candids, an excellent lens is a zoom telephoto in the 70mm to 210mm range; it allows you to remain unobtrusive while the telephoto lens draws the subject closer. And for portraits, a telephoto can be used effectively as close as 2 or 3 feet.

For authenticity and variety, select a place likely to produce interesting subjects. The *Faneuil Hall Marketplace* is an obvious spot for visitors, but if it's local color you're after, visit Chinatown or one of the North End's Italian street festivals, sit at a Newbury Street café and watch the fashion parade, or walk around the Common, where everyone from elderly Brahmins to college students to street people flock to enjoy a sunny day. Aim for shots that tell what's different about Boston. In portraiture, there are several factors to keep in mind. Morning or afternoon light will add richness to skin tones, emphasizing tans. To avoid the harsh facial shadows cast by direct sunlight, shoot in the shade or in an area where the light is diffused.

SUNSETS When shooting sunsets, keep in mind that the brightness will distort meter readings. When composing a shot directly into the sun, frame the picture in the viewfinder so that only half of the sun is included. Read the meter, set, and shoot. Whenever there is this kind of unusual lighting, shoot a few frames in half-step increments, both over and under the meter reading. Bracketing, as this is called, can provide a range of images, the best of which may well be other than the one shot at the meter's recommended setting.

Use any lens for sunsets. A wide-angle is good when the sky is filled with color-streaked clouds, when the sun is partially hidden, or when you're close to an object that silhouettes dramatically against the sky.

Telephotos also produce wonderful silhouettes, either with the sun as a backdrop or against the palette of a brilliant sunset sky. Bracket again here. For the best silhouettes, wait 10 to 15 minutes after sunset. Unless using a very fast film, a tripod is recommended.

Red and orange filters are often used to accentuate a sunset's picture potential. Orange will help turn even a gray sky into something approaching a photogenic finale to the day, and can provide particularly beautiful shots linking the sky with the sun reflected on the ocean. If the sunset is already bold in hue, however, the orange will overwhelm the natural colors. A red filter will produce dramatic, highly unrealistic results.

NIGHT If you think that picture possibilities end at sunset, you're presuming that night photography is the exclusive domain of the professional. If you've got a tripod, all you'll need is a cable release to attach to your camera to assure a steady exposure (which is often timed in minutes rather than fractions of a second).

For situations such as evening concerts on the Esplanade or nighttime harbor cruises, a strobe does the trick, but beware: Flash units are often used improperly. You can't take a view of the skyline with a flash. It may reach out as far as 30 feet, but that's it. On the other hand, a flash used too close to a subject may result in overexposure, resulting in a "blown out" effect. With most cameras, strobes will work with a maximum shutter speed of 1/125 or 1/250 of a second. If you set the exposure properly and shoot within range, you should come up with pretty sharp results.

CLOSE-UPS Whether of people or of objects such as antique door knockers, close-ups can add another dimension to your photography. There are a number of shooting options, one of which is to use a 70mm or a 210mm lens at its closest focusable distance. Unless you're working in bright sunlight, a tripod will be worthwhile. If you are very near your subject and there is a good deal of reflective light, it may pay to underexpose a bit in relation to the meter reading.

If you do not have a telephoto lens, you can still shoot close-ups using a set of magnification filters. Filter packs of one-, two-, and three-times magnification are available, converting your lens into a close-up lens. Even better is a special macro lens designed for close-up photography.

A SHORT PHOTOGRAPHIC TOUR

Here are some of Boston's great pictorial perspectives.

PUBLIC GARDEN Stand at the head of the Commonwealth Avenue mall (in the center park area on Commonwealth Avenue), with the *Ritz-Carlton* hotel to your right and the tricolor flying from the French Consulate to your left. The view east to the Public Garden is, perhaps, the city's best photo op. Picture this: Sitting high atop his steed and checking troop movements to the south is the robust, yet graceful, equestrian statue of General George Washington. At his feet (in the spring) are circular beds of tulips. Behind the good general is the Public Garden's suspension bridge, fringed by elms and gas lamps, which gives way to the upward, verdant slopes of the Boston Common. The trees of the Common enshroud all but the tops of a jungle of financial district high-rises. Their aircraft warning lights flicker just above the treetops. The pure white steeple of the Park Street Church reaches for the heavens to the left. From this angle, Boston seems an Emerald City. Snap one with the focus on the background and one with the focus on General Washington.

BAPTIST CHURCH/HANCOCK TOWER Stand again on the Commonwealth Avenue mall, this time just past the corner of Clarendon Street and Commonwealth Avenue. Face south to gaze upon the First Baptist Church. This antiquated place of worship earned the name the "Church of the Holy Bean Blowers," because of the trumpeting angels sculpted into the church's soaring tower, which was created by Auguste Bartholdi, the French sculptor also responsible for the Statue of Liberty. With your lens pointed toward the upper reaches of the church (you may want to go vertical on this one), capture the ivy creeping up the church's puddingstone façade, the intricate detail of the trumpeting angels (on which you may want to focus), and the stark contrast of the glistening Hancock Tower in the background.

TRINITY CHURCH/HANCOCK TOWER From Copley Square on a sunny day, the sight of the deep red sandstone of the Trinity Church reflected in the light blue panes of mirror window of the gargantuan Hancock Tower seems to exemplify all that Boston is about — from solid old spirituality to the towering heights of the modern high-tech world. Find the right angle and the entire history of Boston can be told in the click of a shutter.

STATE HOUSE Probably the best view of the golden dome of the State House, which Oliver Wendell Holmes called "the hub of the solar system," is from the Brewer Fountain, a bronze replica of a Parisian fountain just next to the Park Street *T* stop in Boston Common. Standing on the sidewalk that runs along Tremont Street you can get the fountain, one of the Common's most beautiful ornaments, in the picture's foreground. Beyond the fountain is a plush strip of turf, resembling a bowling green, which rises higher and higher until it tucks into Beacon Street at the foot of the State House. The dome is most picturesque when it glistens in the midday sun. If one of the park's several mounted police are in the area, they are usually game for a pose.

ACORN STREET This is Beacon Hill's most photographed street. Steep and narrow, charming, and petite (it's really more an alley than a street), this was once home to coach drivers, servants, craftsmen, and a couple of stables. Grass can be seen sprouting in the cobblestone street, and its gas lights at dusk set the jet black shutters aglow. Whatever the angle, this shot's bound to be a keeper.

Directions

Introduction

There are many reasons why walking is the best means of transportation for seeing Boston. Most of them, however, have less to do with sightseeing than with the total impracticability of driving a car in Boston proper, where parking spots are an endangered species, the chance of getting your car stolen is eclipsed only by the likelihood of its being ticketed, and driving is an anarchic battle of wills largely ungoverned by any higher authority. (Boston's police force has a full bag of problems that prevent it from being overly picky about most moving violations.)

Happily, Boston is (for the most part) a pedestrian-friendly city. The Freedom Trail, the Heritage Trail, the Emerald Necklace, and the South End's Southwest Corridor are examples of how walkers have figured prominently in city planning. Confusion does arise, however, when visitors learn that there is both a South End and a South Boston, a West End that no longer exists (when it did it was actually north), a North End but no North Boston, and an East Boston but no East End. Visitors (and locals) are also baffled by the haphazard placement of the city's streets. In fact, Boston may have the most illogical avenue layout of any major US metropolis: Manhattan has numbered streets, after all; finding a location in Los Angeles is as easy as working the card catalogue in a library; and Washington, the American city that comes closest to Boston's well-shuffled deck of asymmetrical streets, was at least the intentional chaos of a French planner.

But what the city lacks in order, it makes up for in intimacy. Boston is remarkably condensed; one can get from the southernmost brownstone in the South End to the northernmost pier in the North End in a brisk, 25-minute walk, and with some fancy footwork, the entire city can be traversed in a day.

Just because the locals are flitting about at breakneck speed, however, doesn't mean you have to keep up; in fact, you're better off not even trying. (A recent study deemed Boston the fastest-paced city in America, with Manhattan — home of the fabled New York minute — downright sluggish by comparison.) While traipsing along the routes outlined in the following seven walking tours and one driving tour to Cambridge, Lexington, Concord, and Lincoln, linger amid the blooming magnolia trees and stalwart statues of the Commonwealth Avenue mall, ruminate over cannoli and cappuccino in the North End, poke around the shops of the *Faneuil Hall Marketplace,* dawdle about the 18th-century homes of Beacon Hill, and loll under the midday sun in Boston Common.

The seven walking routes and one drive, which are presented in geographical order (roughly west to east), have been designed to guide visitors past the lion's share of historic Boston landmarks, into intriguing shops, around common traffic quandaries, and away from questionable areas (assuming you don't travel heavily armed), all the while considering appetite and the primal American lust for occasionally wandering off the beaten path. This is not to say you should take leave of your street smarts, however. Boston is a big city, and like any big city, it's hopelessly congested with more people, places, and (potentially dangerous) things than should be situated on such a small chunk of real estate, so stay alert.

One more thing to consider before stepping out into a Boston intersection: A taxi cab was spotted recently with a bumper sticker reading, "So many pedestrians. So little time."

Walk 1: The Fens

In the 19th-century frenzy to fill in the putrid marshes of the Back Bay and turn them into a posh residential area, it is remarkable that Boston city planners had the foresight to realize that enough was enough. Deciding that some of the original marshland should remain undeveloped, they hired the renowned landscape architect Frederick Law Olmsted to work his magic on a marshy area in the southwest of the city. Olmsted, romancing and subtly manicuring nature as only he could do, created a park that retains the original feel of the salt marshes and tidal flats that it replaced — clusters of reeds rise above still ponds, irregular pools are scattered amid meadows and flower gardens — while it also serves as a pleasant greenspace where the city's residents may stroll, play, and enjoy the outdoors.

Today, the Fens Park is the centerpiece of an area of Boston that includes Kenmore Square and *Fenway Park* to the north, *Symphony Hall* and Northeastern University to the east, the *Museum of Fine Arts* and the *Isabella Stewart Gardner Museum* to the south, and the Longwood Medical Area to the west. Though portions of the Fens have given way to crime and urban blight of late (don't wander its paths after dark), it still remains a godsend to neighborhood residents seeking a natural oasis and a crucial link in what is known as the Emerald Necklace, 8 miles of Olmsted-designed parkland that stretches from Boston Common to Roxbury's *Franklin Park Zoo.*

Our walking tour of the Fens area (allow about 2 hours) begins at *Symphony Hall,* at the corner of Massachusetts and Huntington Avenues. This grand hall of Boston music, built in 1900, is considered one of the world's best; the acoustics are so fine that there's not a bad seat in the house. Just loitering about the foyer watching the crunch of Brahmins bedecked in furs, sequins, and black-tie formal wear rushing to take their seats is a memorable experience. *Symphony Hall* is home to the venerable *Boston Symphony Orchestra* and the *Boston Pops,* and it frequently hosts guest performances. Tours are offered by appointment; ask for the volunteer office (phone: 266-1492).

Music permeates the area surrounding the Symphony stop on the *MBTA's Green Line.* Two blocks down Huntington Avenue (to the west) is the New England Conservatory (NEC), the training ground for many of the musicians who have taken their seats down the street with either the *Boston Pops* or the *Boston Symphony Orchestra.* The NEC's *Jordan Hall* is the venue of many acclaimed local musical groups. Walk up Massachusetts Avenue to the north to see musicians of a different ilk. Here a trendier crowd sits on stoops drumming their knees, grooving to Walkmans, and perfecting their existential looks. This is the Berklee College of Music, the

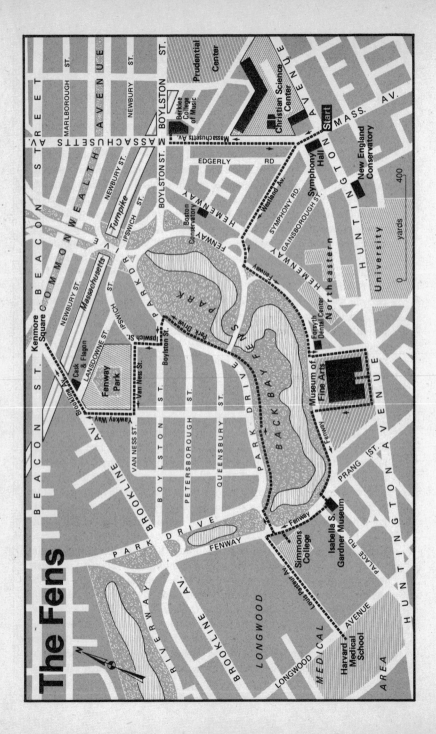

Juilliard of jazz and rock music education (though jazz purists claim the latter has been holding sway of late).

Walk back down Massachusetts Avenue ("Mass. Ave." in local parlance) in the direction of *Symphony Hall.* On the right is *Bangkok Cuisine* (177A Massachusetts Ave.; phone: 262-5377), an excellent Thai restaurant. It has some of the tastiest, most moderately priced Thai food in Boston. Try the extra spicy *tom yum kong* soup — if you dare.

Continue down Mass. Ave. past the Christian Science Church headquarters and reflecting pool on the left (see *Walk 2: South End*). Make a sharp right on Westland Avenue. From here the Fens Park is straight ahead. The lights of *Fenway Park* are visible, peeking over the treetops. Nearby is Kenmore Square, this tour's ultimate destination; should you lose your bearings, just head for the neon Citgo sign that hovers over this busy square (more on this unlikely landmark later).

First cross Hemenway Street — primarily the site of student housing for Northeastern University — and proceed between the two columns that offer a stately entrance to the Fens. Walk diagonally across the grassy area to the Fenway, the road that traces the east boundary of the Fens Park. Be sure to look both ways (several times) before negotiating this street, since you're crossing at a bend and every other car is likely to be driven by a college student, who considers the roadway surrounding the park a convenient racetrack. Once safely across, walk left along the lower path under the magnolia trees. If it's a nice day, an artist may be adjusting the position of his easel, trying to find just the right angle to capture the glint of sunlight on the water, the frolicking ducks, or one of the miniature bridges that span the still pond. From this vantage point, it's easy to appreciate what Olmsted had in mind when he chose simply to enhance the marsh rather than radically transform it.

Across the Fenway are a handful of the buildings that house dorms, classrooms, and administrative offices of the sprawling Northeastern University, which with a student body of 35,000, is one of the largest cooperative-plan schools in the country. (Students alternate classroom instruction with paid employment in their chosen profession.) As the Fenway bends, the ornate building on the left is Forsyth Dental Center, which sits across Forsyth Way from the *Museum of Fine Arts (MFA).*

The *MFA,* housed in this magnificent building since 1909 (it first opened in Copley Square in 1870), has developed into one of America's finest cultural institutions. Many consider it second only to New York's *Metropolitan Museum of Art.* Follow the Fenway along the back of the building, then turn left on Museum Road, which leads to the main entrance, in the newer west wing, designed by architect I. M. Pei. Be sure to walk around to the front of the building to see Cyrus Dallin's statue *Appeal to the Great Spirit.* In the *MFA*'s grand halls is a vast array of American works, an impressive number of paintings by the French Impressionists (including 38 Monets), some of the Western world's best Oriental art, and possibly the largest collection of Egyptian art outside Egypt. The museum merits at least a half-day visit, so you may want to skip it for now and return when time allows. Closed Mondays; open late on Wednesdays. Admission charge. 465 Huntington Ave. (phone: 267-9300). Also see *Special Places* in THE CITY.

Leaving the museum, be sure to stop in the Tenshin Garden, a Japanese design fused with New England flora that elevates gardening to an art form. Just past the garden is the Japanese Temple Bell, given to Boston by the Mayor of Kyoto, Japan, as a symbol of friendship. From here walk to the home of the flamboyant "Mrs. Jack," the *Isabella Stewart Gardner Museum.* Take a left on the Fenway and follow it around; at the bend is the School of the Museum of Fine Arts; directly ahead and to the left is the *Gardner Museum.*

This 4-story yellow brick Venetian palazzo may not look spectacular from the outside, but inside is one of the best private galleries in the country, including works by Titian, Matisse, Botticelli, and Rubens. It's easy to spend several hours perusing the art and antiques (make sure to purchase a museum guide upon entering) and enjoying the blooms in the serene courtyard.

Security at the museum is tight, following the still unsolved robbery of 13 works, including some by Rembrandt, Degas, and Vermeer, in a highly publicized heist in March 1990. There's also a pleasant café that serves light bistro fare during lunch hours. Closed Mondays. Admission charge for the upper galleries. You can stroll through the spectacular courtyard for free. 280 The Fenway (phone: 566-1401). For more information, see *Special Places* in THE CITY.

Continue left along the Fenway to Simmons College. Take a short detour and visit the majestic Harvard Medical School building located in the Longwood Medical Area, one of the world's foremost medical complexes. Or cross back to the park side of the Fenway, and follow the path to the right over a stone bridge to the road that borders the other side of the Fens. This part of the Fens, site of several baseball diamonds, basketball courts, and a running track, is admittedly unattractive. But forge ahead. A bit farther along the path, in an enclosed area on the right, is the Rose Garden, which blooms in the summer months with thousands of wild and cultivated varieties of roses. There are also monuments in this area to local soldiers who died in World War II, the Korean conflict, and Vietnam.

Continuing along the edge of the park, just beyond the Rose Garden are the Victory Gardens, where city dwellers can be found cultivating small plots of vegetables and flowers. When World War II sent food prices soaring like German bombers over London, 4½ acres of the Fens Park were cleared so that city residents could grow their own vegetables. Though the area since has been reduced, 100 plots now are maintained by the Fenway Garden Society, which parcels them out to soil-starved urbanites.

From here the tour leads to *Fenway Park,* the home of the *Red Sox.* Walk past the Victory Gardens and cut across the grassy triangle, heading north from the Texaco station. Cross Boylston Street and take a quick right onto Ipswich Street. Directly ahead is *Fenway Park,* built in 1912. Make a left on Van Ness Street; walk along the side of the stadium for 1 block, then turn right on Yawkey Way (where autograph seekers lurk after games and try, not always successfully, to get the signatures of players leaving the *Red Sox* parking lot). This street was named after Tom Yawkey, the late owner of the *Red Sox,* who bought the team in 1933 as a 30th-birthday present for himself and, until his death in 1976, tried unsuccessfully to win the *World Series* (the *Red Sox* haven't won a *World Series* since 1918). On the left are *Red Sox* souvenir shops and a candlepin bowling alley, a strange form of the game that's indigenous to New England and uses down-scaled pins and balls.

Turn right on Brookline Avenue. At the corner of Brookline Avenue and Lansdowne Street is the very nerve center of game days, the *Cask and Flagon* (phone: 536-4840). The *Cask* was for many years a smoke-filled, low-key watering hole with pool tables. Since catching the sports bar bug several years ago, it has become downright flashy. Along with some solidly American food, there's an original team photo of the 1948 *Red Sox* and the blueprints for *Fenway Park* on the wall. When emerging from the *Cask,* look left down Lansdowne Street. On the right looms the Green Monster, Fenway's inordinately tall left-field wall, which has contributed to so much baseball lore. Lansdowne Street could also be called Nightclub Row: It's where the city's young and hip come to dance at places such as *Axis* (No. 15) and, the latest, *Alley Cat* (1 Boylston Pl.).

If the *Sox* are in town, it's worth trying to get tickets (2 Yawkey Way; phone: 267-1700). Even if you don't like the game (or if you're a *Yankees* fan), there's nothing like the ambience of this grand old ball field. (Also see *Quintessential Boston* in DIVERSIONS.)

Follow Brookline Avenue toward the Citgo sign into Kenmore Square. This big lug of a neon sign, an unusually ambitious example of self-promotion even for a large corporation, has been saved several times from destruction by preservationists. It's there to stay, it seems, a landmark as much identified with Kenmore Square as its horrendous evening traffic jams. (In the spirit of Rome, Kenmore Square consists of a harrowing convergence of five streets.) *Pizzeria Uno* (1 Brookline Ave.; phone: 262-2373), on the corner to the left, serves up a formidable deep-dish pizza and good pasta dishes and salads.

Though Kenmore Square is largely a collection of fast-food joints, music stores, and quick-cash machines (Boston University is a block down Commonwealth Avenue to the west), there are a few places of note. The *Boston University Bookstore* (660 Beacon St.; phone: 267-8484), a 5-story building on the other side of Kenmore Square, is the one of the largest bookstores in New England. If you're hungry or parched, *Souper Salad* (524 Commonwealth Ave.; phone: 536-7662) has a bounteous salad bar, and *Cornwall's* (510 Commonwealth Ave.; phone: 262-3749) is a handsome pub and restaurant with a wide variety of ales and a dart board atop a wooden stand in front of the kitchen. Either one will provide a pleasant epilogue to your walking tour of the Fens.

Walk 2: South End

During the warm months, stoop sitting is a common weekend pastime in Boston's South End. Walk down any of several South End streets on a balmy day and see a rainbow coalition of residents gathered on the steps of their Victorian brownstones and red brick townhouses, taking in the sun, snapping photos of their kids, swapping recipes and tales of urban life. Blacks still live next to Hispanics here, gentiles next to Jews, and Irish alongside Armenians, creating a sense of tolerance unmatched in any other part of Boston. This synthesis of colors and creeds gives the South End its identity.

Boston's South End has been many things to many people since 1855, when it was claimed from the marsh along a narrow neck of land connecting the Boston peninsula to the mainland. It went into a tailspin from nouveau riche to lower middle class to skid row about as fast as you can say "capital flight." Only recently has it rallied back to respectability.

The South End makes for an attractive and interesting walk, offering visitors a look at a side of the city that many tourists never see. The neighborhood has neither downtown Boston's concentration of historic sites nor the Back Bay's homes of famous old families. Rather, the South End offers a living testament to Boston's ethnic diversity, to the wave after wave of immigrants that have kept the city vibrant. And then there is the architecture. Even during the worst of times, it was said that the South End was the "most beautiful slum in the world."

This walk should take about 2½ hours. Begin on the Boylston Street side of the Prudential Center (the "Pru"). The Pru and Copley Square Plaza separate the South End from the rest of Boston, with the Pru serving as the boundary between the Back Bay and the South End. To cross over from the Back Bay, ascend the escalator just beyond (and slightly to the left of) the outstretched arms of the statue *Quest Eternal* in front of the Pru. Walk the length of the plaza (there is an *Au Bon Pain* here for coffee or a croissant for sustenance) and descend the escalator on the other side. Voilà! The South End is before you.

Before crossing Huntington Avenue and plunging in, first visit the life's work of Mary Baker Eddy, founder of the Church of Christ, Scientist (better known as the Christian Science Church). The vast Christian Science World Headquarters complex sits at the juncture of the South End, the Fens, and the Back Bay.

Just across Belvedere Street is the complex's fountain and reflecting pool, a popular spot on steamy summer days, when local youth take turns maneuvering their skateboards and bicycles through the spouting water (it's better than opening a fire hydrant on a busy street). Take a stroll around the 670-foot rectangular pool — it continually circulates water so

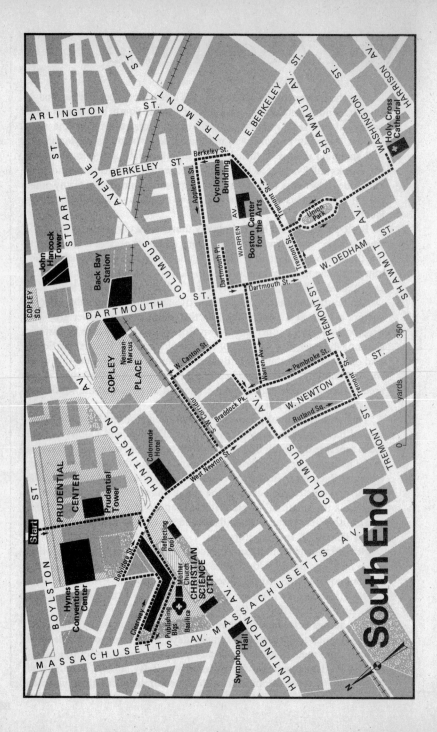

South End

that it gently rolls over the pool's rounded inner edge. Someone walking on the outer ledge of the opposite side of the pool appears to be walking on water. Before giving in to the impulse to convert or to try it yourself, be forewarned — it's just an illusion.

The original church, built in 1894, is on the right at the end of the pool. Today, the granite building is enveloped by an immense basilica, which is best viewed from the sidewalk on Massachusetts Avenue. It's even more dazzling at night. All the other contemporary buildings in the area are administrative offices for the Christian Science Center and were designed by architect I. M. Pei.

Turn right after reaching the basilica. The Christian Science Publishing Society Building, which houses the offices of the *Christian Science Monitor,* is straight ahead. The *Monitor* is read in 147 nations. The offices of *Monitor Radio* are located in the Christian Science Broadcast Building.

The most interesting aspect of the Christian Science Publishing Society Building, however, is the Mapparium (no need to run to *Webster's*; the word was coined here). A stained glass globe built in 1935, the Mapparium is hopelessly stuck in the Old World Order — there are only 70 countries depicted, Sri Lanka is labeled Ceylon, and Laos and Vietnam are listed as French Indochina. Though anachronistic, the globe has one appealing quality — you can walk through it. But it's not the best place to pass national security secrets or make dirty confessions — the acoustics are incredible. A whisper at one end can be heard loud and clear on the opposite side. The Mapparium is open Tuesdays through Saturdays, 9:30 AM to 4 PM. Remember to pick up a free issue of the *Christian Science Monitor* on the way out.

Once outside, Mass. Ave. is on the right. Follow the sidewalk to Clearway (the first street), a charming little thoroughfare with narrow, red brick buildings and gas lamps. Follow this street to the rear of the church complex, then veer left onto Belvedere Street and turn right. The hotel on the left is the *Sheraton,* where the doormen dress, inexplicably, like British military officers during the Boer War. The *Hilton* is across the street.

When Belvedere crosses Huntington Avenue, it becomes West Newton Street. The *Colonnade* hotel (phone: 424-7000), on the left, is known for its Old World European luxury. A jazz trio blows some cool riffs in the hotel's *Zachary's* bar on weekend nights.

At the end of this first block on West Newton (which becomes a veritable wind tunnel and, consequently, an umbrella graveyard when the weather is foul) is *St. Botolph* restaurant (99 St. Botolph St.; phone: 266-3030), with excellent continental fare.

Just past St. Botolph Street is a wide, well-manicured corridor with shrubs, trees, and wrought-iron gates. This is the Southwest Corridor, a pleasant pedestrian avenue that stretches from the Back Bay *T* stop on the *Orange Line* (behind *Neiman Marcus* near Copley Square) all the way to the Forest Hills station (the other side of Massachusetts Avenue). The fact that one can stroll casually down this mall is a tribute to the tenacity of local residents. The space had originally been carved out for what was to have been the Southwest Expressway, a highway that would have been as damaging to the South End as the Southeast Expressway is to the North End today. The neighborhood's savvy residents, whose civic activism has been honed through countless battles over the past 2 decades, put their collective foot down on this plan.

Past the Southwest Corridor, at the corner of West Newton and Columbus, is the Union United Methodist Church, its mossy pudding stone plush and inviting. The church's leader, Rev. Charles Smith, is an influential voice in Boston's black community. Built in 1872, it originally served the Universalist congregation that migrated to the South End. Across Columbus Avenue and to the right is Rutland Square, a quiet block with a small fenced-in mall — little more than a tiny sliver of grass adorned with pink-and-white magnolia trees. The Italian bowfront houses in this block, which date from the 1860s, are more modest than in larger South End squares like Union Square (see below). But Rutland Square remains much more ethnically diverse than Union Square. The area, however, is in a state of flux. Using front doors as a guide, it's possible to determine which buildings are homes to lower-income families, which are being gutted, and which house wealthier former suburbanites who recently moved in, part of the gentrification movement in the South End.

Walk along Rutland Square to Tremont Street, noting the twin-towered New Hope Baptist Church across the way. On Sundays, cars sometimes are parked three-deep at the curb. Sermons are frequently interrupted by distressed car owners hemmed in and late for brunch. As the church doors open, the sweet sound of the gospel choir floods the street.

Turn left on Tremont, the South End's spinal column. The astonishing array of ethnic restaurants on or close to Tremont Street is a key indicator of local demographics. There are eateries offering the following fare: soul, West Indian, continental, Puerto Rican, Brazilian, Irish, Cajun, Italian, Ethiopian, Greek, Lebanese, Korean, and Chinese. These aren't just yuppie caterers, either. Each place has a sizable ethnic clientele.

One block south down Tremont Street is West Newton, where residents exult in painting their doors bold reds, deep greens, or stately blues. One can quickly determine if a building has been restored or gentrified by the condition of its front door. Street fairs are frequently held here, community events during which the whole block is closed to automobile traffic and members of the South End's large artistic community display their arts, crafts, and bric-a-brac.

Along with the hodgepodge of ethnic groups and wealthy, socially aware liberals, many gays live in this area of the South End. They staked their claim long ago, as part of the first wave of renovators in the ongoing gentrification process that began in the early 1970s. Politically, South End gays are a very cohesive bunch. They have their own newspaper, *Bay Windows,* and are a force to be reckoned with on local issues.

The next block south is Pembroke Street; turn left. If it's a nice day, you will likely see a portly fellow squatting on his stoop in his undershirt, bantering with a neighbor in a jackhammer voice that can be heard for blocks. His name is Al, but he is known throughout the block as the "Mayor of Pembroke Street," one of the area's old guard. The "mayor" bought his 4-story townhouse for $25,000 in 1957 and has been running it as a boardinghouse ever since. With the South End's brilliant comeback and decades of soaring property values, he needs to do little else but stoop-sit.

Follow Pembroke Street to its intersection with Columbus Avenue. Braddock Park is on the left. At the end of the block on the opposite side of the street is *Charlie's Sandwich Shop* (429 Columbus Ave.; phone: 536-7669). *Charlie's,* a family-run operation for more than 50 years, is a South End institution. Open for breakfast and lunch every day except Sundays, it is beloved for its cranberry pancakes, western omelettes, home fries, and sweet potato pie.

Backtrack to Braddock Park. On most days there are a few people hanging out in front of *Braddock Drug* (437 Columbus Ave.; phone: 266-6445), since it has to be the only pharmacy in the city that sells beer.

Make a sharp left onto Warren Avenue, an attractive residential street that passes several small, typical South End squares along its unhurried route to Tremont Street. On the right is the Concord Baptist Church, built in 1869. While townhouses in the Back Bay are influenced by French design, those in the South End reflect English architectural styles. When these buildings were single-family homes, the kitchens and dining rooms were tucked under the stoops on the buildings' first floors (called English basements), while the steps rose a full story to the second floors. This design made them easy to convert into multiple-family dwellings when, in the 1930s, the South End began its decline and Mayor Jerome Smith concluded that the neighborhood "should be opened to mechanics of limited means."

At Dartmouth Street, a short walk to the left leads to Dartmouth Place, a cute-as-a-button cul-de-sac. These brick row houses all have second-story bay windows that face the rear gardens of the Appleton Street houses.

Backtrack down Dartmouth Street to Tremont. The residents of the section to the right, beyond Tremont Street, are predominantly Hispanic. Across this intersection, in the first block of West Dedham Street, is Villa Victoria, an award-winning experiment in low-income housing. The complex consists of nearly 200 three-family units with private entrances that don't smack of public housing. Once in fear of displacement, this community now has housing it can be proud of. Across the street is the *Buteco II* restaurant (57 W. Dedham St.; phone: 247-9429), which serves authentic Brazilian food.

Two blocks to the right off Tremont is Union Park, a real South End treasure. The first square to be completed in the neighborhood, this is some city residents' favorite spot in the Hub (though Bostonians are prone to fall in love with anything that isn't too common). Its plush greenspace, fountains, and ample foliage make for a resplendent foreground to the large Victorian brick row houses. At the end of the street on the left is *On the Park* (315 Shawmut Ave.; phone: 426-0862), an intimate café that serves some of the finest shepherd's pie in town. The turkey pot pie is another good choice, and inexpensive, too. The restaurant's owner is also one of the city's best-known caterers; his *East Meets West to Go* sandwich shop and bakery across the street (314 Shawmut Ave.; phone: 482-1015 or 426-3806) is rife with unusual entrées, salads, and cookies.

On the corner of Union Park and Washington Street, a block past Shawmut, is the Cathedral of the Holy Cross. As the largest Catholic church in the country at the time, it was the reason that many Irish immigrants crowded into this area in the late 1870s. The cathedral is located on the site of the old town gallows, on what was formerly the neck of land connecting Boston to the mainland.

For decades, Washington Street lay in the shadow of the unsightly "El" (for elevated train track), which was built at the turn of the century and hastened the South End's rapid early decline. The El was dirty and noisy, and it created blight along its path. A number of disreputable establishments emerged in its shadows. Like any skid row, it was home to many Boston alcoholics. Fortunately, the El was put out of its misery when the new *Orange Line* was built in 1987; the last remaining sections of the El were taken down in 1990.

Cut back through Union Park to return to Tremont Street. In the several blocks in both directions along Tremont are a number of establishments worthy of attention. Dining spots are dense here. *Azita's* (560 Tremont St.; phone: 338-8070) is a petite subterranean restaurant with slick, black tables and indirect lighting. The Cornish game hen with rosemary is delicious. Farther up the street is *Hamersley's Bistro* (578 Tremont St.; phone: 267-6068), which serves up hearty, home-style meals to the suit-and-tie crowd.

Across the street is *St. Cloud* (557 Tremont St.; phone: 353-0202), a favorite of the glitterati; with three walls of glass, it's not a place for shy types. For flashy ambience, though, it can't be beat. Its extensive, light, café menu is easy on the wallet. *Botolph's on Tremont* (569 Tremont St.; phone: 424-8577) is the more moderately priced cousin of the *St. Botolph* restaurant. (The word "Boston," by the way, is derived from the saint's name.)

Across the street from *St. Cloud* is the *Boston Center for the Arts* (539 Tremont St.; phone: 426-5000 or 426-7700), the highlight of which is the

Cyclorama Building, which is listed as a national landmark. The structure was built in 1884 to house a 400-foot-long circular painting of the Battle of Gettysburg by Paul Philippoteaux, a famed chronicler of the Civil War. After the painting was sent to Philadelphia, the Cyclorama Building became, in succession, a bicycle riding academy, a wholesale flower market, a garage (in which Alfred Champion invented the spark plug), and finally, art exhibition space. During warm-weather months, the *St. Cloud* uses the plaza area for outdoor dining; it's always festive in the summer. The arts complex also has a gallery (*Millis*), three theater spaces, and artists' studios. On any given day, there may be something worth checking out.

Turn left on Berkeley. At the corner of Berkeley and Appleton Streets is a grand old building which houses the Franklin Institute. Founded with money from Benjamin Franklin, whose will grants funds to "the city of Boston's needy youth," it offers associate degrees in industrial and engineering technology.

Turn left onto Appleton, the South End's most sought-after residential street. After 3 blocks, cross Columbus to West Canton, a small thoroughfare that leads to the Southwest Corridor. Turn left at the corridor and walk 3 blocks to West Newton Street; turn right to the Prudential Center area. The Skywalk at the top of the Prudential Tower offers an excellent overview of the city and is a fitting place to conclude this walking tour of Boston's South End.

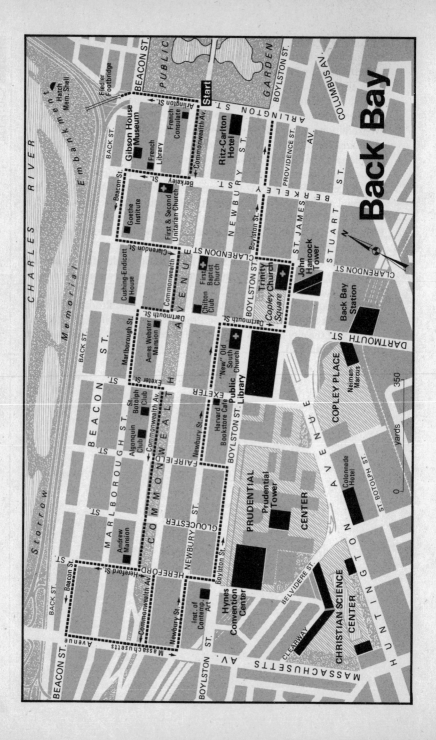

Walk 3: Back Bay

In the first half of the 19th century, the Back Bay section of Boston was a reservoir of trapped tidal backwater crisscrossed with railroad beds and a mill dam. It reeked of sewage and dumped refuse and was considered an eyesore and a health menace. By the turn of the century, however, many elite Boston families called Back Bay home.

Today, Boston's Back Bay is a posh area that is a living, breathing museum of residential Victorian architecture. With wide Commonwealth Avenue — reminiscent of a Parisian boulevard — a gridwork street layout, and its alphabetized cross streets, this section of the city couldn't be more different from downtown's random jumble of narrow, crooked byways.

The filling in of Boston's Back Bay was a remarkable achievement for its time. In roughly 30 years, beginning in the 1850s, Boston nearly doubled in size, growing from a crowded, pear-shape peninsula to a bustling Victorian city with easy access to new parks and expanding suburbs. Almost as soon as land emerged in the Back Bay, upper-crust Bostonians began their migration from Beacon Hill, the North End, and downtown. Churches, social clubs, and other institutions were soon to follow.

The process of creating a neighborhood from a marsh, however, was not without its headaches, some of which persist today (the area's rat problem is notorious, and at least 1 block of Back Bay is thought to be sinking). But Back Bay was and is worth the trouble. An afternoon spent walking along its magnolia-lined streets can be surprisingly relaxing for a big-city excursion.

The starting place for our Back Bay walk is the head of Commonwealth Avenue, where this wide boulevard meets the Public Garden. The tour — which will take about 3 hours if done at a leisurely pace — begins with a stroll around the Public Garden.

Though Bostonians tend to think of the Public Garden and Boston Common as one, they have vastly different histories. The Common has been green for time immemorial, while the Public Garden was a salt marsh before it was transformed by the Back Bay landfill project into the nation's oldest botanical garden. The Common and Public Garden are divided by Charles Street, just over and beyond a bridge that spans the Garden's pond. The fabled, pedal-driven Swan Boats leisurely cruise the pond from mid-April to late September (remember to bring bread for the ducks).

The Public Garden is home to a variety of native and European trees. An abundance of flowers are planted along the garden's many footpaths and in plots near the Arlington Street entrance. The carefully tended beds are changed with the seasons — the spring tulips are particular favorites among locals and visitors alike.

On the Arlington Street (west) side of the Public Garden is Thomas Ball's statue of General George Washington atop his spirited horse (the sculptor's model was the steed ridden by the Prince of Wales during a visit to Boston in 1860). To the north is the red marble and granite Ether Monument, which commemorates the first successful use of ether as a painkiller during surgery at nearby Massachusetts General Hospital in 1846. Also of interest (to the statue fanatic) are the likeness on Charles Street of Edward Everett Hale, author of the disturbing novel *The Man Without a Country*; the sculpture depicting Unitarian preacher William Ellery Channing, which faces his Arlington Street church; one of abolitionist Senator Charles Sumner, which stands on Charles Street; and the statue of Civil War hero Colonel Thomas Cass, located on the Boylston Street side of the park.

More enjoyable than statue seeing, however, is simply lounging on a Public Garden bench and absorbing the sights, sounds, and scents of this small enclave of nature in the urban jungle. Notice the sudden serenity of those entering the Public Garden; even the most uptight Bostonians become downright thoughtful here. The sanity of many a Back Bay resident rests on the walk home from the office through the Common and the Public Garden. It's an ideal way to unwind — and much healthier than a double martini. The Public Garden is open daily from dawn to 10 PM.

The Back Bay is roughly rectangular in shape. The rest of this walk weaves back and forth among Commonwealth Avenue and Marlborough and Beacon, the streets of the residential area to the north; then explores Newbury and Boylston Streets to the south, winding up at the John Hancock Tower near Copley Square.

Cross Arlington Street at the southern foot of the Public Garden. The grande dame of Boston hotels, the *Ritz-Carlton* (phone: 536-5700) sits elegantly on the southwest corner of Commonwealth and Arlington, its doorman keeping a vigilant watch for limousines. Though attire appropriate for a walking tour is not exactly appropriate for afternoon tea at the *Ritz* (jackets are required for men), it is an experience that shouldn't be missed. This daily ritual (from 3 to 5:30 PM) in the second-floor *Tea Lounge* has been a traditionally Bostonian event since the hotel opened in 1927 (see *Quintessential Boston* in DIVERSIONS). The downstairs bar is a stately place for a drink, albeit a costly one (the *Ritz* still makes the best martini in town). With jazz performances nightly, this Boston institution may even be loosening up a bit.

While the blue blood is still coursing through your veins, have a peek inside *Firestone and Parsons* (phone: 266-1858) in the *Ritz* building around the corner. The ultimate old-guard jewelry store, it is known for its antique tea services. Try not to knock anything over. Farther up Newbury Street (don't stray too far since the route heads in the other direction) is a row of sumptuous fur and jewelry shops. After browsing (or buying), return to Commonwealth Avenue.

Cross Commonwealth Avenue (the locals just say "Comm. Ave.") to the center mall area near the statue of Alexander Hamilton. Look back in the direction of the Washington statue for one of Boston's most attractive views. The general sits high upon his mount just beyond the wrought-iron fence of the Public Garden. The white tower of the Park Street Church can be seen beyond him, and the skyscrapers of the financial district are beyond that.

Across the street are a pair of venerable buildings. On the corner of Commonwealth Avenue and Arlington Street is the Harbridge House, the grandest of the surviving houses on Arlington. Currently home to an international consulting firm of the same name, it was built in 1860 by Arthur Gilman, who also designed the Arlington Street Church. *Atlantic Monthly* magazine, one of the nation's oldest journals, was published in the homogeneous buildings at 8-11 Arlington Street until 1989. (The magazine is now located at 745 Boylston St.)

Walk straight ahead to where Arlington intersects Beacon Street. If the year were 1830, you would now be standing on the old Mill Dam, built across Back Bay in 1814 to harness energy from the tides for mill power. The dam extended westward along what is now Beacon Street to what today is Kenmore Square, home of the mammoth Citgo sign and *Fenway Park*. Bostonians used the 50-foot-wide dam for winter sleigh rides and summer evening strolls. It was filled in with the rest of Back Bay during the second half of the 19th century.

Ahead is a brown ramp leading over Storrow Drive to the Esplanade, an elongated park along the Charles River. This ramp is the *Fiedler Footbridge*. Named after the late, legendary *Boston Pops* conductor Arthur Fiedler, it is the best route from Back Bay to the *Hatch Shell*, site of summer concerts and the *Independence Day* performance of the *Boston Pops*, the acclaimed symphony orchestra known for its generally lighthearted repertoire. The Esplanade is packed with hundreds of thousands of people during the enormously popular *July Fourth* celebration, which features a sing-along of all-American favorites, a rousing rendition of the *1812 Overture*, and a truly spectacular fireworks display.

Return to Commonwealth Avenue and turn right. The building with the billowing tricolor flag in front is the French consulate. Beyond that, at No. 5, is the Boston Center for Adult Education (BCAE), an organization that offers more than 500 evening courses, including Beginning Russian, Stand-up Comedy, Fly-Fishing, and Brazilian Cooking.

Visitors are welcome to poke around the BCAE building, originally a mansion built by cotton broker Walter Baylies in 1904. Baylies demolished a house identical to the French consulate building on this site when it was only 40 years old, erecting in its place the present, more fashionable structure. He also built the lavish Louis XIV ballroom on the building's west side in 1912 for his daughter's debut into Boston society (phone: 267-2465).

Turn right on Berkeley Street. Round the corner and notice the Hooper Mansion (25-27 Berkeley St.) over your right shoulder. Once the home of congressman and merchant Samuel Hooper, it has a huge (by Back Bay standards) corner yard.

On the left is the First and Second Unitarian Church (66 Marlborough St.; phone: 267-6730), built by former Puritans in 1867. All that remains of the original structure (after fire ravaged the building in 1968) are the tower and arcade. A statue of John Winthrop, the Massachusetts Bay Colony's first governor, stands around the corner on the Marlborough Street side of the building. Across Marlborough Street is the French Library (53 Marlborough St.; phone: 266-4351). Films and lectures about France and French culture are frequently held in this handsome, 19th-century Victorian mansion, which is surrounded by a tall iron fence.

Continue 1 more block down Berkeley to Beacon Street. This section of Beacon Street has been Back Bay's most blue-blooded since the neighborhood was created. (At the time, a few paces could make a world of difference to Bostonian aristocracy. As a rule, a Beacon Street address meant an old family with money; old families without much money resided on Marlborough Street; and the nouveau riche lived on Commonwealth Avenue.)

For a more in-depth look into Victorian Boston, tour the *Gibson House Museum* (137 Beacon St.; phone: 267-6338). This row house was typical of middle class Back Bay residences. Its Victorian fixtures and furniture were left intact after the departure of its last occupants in the 1950s. Among the 19th-century features of the house are a basement kitchen and a butler's pantry complete with a dumbwaiter. Tours are offered Wednesdays through Sundays from May 1 to November 1 and on Saturdays and Sundays during the rest of the year. Admission charge.

Walk west on Beacon to the French Library's Saxon counterpart, the Goethe Institute (170 Beacon St.; phone: 262-6050). This German cultural center for New England is a branch of the Goethe Institute in Munich. Once a relatively sleepy organization, enrollment in language and other cultural programs is up since German reunification.

The stark metal-and-glass monstrosity at the corner of Beacon and Clarendon Streets is a housing complex completed in the 1970s. Its institutional feel scared the daylights out of local supporters of historical preservation, who have since redoubled their efforts to regulate construction in the area. They now seem to have the upper hand in Back Bay development.

On Clarendon Street, turn left and walk down to the central mall on Commonwealth. Designed by landscape architect Frederick Law Olmsted (who also designed New York's Central Park), the mall is one link in a chain of parks, including the Common and the Public Garden, that stretches west for 8 miles. Known as the Emerald Necklace, it is the longest stretch of urban parkland in the United States.

Ahead is another landmark that merits at least one photograph. The First Baptist Church (phone: 267-3148), designed by architect H. H. Richardson (who also designed Trinity Church — see below), sits on the corner of Commonwealth and Clarendon. Ivy climbs between the rounded windows of the pudding-stone façade. A frieze at the top of the tower was designed by Auguste Bartholdi, who also sculpted the Statue of Liberty. Built in 1871, the building quickly earned the nickname the "Church of the Holy Bean Blowers" because of the trumpeting angels on the corners looking down over Back Bay. The church is especially photogenic when contrasted with the ultramodern Hancock Tower in the background.

Notice the sturdy building at the end of the block to the left (152 Commonwealth Ave.). This is the home of the *Chilton Club,* the female counterpart to Boston's stuffy, formerly all-male clubs. At one time it had three separate entrances — one for members, one for members with guests, and one for the help — and was known more for its inner, rather than outer, decorum.

Two more noteworthy buildings face each other from different sides of Commonwealth Avenue at the beginning of the next block to the right. On the south side is the *Vendome* hotel. This once-proud establishment boasted General Ulysses S. Grant, President Grover Cleveland, P. T. Barnum, Mark Twain, Oscar Wilde, and Sarah Bernhardt as its guests. Today, it plays host to a legion of yuppies who work within its high-tech interior. No need to go inside — the interior retains hardly a trace of its former opulence. There's a basement restaurant with an outdoor dining area just below street level. Its current incarnation is *Spasso* (phone: 536-8656), a charming Italian bistro.

Across Commonwealth Avenue is the Ames-Webster Mansion (its address is actually 306 Dartmouth St.), at one time among the most spectacular residences in Back Bay. Members of Boston society once would clatter up to the wrought-iron gate on the Dartmouth Street side in carriages. Men would debark and enter through the doorway to the left; ladies would be driven through the porte cochère to a rear door where they would ascend to a second-floor powder room via elevator. Once properly powdered, they could make their grand entrance to the first floor down an elaborately carved staircase. The mansion is now an office building, having narrowly escaped the perils of student housing in 1969. Much of its inner grandeur has been revived.

Proceed north (right) on Dartmouth to Marlborough Street. At the northeast corner is the noteworthy Cushing-Endicott House. Built in 1873, it's named after two old Boston families that were the house's only residents until 1953. The great American painter John Singer Sargent used one of its bedrooms as his studio at the turn of the century. It was subdivided into six condominiums in the mid-1980s; the largest one was recently on the market for $1.35 million.

Head west (left) down Marlborough. At the corner of Marlborough and Exeter, turn right and walk 2 short blocks for a panoramic view of the Charles River. Across the river, the granite building with the rotunda is the main administration building of the Massachusetts Institute of Technology (MIT).

Return to Commonwealth Avenue via Exeter and turn right. This block is home to two of Boston's most elite social clubs. On the right is the *St. Botolph Club* (199 Commonwealth Ave.), an august establishment of "men of letters." It is so proper that, according to legend, a member sat dead in his club chair for 2 days before his death was noticed. The gentleman was thought to be asleep and no employee was so brash as to speak to him before being spoken to first. From the street, the balding heads of club members may be visible above their leather, high-back chairs through the first-floor bay window.

The statue on the Commonwealth Avenue mall of a pensive man dressed in a raincoat and seated on a bluff overlooking the sea is of the noted American historian Samuel Eliot Morison, a member of the St. Botolph Club. His casual appearance and posture contrast markedly with the other formal statues on the mall.

Farther down the block on the right is the *Algonquin Club* (217 Commonwealth Ave.) — identified by its blue-and-white banner and limestone façade — another stockyard for Boston Brahmins. From the second-floor windows, business types can be seen nursing their brandies and exchanging the news of the day.

The 9-room hotel known as *267 Commonwealth* (phone: 267-6776) offers intimate Victorian lodging; try to convince the manager to give you a tour of the hotel's suites, which feature working fireplaces, ornate woodwork, and floral print papers similar to the original Victorian patterns.

In the next block, on the northeast corner of Commonwealth and Hereford, is the Andrew Mansion, an Italian Renaissance Revival structure with a wrought-iron balcony on the third floor that comes from the Tuileries Palace in Paris, which was burned down in 1871. Today, passersby may see somebody hanging by their feet from that balcony, since the mansion is now an MIT fraternity house. The fraternity, to be fair, maintains this building proudly.

At this point, architecture buffs may want to take a small side trip to see an outstanding (and unusual) example of a church-gone-condo. Turn right on Hereford and cut over to Beacon Street, then turn left. Church Court, a complex of condominiums on the corner of Beacon Street and Massachusetts Avenue, was the Mount Vernon Church before it was ravaged in a spectacular fire in 1978. Portions of the church are brilliantly blended into an L-shape building that now houses 42 condominium units. (Turn left on Massachusetts Avenue to rejoin the route.)

Otherwise, follow Commonwealth Avenue to Massachusetts Avenue, noting the Burrage Mansion (314 Commonwealth Ave.) to the right. It is one example of New York architectural flamboyance that slipped through the cracks of the more conventional Back Bay. The limestone palace seems to have been inspired by the Vanderbilt mansion in New York. Today, it is the Boston Evening Clinic, which provides health care during "off" hours for workingpeople. It has become the workhorse in Massachusetts's attempt to ensure quality health care for those with or without health insurance.

Turn left on Massachusetts Avenue. *Newbury's Steak House* (94 Massachusetts Ave.; phone: 536-0184), located about mid-block, is an excellent choice for a hearty New York strip steak or prime ribs in an old Boston atmosphere at a reasonable price. Around the corner is the new *Capital Grille,* a classic steakhouse that ages its own meat (359 Newbury St.; phone: 262-8900). Across Mass. Ave. and roaring below is the "Mass. Pike" (Massachusetts Turnpike), running from downtown Boston across the state to the New York border.

Turn left at the next corner onto Newbury Street, where antiques shops, record stores, hair salons, art galleries, trendy restaurants, designer boutiques, jewelry stores, fur salons, bridal shops, bookstores, sidewalk cafés, "vintage" clothing shops, imported gift emporiums, florists, and purveyors of countercultural comic books all stand side by side in the basement and first-floor retail spaces of attractive brownstone buildings. Boston's most fashion-conscious byway, Newbury Street features an endless parade of people, with personal styles ranging from Bohemian to preppy, Eurochic to yuppie.

Of particular interest in the first block of Newbury Street is *Trident Booksellers & Café* (338 Newbury St.; phone: 267-8688), on the right, one of two such hybrid establishments on Newbury Street. After browsing through the books, including an extensive selection of works on Eastern religions, relax with a cup of herbal tea and a muffin.

Across the street is *Genji* (327 Newbury St.; phone: 267-5656), which serves excellent traditional Japanese food. Though the dinner menu is expensive (some guests initially think it's quoted in yen), the food is excellent. Sushi orders are reasonably priced, and the luncheon menu is downright inexpensive. The decor is soothing, understated, and elegant (except for the sushi clock, which has California rolls where the numbers should be).

On the right is the home of the *Hellenic Chronicle,* a newspaper that serves Boston's sizable Greek population. Appropriately, *Steve's* (62 Hereford St.; phone: 267-1817), an informal, authentic Greek restaurant, is on the northeast corner of Newbury and Hereford. It serves first-rate Greek salads and *spanikopita* (pastry filled with spinach and cheese).

Turn right on Hereford Street. The colossal building ahead is the *Hynes Convention Center,* a state-owned complex that hosts conventions for groups ranging from wood-siding manufacturers to members of the clergy.

Head right on Boylston Street past a fire station to the *Institute of Contemporary Art (ICA;* 955 Boylston St.; phone: 266-5152). The museum/gallery, which features the work of local artists and hosts traveling exhibitions, was once a police station. Closed Mondays and Tuesdays; admission charge. Next door is *Division Sixteen* (phone: 353-0870), an informal, trendy restaurant named after the building's former occupant, a fire station.

Turn around and head back down Boylston Street (named after Dr. Zabdiel Boylston, who fearlessly began smallpox inoculation in America in the early 1720s). On the corner of Boylston and Hereford is the *Cactus Club* (phone: 236-0200), a Santa Fe–style restaurant with reasonably good Tex-Mex food (considering that it's in the "home of the bean and the cod"). The decor, featuring a real stuffed buffalo over the bar, is worth the visit.

The tall building across the street is the Prudential Center (the "Pru" among locals), an overgrown (52-story) tower built 26 years ago to replace some unsightly railroad yards (many feel the Pru isn't any more sightly). The shops in the plaza are lackluster, but they are currently being renovated. Donald DeLue's statue of a man reaching for the heavens in front of the Pru, titled *The Quest Eternal,* was the old finish line for the *Boston Marathon.* When the John Hancock company became the primary sponsor of the grueling 26.2-mile April race, it moved the finish line closer to its own building, several blocks from here. A must on any itinerary is the *Top of the Hub* (phone: 536-1775), a restaurant and bar on the building's top floor that offers a breathtaking view of the city. The Skywalk on the 52nd floor offers the best view of the Christian Science Center and its reflecting pool.

At 777 Boylston is the *Atlantic Fish Co.* (phone: 267-4000), a restaurant that serves an array of seafood rivaled in scope only by the *New England Aquarium* (where they are not for consumption). The restaurant — not the aquarium — offers outdoor dining in summer. *Lord & Taylor* (phone: 262-6000), a fine department store, is across the street.

Now turn left on Fairfield and then take a right to head down Newbury Street for a short stretch. This block features a number of acclaimed art galleries, such as the *Randall Beck Gallery* (263 Newbury St.; phone: 266-2475), which is highly regarded for its contemporary prints.

Stroll to the *Harvard Bookstore Café* (190 Newbury St.; phone: 536-0095), on the corner of Exeter and Newbury. Like the *Trident,* this hybrid bookstore/café is a wonderful place for coffee, pastries, and nouvelle (or is that novel?) cuisine. Sunday brunch is a real treat, featuring some of the best croissants around. Good food, a leisurely, literary ambience, a great selection of books, outdoor dining (weather permitting), exhibits by local artists, and frequent book signing parties featuring well-known authors, all combine to make the *Harvard Bookstore Café* one of Newbury Street's cherished spots. If for some reason you can't find what you want here, cross the street to the *Waterstone's Bookstore.* Within the cloistered halls of this once-upon-a-time theater is one of the city's largest collections of books.

Two notable galleries on this block are the *Pucker-Safrai* (171 Newbury St.; phone: 267-9473), with a permanent collection of works by New England, European, Israeli, and other artists, and the *Nielsen Gallery* (179 Newbury St.; phone: 266-4835), which shows the work of a stable of talented young artists. If the weather is good, you may find another type of art exhibit beneath your feet. Sidewalk Sam, an irrepressible Boston-based artist, has created more than 1,000 perishable works — elaborate chalk murals, often copies of well-known masterpieces — on Boston walkways. You may even run across Sam Guillemin himself laboring over a work in progress.

Turn right on Dartmouth, and walk to the "New" Old South Church at the corner of Dartmouth and Boylston Streets. This northern Italian Gothic-style church was built in 1877, and was the successor to the Old South Meeting House of Tea Party fame downtown. Open daily.

Directly ahead is Copley Square. Cross Boylston Street at this point (which, incidentally, is the current *Boston Marathon* finish line) to come to the Boston Public Library (666 Boylston St.; phone: 536-5400). This grandiose Renaissance Revival building, built in 1895, serves to underscore the premium that Bostonians place on education. Inscribed in stone over the library's east (and oldest) entrance is "Free to All." Many of Boston's homeless take this motto to heart, spending endless winter days at the library's long tables. As long as they sit upright and look busy, they are not told to move along. Consequently, the BPL's clientele is somewhat motley. The former main entrance in the old half of the building is flanked by seated statues of Arts (on the left) and Sciences (on the right). The huge bronze doors just inside the outer doors were created by Daniel Chester French, sculptor of the Lincoln Memorial. But the oldest section is under renovation (scheduled to continue until the end of the century), so visitors must enter through the blocky new addition, designed by Philip Johnson and built in 1972. Once inside, turn left and go up a few stairs. Turn left and quickly right and you'll find yourself in a beautiful courtyard. Rest a while or continue across the courtyard to the older section, which is decorated with work by some of the greatest painters of the day. Murals by Puvis de Chavannes, Edwin Abbey, and John Singer Sargent adorn the walls of the second and third floors. The barrel-vaulted Bates Hall reading room is simply breathtaking. It looks and smells like everything a library should be. As Robert Parker, Boston-based author of the not-as-popular-now "Spenser" detective series, remarked, "Even when I went in to look up Duke Snider's lifetime batting average, I felt like a scholar." Open daily (phone: 536-5400).

Down Dartmouth Street past the library's main entrance is *Copley Place,* a shopping magnet. As the first indoor mall to be erected inside

Boston's city limits, it was a controversial project. Development critics suggested it would cheapen the surrounding architecture of Copley Square. Yankee shoppers, who are quite content to wear the proverbial old hat passed down from generation to generation, complained it would be too expensive. Nonetheless, *Copley Place* has gotten along just fine with upscale names such as *Tiffany* and *Neiman Marcus.* There's even *Le Chapeau,* which carries a staggering variety of hats (perhaps the Yankee stereotype itself is becoming old hat).

Across Dartmouth Street from the shopping center is the *Copley Plaza* hotel (phone: 267-5300), a stately structure that has hosted presidents, royalty, and numerous gala social events in its venerable career. Afternoon tea is served from 3 to 5 PM among the potted palms in the hotel's lobby.

Cross St. James Avenue in front of the hotel. At the end of the wide plaza is Trinity Church, one of the most impressive churches in America. The masterwork of H. H. Richardson, this 1877 building was, interestingly, built on wetlands. Since the tower alone weighs in at a hefty 12½ million pounds, the church was built on 4,500 wood pilings that must be constantly kept wet to avoid dry rot. The water level is checked periodically from a hatch in the church's basement. With its beautiful medieval decorations and its awe-inspiring sense of enormity, Trinity Church deserves an extended visit. Guidebooks and brochures are available inside. Open daily (phone: 536-0944). Also see *Historic Churches* in DIVERSIONS.

Across St. James Avenue from Trinity Church is the entrance to the observatory of the 62-story John Hancock Tower, a mirrored marvel designed by I.M. Pei that contains more than 13 acres of glass. When the building opened in 1975, the glass windows kept popping out, much to the dismay of pedestrians on the street below. Just as all the glass was finally replaced, employees in the upper floors complained of a terrifying sway when the wind blew. The building was found to have a flaw that prompted one German consultant to remark that it could blow over on its side like a book. Thanks to the bad publicity, that problem was fixed in a hurry. But the saga continues — now the construction of the tower is found to have done serious structural damage to the beloved Trinity Church next door. Nonetheless, the 60th floor is a spectacular place to learn about the development of Boston, see a scale model of the city as it was in 1775, and relive your tour of Boston's Back Bay. Open daily; admission charge (phone: 247-1977).

To return to the Public Garden, just walk 1 block north to Boylston Street or 2 blocks to Newbury Street, and head right (these remaining blocks feature many lavish clothing boutiques and furriers).

Walk 4: Boston Common

All kinds of people have long enjoyed Boston Common, America's oldest public park. Those who do — Beacon Hill socialites, Frisbee-hurling college students, street people, soapbox pontificators, hand-holding couples, families on picnics, tourists from Japan, skateboarding adolescents, Christian proselytizers, political rally participants — all owe this calming stretch of greenery to an eccentric Anglican clergyman who loved books, madeira wine, and the anger these two passions incited in the uptight Puritans of the 17th century.

The clergyman, William Blaxton (pronounced, and sometimes spelled, *Blackstone*), was Boston's first settler, having put down stakes on the land that would become Boston Common in 1630. But when the Puritans tried to convert him, he headed south to the more permissive Rhode Island. He could easily afford the move since he had sold the 50-acre Common to Royal Governor John Winthrop and his band of Puritans at the then-exorbitant price of 30 pounds. Winthrop thought it was a great deal, however, because it provided plenty of space for cattle grazing and military training. For all the good that Bostonians over several centuries have gotten out of their park (even after cattle were banned from the Common in 1830 to avoid the nuisance to female pedestrians), it was a steal.

The best place to begin a tour of the Common (this one will take about an hour and a half) is the visitors' information center along Tremont Street. The attendants in this big blue booth, halfway between the Park Street and Boylston *T* stops, can accurately answer almost any Boston-related question (except when the *Red Sox* will end their *World Series* drought). Trolley tours offered by several companies originate here. Across the street is the *Boston Welcome Center* (phone: 451-2227), which has every conceivable Boston souvenir, book, postcard, or gift. Free maps are available.

Adjacent to the visitors' center is Parkman Plaza, a lovely place to sit, though it tends to be a gathering spot for the down-and-out. The plaza's namesake, George Parkman, lived up to his surname — he bequeathed $5 million to the Common and other city parks, no small chunk of change in 1908. Parkman's house still stands on Beacon Street (see *Walk 5: Beacon Hill*).

Cut through the middle of the plaza and walk to the *Parkman Bandstand,* a neo-classical structure tucked in the shade of the surrounding elm trees and reached by any one of a number of paths. No longer used for concerts, the bandstand, which has reasonably good acoustics, is now the

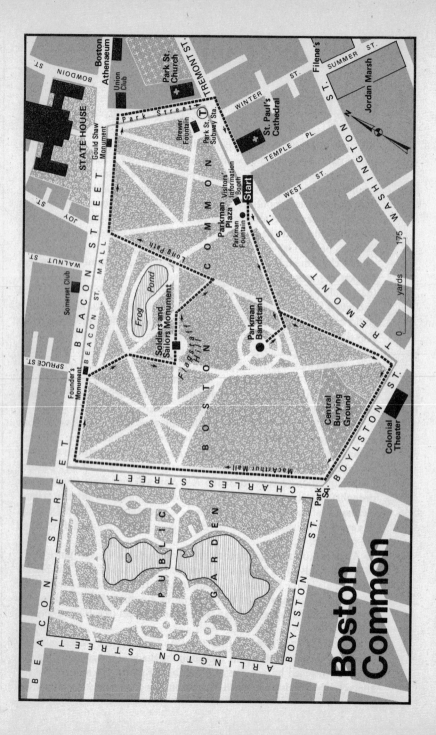

Boston Common

STATE HOUSE

Boston Athenaeum

Union Club

Park St. Church

TREMONT ST.

Gould Shaw Monument

Brewer Fountain

Park Street

Park St. Subway Sta.

WINTER ST.

St. Paul's Cathedral

Filene's

SUMMER ST.

Jordan Marsh

BOWDOIN ST.

JOY ST.

TEMPLE PL.

WASHINGTON ST.

WEST ST.

Visitors Information Booth

Parkman Plaza

Parkman Fountain

Start

Long Path

BEACON STREET

BEACON ST. MALL

WALNUT ST.

Somerset Club

SPRUCE ST.

Founder's Monument

Frog Pond

Soldiers and Sailors Monument

Flagstaff Hill

BOSTON COMMON

Parkman Bandstand

Central Burying Ground

BOYLSTON ST.

Colonial Theater

TREMONT ST.

175

yards

0

MacArthur Mall

CHARLES STREET

Park Sq.

BOYLSTON ST.

PUBLIC GARDEN

BEACON STREET

ARLINGTON STREET

BOYLSTON

venue for the raspy singing and late-night howls of the crowd who call the Common home. (It's safe here by day, but don't get caught in this area after sundown.)

Concerts on the Common, performances occasionally held on summer evenings, take place in a big, wooden pen erected just to the north of the bandstand. Many Bostonians to whom sound is more important than visuals enjoy the music of topnotch performers while picnicking outside the concert area. There are usually more listeners outside than in, since it's less expensive (free) and there is more legroom (50 acres). The music can be heard for blocks (which is why area neighbors have fought — successfully — to reduce the number of concerts presented each year).

Work your way through the intricate web of paths to the extreme south section of the Common, the location of the Central Burying Ground. This is best done via a path called Railroad Mall, which runs parallel to Tremont Street about 50 to 100 feet inside the Common. Along the way is a monument commemorating the Boston Massacre, which occurred at the Old State House not far from here (see *Walk 6: Downtown*). At the burial ground, the baseball field and tennis courts will be on the right.

Today, a burial ground in a public park and at a busy intersection seems at best poorly planned, at worst disrespectful. Not part of the original Common grounds, this area was an obscure piece of real estate purchased in 1756 after gravediggers complained that the downtown cemeteries (the Old Granary and King's Chapel) were so crowded that bodies had to be buried four-deep. The burial ground's most famous occupant (in an unknown grave site) is Gilbert Stuart, portraitist of George and Martha Washington, Paul Revere, and other early American patriots.

Across Boylston Street is the *Colonial Theatre* (106 Boylston St.; phone: 426-9366), which marks the northern edge of Boston's theater district. If time allows, round the corner to Tremont Street, where a number of old theaters and the *Stage Deli* (275 Boylston St.; phone: 523-DELI), Boston's best delicatessen, are located. The *Colonial,* built in 1900, is the oldest theater in the city to survive, intact, under the same name; its period decor has been painstakingly restored. The *Colonial* has been the setting for many theatrical debuts, from Irving Berlin and the *Ziegfeld Follies* to Rodgers and Hammerstein. (Also see *Inside Boston's Theaters* in DIVERSIONS.) Here also are a number of music stores, including *Carl Fischer Music* (156 Boylston St.; phone: 426-0740), *M. Steinert & Sons* (162 Boylston St.; phone: 426-1900), and around the corner, the *Boston Music Co.* (172 Tremont St.; phone: 426-5100), all wonderful places for browsing. At the end of the block in a former bank building is *Remington's* (124 Boylston St.; phone: 574-9676), a restaurant and pub that has excellent burgers and ale.

A plaque on the building at 176 Boylston Street, at the corner of Carver Street, marks the birthplace in 1809 of Edgar Allan Poe (the actual house at 62 Carver no longer stands). The writer, who seemed to be miserable everywhere, made no bones about disliking Boston. Perhaps his only kind comment about the city was when he remarked that Boston Common was "no common thing." Nonetheless, Poe always said he was "heartily ashamed" to have been born here.

Farther down is Park Square, where Boylston meets Charles Street. Follow the path around the bend and walk parallel to Charles Street. This is MacArthur Mall, which before Back Bay was filled in, was a seawall that prevented tides from rolling across Back Bay. Below the seawall was the site of many gallows executions. Instead of being given a decent burial, the bodies of the executed were just allowed to wash out to sea.

This area, with its greenery cleared to accommodate a baseball field, bleachers, and a chain-link fence, is the Common's least attractive. Street vendors usually peddle pretzels, fried dough, and Italian sausages along here. Across Charles Street is the lovely Public Garden (see *Walk 3: Back Bay*). After rounding the next bend, you're plunged into the heart of the Common.

There is a plaque along MacArthur Mall, about halfway to Beacon Street ahead, which commemorates the place where in April 1775 the redcoats embarked on their fateful voyage across the Charles River and on to Lexington and Concord. Though their "oars were muffled to prevent noise," as the plaque says, the attack was no surprise to the colonists.

Past the plaque on the right are the Parade Grounds, the former site of military training, which was one of the Common's original purposes. In fact, MacArthur Mall was built large enough to hold a full column of soldiers. America's oldest military order, the Ancient and Honorable Artillery Company, founded in 1638, sometimes holds elaborate ceremonies in full regalia here. (The company has a museum on the top floor of *Faneuil Hall.*) In 1979, thousands gathered on the Parade Grounds for an outdoor mass conducted by Pope John Paul II. A granite marker commemorates the event.

At the corner, Charles Street intersects with Beacon Street, the southern boundary of Beacon Hill. Turn right on the Beacon Street Mall. A short jaunt uphill opposite Spruce Street leads to a monument to William Blaxton (a.k.a. Blackstone), founder of the Common and Boston's first settler. The statue depicts an ebullient Blaxton (who must have been desperate for companionship since he didn't like the Puritans any more than the English Lord Bishops from whom he fled) inviting Governor John Winthrop onto the Boston peninsula to share its beauties and ample springs.

Take a path on the right leading up to Flagstaff Hill, the highest point on the Common. At the top is the Soldiers and Sailors Monument, which honors those who fought in the Civil War. While graffiti artists have since added some of their own commentary to the monument, the hilltop is still a wonderful place to view a panorama of the Common or to enjoy a picnic on one of the benches.

Downhill to the north is the Frog Pond, which has no frogs and is scarcely even a pond since it is lined with concrete. Formerly a watering place for cattle, today the pond is a children's wading pool in the summer. During the early spring, when there is no water, the empty pool is the domain of skateboarders and roller skaters.

A shade-drenched walkway skirts the edges of the Frog Pond, then intersects with a path that leads back to Beacon Street. Head down this walk — called the Long Path because it stretches diagonally across the Common from Beacon to Tremont Street — away from Beacon Street. At the intersection of three paths, in the "V" that opens up to Flagstaff Hill, once stood the Great Elm. A mammoth tree (over 70 feet tall, with branches that spread out 100 feet), the Great Elm was the site of many executions, including that of Mary Dyer, a Quaker who was hanged here in 1660 for her religious beliefs. Though the tree died in 1876, it lives on as a symbol of stern Puritan justice.

Backtrack to the Beacon Street Mall along the Long Path, also called Oliver Wendell Holmes Walk, after the author, doctor, and father of Justice Holmes, who so loved to stroll along this route (the Long Path was the site of a famous romantic scene in Holmes's celebrated *Autocrat of the Breakfast Table*). The 19th-century British author William Makepeace Thackeray likened this elm-studded portion of the Common to the promenades of Windsor Castle.

At the top of the path, on the left, is the Robert Gould Shaw Memorial, designed by Augustus Saint-Gaudens. Shaw, the 26-year-old son of a prominent Boston family, died while leading the 54th Regiment — the first regiment of free blacks — into battle during the Civil War. Shaw and the regiment are the subjects of the 1989 film *Glory*.

Now turn right and head downhill along the red strip in the middle of the pavement (which indicates the Freedom Trail). This path is usually busy with State House employees walking to and from Park Street Station, the site of the country's first underground trolley (a.k.a. "subway"). At the top of the hill, on the corner across from the State House, is the Ticknor Mansion, built in 1804 but heavily rebuilt to accommodate offices and an excellent antiques shop on the corner. Farther down Park Street is the exclusive *Union Club* and the Roman Catholic Paulist Center. Walk downhill, with Park Street on your left. The trees along this walk and those in the rest of the Common are resplendent with sparkling lights at *Christmastime*. It is wise not to get too engrossed in the natural beauty or the architecture, however; keep a lookout for stray Frisbees and boomerangs in this most boisterous area of an otherwise peaceful Common.

The corner of Tremont and Park Streets is one of Boston's busiest intersections. Heavy traffic merges with rabid shoppers jaywalking across Tremont Street in droves, their eyes fixed on the shops of Winter Street and the Downtown Crossing retail district beyond. Complicating matters are the usual array of protesters, sidewalk evangelists, pretzel vendors, and street people. Overseeing this jumble of humanity is the Park Street

Church, across Park Street, with chimes that thrice daily attempt to calm the madding crowd.

Just behind the granite Park Street *T* stop entrance and exit is the Brewer Fountain. Clear a path through the pigeons and pause to enjoy this beautiful monument, a bronze replica of a Parisian fountain that was quite the rage at the *Paris Exposition* of 1855. The view beyond the fountain up the lawn to the gold dome of the State House is arresting.

Jaywalk (carefully) across Tremont Street with the shoppers to the rather gloomy, seemingly unfinished St. Paul's Cathedral. St. Paul's has a generic feel from the outside because the pediment over the porch is blank. It was supposed to be graced with rich ornamentation, but lack of funds prevented any further work. Colorful — and slightly incongruous — banners are hung from the outside columns to jazz the place up. But don't be fooled by the plain façade; inside, this Episcopalian church, built 10 years after the Park Street Church, is sumptuously decorated. Cross the street once more to return to the visitors' information booth, the last stop on the Boston Common walking tour.

Walk 5: Beacon Hill

The hub of activity in the Hub is the corner of Park and Tremont Streets on Boston Common's east boundary, a bustling area that revolves around the Park Street subway station. The country's oldest subway station, where in 1897 a trolley car first operated underground, today it is the intersection of the *Red* and *Green Lines* of Boston's famed (some residents say infamous) *Massachusetts Bay Transit Authority* (*MBTA,* or just "the T"). The walking tour of the Beacon Hill historic district, which will take approximately 4 hours at a leisurely pace, begins here.

Take a few moments to enjoy the panoramic view from this spot. As you look up toward the gold dome of the State House, the seat of Massachusetts government, you'll also see the Boston Common, the nation's oldest park, stretching out before you and to the left. The road at the right, Park Street, runs down from the foot of the State House to Tremont Street. Turn to the right to view the historic Park Street Church at the intersection of the two streets, then turn farther to face Tremont. To the right is Winter Street, which leads downtown to the city's financial and retail districts.

The spot where you are now standing is Brimstone Corner, which takes its name from an active ingredient — also known as sulfur — in the manufacture of gunpowder. Some Bostonians say that the name derives from a sizable cache of gunpowder that was stored in the basement of the Park Street Church during the War of 1812. As with nearly every issue, other city residents beg to differ. They say the source of the corner's colorful name is the "fire and brimstone" speechifying that used to sally forth from the church's pulpit, such as the attack mounted on the evils of slavery by William Lloyd Garrison, the great abolitionist, in 1829. At 9 AM, noon, and 4:45 PM, the church's chimes ring out familiar hymns. The church is closed Mondays (phone: 523-3383). Also see *Historic Churches* in DIVERSIONS.

The plaza area near the entrance to the Park Street *T* stop is reminiscent of London's Hyde Park. Though free speech is never in short supply here, your patience may be. If you haven't been handed a pamphlet, asked to sign a petition, urged to boycott a product, or coaxed to write to your congressman, it's probably raining. And even rain doesn't dampen the zeal of a group of Quakers who regularly bear witness to sinful acts and exhort passersby to mend their ways.

Panhandlers also work this area with aplomb. They congregate on the steps down to the *T* where hurried commuters fumble for subway change (85¢). Here a scruffy fellow once delivered one of the greatest lines in the business: "Hey buddy, can you spare a thousand dollars? Well, no problem. If you've got a quarter, I can make up the rest."

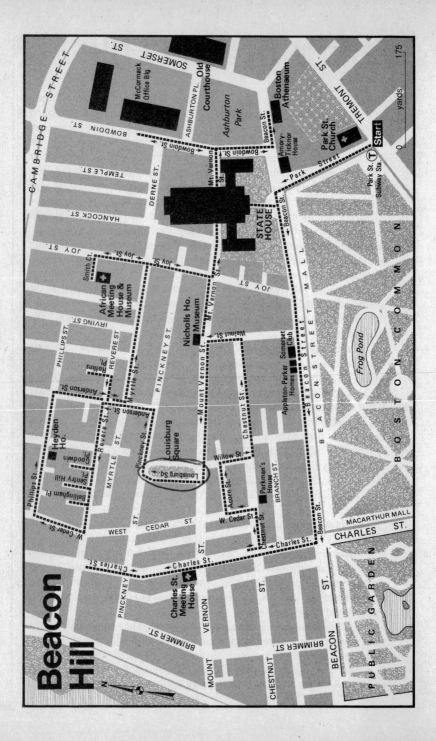

This corner is also home to a number of vendors who peddle everything from hot pretzels to jewelry. Try a monster pretzel, slathered with a generous dose of mustard. Many a relationship has been saved by the resident flower vendor (forgotten birthdays, anniversaries), whose business blooms during rush hour.

Following the Freedom Trail, which is marked by a painted red line on the sidewalk, start up the hill toward the State House. On the right is Park Street, which began as a pathway through the Common to the beacon, a signal lantern atop a pole that warned townspeople of any danger, and gave this hill its name.

The row of 19th-century, Federal-style buildings on Park Street was once called Bulfinch Row because most were designed by the famous architect Charles Bulfinch. The only Bulfinch building still standing on Park Street is the Amory-Ticknor House, on the corner of Park and Beacon. The house was built for Thomas Amory, a merchant who went broke before he got a chance to move in.

Follow the Freedom Trail up the walkway to the steps that climb to Beacon Street. In between the two sets of steps is the Robert Gould Shaw Memorial. (See *Walk 4: Boston Common.*)

Clamber up the steps to see the crowning glory of Bulfinch's many Boston landmarks, the Massachusetts State House, completed in 1798. Oliver Wendell Holmes (the author, doctor, and father, not the justice son) remarked that the "Boston State House is the hub of the solar system," a remark that spawned the city's nickname, "the Hub." The original State House building is the ornate, red brick structure with white marble trim and a great golden dome. The various wings-come-lately are uninspired afterthoughts by comparison. If you squint just right you can block them out of view and see the building as James Monroe did in 1817. The president was so impressed that he put Bulfinch in charge of the reconstruction of the nation's Capitol in Washington, DC, where the architect repeated the rotunda and dome motif. Some final notes about the dome: Its original whitewashed shingles were replaced with copper in 1802 by a Grand Master of the Masons, a fellow by the name of Paul Revere. It has since been gilded, though it was painted gray during World War II to hide the building from possible Axis bomb attacks.

The governor's office is on the third floor, just left of the columns and behind the statue of Horace Mann, the great advocate of public education. The location has its pros and cons for the current governor, William Weld, the first Republican to occupy the office in 18 years. Although it's far removed from the offices of the state legislators (mostly Democrats), it overlooks an area commonly used for political demonstrations.

There is a closer look at the State House and its inside attractions later in the walk. For now, cross the intersection and turn left. A small park of statues on the right features likenesses of statesman Henry Cabot Lodge, who lived not far from here; Anne Hutchinson, who was banished from the Massachusetts Bay Colony for her 82 heretical opinions, "some blasphemous, others erroneous, and all unsafe"; and President John F. Kennedy, who is captured in his familiar, confident stride.

Begin down Beacon Street, an old thoroughfare steeped in history. Though it was called "Poor House Lane" in the 17th century because of an almshouse nearby, by the end of the 19th century, Oliver Wendell Holmes had dubbed it "the sunny street that holds the sifted few."

By now some of the high-rises of the Back Bay should be visible ahead in the distance. Next to the blue glass Hancock Tower is an older building with a vertical row of colored lights on its spire. This is the old Hancock Building; its lights forecast the weather. This epigram tells it all: "Steady blue, clear view. Flashing blue, clouds are due. Steady red, rain ahead. Flashing red, snow instead." (Flashing red lights in the summer indicate that the *Red Sox* game has been canceled, but no one yet has been able to fit that into the rhyme.)

Stroll down Beacon Street and note the purple glass in some of the windows. These purple panes, of which their owners are very proud, were really a big mistake. The violet hue is the result of imperfections in a type of glass shipped from Hamburg, Germany, around 1820. Brought out by the sunlight, this flaw must have caused quite a row among proper Bostonians when it was detected. Today, however, purple panes of glass mean old, which is synonymous with "status" in Beacon Hill parlance.

Nearly every building along Beacon Street figured prominently in the history of Boston. Two of the most interesting are the Appleton-Parker homes (39-40 Beacon St.), a stately pair of early Greek Revival bowfront houses. Nearby is the *Somerset Club* (42 Beacon St.), a 3-story granite house; now a social club, it's strictly private — and profoundly conservative. The *Somerset* was Daniel Webster's favorite haunt. Also note the former home of the Cabot family (34 Beacon St.) and the Third Harrison Gray Otis House (45 Beacon St.), built for the patriot and Mayor of Boston. At 55 Beacon Street is the William Prescott House, former home (from 1845 to 1849) of the grandson of Colonel William Prescott, who commanded the colonial troops at the Battle of Bunker Hill. The younger Prescott, who was blinded in an accident while he was a student at Harvard, was a historian who also devised a system of reading and writing for the blind that preceded Braille. The building is now headquarters for the National Society of Colonial Dames.

Children may be better qualified to recount what happened at the intersection of Beacon and Charles. In Robert McCloskey's *Make Way for Ducklings!,* it is here that Officer Clancy and four fellow Boston policemen held up traffic so that Mrs. Mallard could escort her eight ducklings, single file, into the Public Garden to reunite with Mr. Mallard. On the path to the pond in the Public Garden are bronze statuettes of Mrs. Mallard and her offspring.

Most visitors to Boston want to see *Cheers,* the bar made famous by the long-running television series (now only in reruns), and most people are disappointed with what they find. The one on TV used only the façade of the one on Beacon Hill, which is actually called the *Bull & Finch* pub (84 Beacon St.; phone: 227-9605); the interior looks altogether different. Nonetheless, scads of tourists swarm the place to lap up overpriced beer and buy $20 sweatshirts with the "Cheers" logo. If this sounds appealing, cross the intersection and continue down to where Beacon Street levels out. (The place is so popular that it has expanded from its original basement location and now also includes part of the first floor.)

The *Hampshire House* (phone: 227-9600), located upstairs at 84 Beacon Street, is an entirely different matter. The dining room of this 19th-century mansion overlooking the Public Garden is conservative, elegant, refined, reserved, and all those other fancy adjectives that describe things Bostonian.

Head back on Beacon to Charles Street, turn right, then stand for a few moments to let the Old World feel of this beloved Boston street sink in. If you stood in this precise location 180 years ago, charm would not be the only thing sinking in; you would be standing knee-deep in the Back Bay. Before it was filled in during the second half of the 19th century, the area west of Boston Common and Charles Street was a bay. The part of Charles Street between the Common and the Public Garden is where British troops embarked for Charlestown in their fateful voyage to Lexington and Concord on April 18, 1775.

Charles Street was originally a residential area. It now serves residents of Beacon Hill with antiques shops, bookstores, pubs, and markets. Even *Christy's,* one link in a ubiquitous New England convenience store chain, seems downright civilized in its elegant Greek Revival building.

Farther down is *Deluca's Market* and an adjacent package store (New England–speak for liquor store), with an excellent wine cask street sign, a Victorian form of advertisement that is, unfortunately, now a rarity. At the end of the block is *Rebecca's* (21 Charles St.; phone: 742-9747), a relaxing restaurant with walls decorated with hand-painted flowers and a menu that features fresh salads and excellent pasta dishes. Try the linguine with plum tomatoes, shrimp, and capers. Farther down Charles Street on the opposite side (west) is a building with a clock tower and belfry. This is the Charles Street Meeting House, one of the first great forums of anti-slavery activity. Built in 1807, this building, which was in succession a temple of worship for Baptists, Methodists, Episcopalians, and Universalists, is now a temple of commerce. The ground level consists of five retail shops. The upper floors are office space for financiers, attorneys, and other professionals.

Continue down Charles Street to see the antiques shops tucked cheek-to-jowl between Revere Street and Charles Street Circle. Have a look through the *Boston Antique Cooperative* (119 Charles St.; phone: 227-9810), a five-owner shop that reflects each owner's specialty. (Also see

Shopping in THE CITY and *Antiques: Boston's Best Hunting Grounds* in DIVERSIONS.) Along the way, pop in for a "pop" (Boston jargon for a beer) at the *Seven's Ale House* (77 Charles St.; phone: 523-9074), a typical Boston drinking haunt. But beware of "walking under the influence" in this hilly neighborhood. An imbiber was once witnessed accelerating so fast down a steep Beacon Hill incline — on foot, mind you — that he body-slammed a parked car. The only injury was a small dent — in the car.

Return to the corner of Charles and Chestnut Streets to begin the trek up Beacon Hill.

The townhouses on Chestnut Street, remarkably harmonious in architectural design, are known for their embellishments. Fanciful boot scrapers, ornamental iron balconies, gas lamps, a cast-iron hitching post, and outlandish brass door knockers are just some of the frills that enhance these dwellings. But first, a quick detour. After passing by the *Harvard Musical Association* at 57A Chestnut (whose remarkable music library is the oldest in the nation, and whose occasional evening concerts feature a pre-concert supper of baked beans and beer for its members), turn left onto West Cedar Street and then take an immediate right. This is Acorn Street, Beacon Hill's most precious byway.

Now the showcase of Beacon Hill, Acorn Street has done some social climbing since the days when servants, coachmen, and traders called it home. Be careful when crossing its cobblestone street; some visitors get to gawking at the photogenic buildings and sprain an ankle. It is such a narrow street that a sign was once hung, with subtle humor, that read, "Please don't block this doorway when parking." At Acorn's crest, go right on Willow Street, then left, to continue up Chestnut Street.

Among the historic houses on Chestnut Street are the home of Edwin Booth, a famous actor and brother of John Wilkes Booth, Abraham Lincoln's assassin (29A Chestnut); the residence of Julia Ward Howe (13 Chestnut), a member of Boston literary circles and author of "The Battle Hymn of the Republic" (inspired by a personal visit with a war-weary President Lincoln in the White House); and the meeting place of the Radical Club (17 Chestnut), which claimed Whittier, Emerson, and Longfellow as regular visitors. Former Secretary of State Henry Kissinger lived at 1 Chestnut Street when he was teaching at Harvard. Look for the gaslight at the foot of its stone steps.

Turn left at the top of Chestnut and walk along Walnut Street to Mt. Vernon Street, the street of mansions; then turn left again. Two houses, both designed by Charles Bulfinch, stand majestically toward the end of this block. The Second Harrison Gray Otis House (85 Mt. Vernon St.) is an exception to Beacon Hill's dense development, reflecting Bulfinch's vision (never realized) of a group of freestanding mansions with landscaped grounds in this area. If the gate is open, walk up the cobblestone drive toward the rear of this private house and see the stable, now a separate dwelling (across the street is a whole row of stables converted into homes), and a fountain with water spurting out of a lion's mouth. Also notice the octagonal cupola on the roof. Bulfinch built the house next door (87 Mt. Vernon St.) for himself and his family. Unfortunately, they never got a chance to live in it, because financial woes plunged the architect into bankruptcy.

Past these homes is Louisburg Square, the Hope Diamond of Beacon Hill gems. This quiet oval park framed by bowfront dwellings is an exquisite reminder of Boston's British heritage. Statues of Aristides the Just and Christopher Columbus, gifts of a former Turkish consul to Boston, stand on either end of the small fenced park. On the northern side of the park once bubbled a freshwater spring. "Blackstone's Spring" (named after William Blaxton, the first settler, who lived not far from here) still seeps into Pinckney Street basements after unusually heavy rainfall. The serene, pensive aura of the square must have been ideal for Louisa May Alcott, the author of *Little Women,* who lived at No. 10 during her last years. Wander slowly around the park, savoring its ample shade. Unfortunately, this carefully tended swatch of green is for the exclusive use of Louisburg Square residents. But if the gate is open . . .

Leave Louisburg Square from the other end and continue up Pinckney Street to the right. This street was an endeavor in defensive city planning. Composed mainly of horse stables behind the Mt. Vernon Street mansions, Pinckney Street was designed in 1802 as a buffer zone between the affluent south slope of Beacon Hill and the seedy north slope or "back of the hill," which had become known throughout the great ports of the world as "Mount Whoredom." Accordingly, the only access to the north slope from Pinckney was Anderson Street, just ahead.

But Pinckney Street has made a brilliant comeback. It was swept clean in 1823 by Mayor Josiah Quincy and his police force, who evicted 300 residents, described by a clergyman of the time as "females wholly devoid of shame and modesty." Now home to literary figures, artists, and academics, it offers Beacon Hill's best view of the Charles River. During the late afternoons of summer, sailboats can be seen tacking to and fro on the Charles, as the river blazes with the light of the setting sun.

Several buildings on Pinckney Street have interesting pasts. Louisa May Alcott and family lived in three dwellings here — Numbers 20, 43, and 81 — in the family's ongoing pursuit of shelter. Her father, Bronson, though he frequently hobnobbed with Emerson and the other transcendentalists, was a hopeless mystic and terribly irresponsible with the family's funds.

Transcendentalist lawyer and publisher George Hillard lived at 62 Pinckney in the 1840s and 1850s. During that time, he became a US commissioner in charge of issuing warrants for the arrest of fugitive slaves, putting him at serious cross-purposes with his abolitionist wife, who hid slaves in the house without her husband knowing.

Head north on Anderson Street (always think of the harbor to get your bearings). Massachusetts General Hospital, where the first successful operation with ether was performed in 1846, can be seen down the hill from around 62 Anderson Street.

Ramble down Anderson to the corner of Revere Street. To the right (about half a block down) is Rollins Place, a cozy, little alley illuminated by gaslights. At the end of the block is a wooden Greek Revival façade; resembling a stage set, it was installed by the owner of the property to prevent the absentminded from toppling off the cliff just behind.

Head back down Revere Street (west) to view Goodwin Place, Sentry Hill Place, and Bellingham Place, private courts and alleys that are among the most sought-after residential areas on Beacon Hill. These cul-de-sacs, built around 1845, are lined with red brick houses and were originally the homes of artisans and traders. If the gates are open, feel free to stroll.

Swing around the block — turn right on the West Cedar Street footpath, then right again onto Phillips Street. The dwelling at 66 Phillips, once the home of Lewis and Harriet Hayden, figured prominently in the abolitionist movement. After the Fugitive Slave Act of 1850 gave slave owners the legal right to recapture escaped slaves, the Haydens became leaders of the Underground Railroad, and their house became a "station" on the way to Canada. The couple reportedly kept several kegs of gunpowder in the basement, vowing to blast the whole building sky-high rather than return a single slave. Luckily, the house was never searched.

With all this climbing and snooping about, it may be time to refuel. Turn right on Anderson, then make a left on Myrtle Street, just past Revere. A short stroll from here is *Primos* (28 Myrtle St.; phone: 742-5458), a latter-day Beacon Hill institution and the best (possibly because it's the only) pizza joint on the hill. The Italian and the eggplant hero sandwiches (they're called grinders in these parts) are quite good. So is the pizza. All in all, it's a fine place for a snack and a breather.

Farther east, Myrtle Street intersects with Joy Street. Turn left on Joy and make another left on Smith Court. The first black church in the United States, the African Meeting House, is here. Founded in 1806, it has long been a gathering place for supporters of abolition and civil rights. William Lloyd Garrison founded the New England Anti-Slavery Society here in 1832. The *Museum of Afro-American History* (phone: 742-1854) is located on the first floor. It's open Tuesdays through Fridays; no admission charge. The home of William Nell, an early black crusader for school integration, is across the street at 3 Smith Court. Built in 1799, this site and others are part of the Black Heritage Trail, a walking tour that explores the history of the black community in Boston. Call the National Park Service Visitor Center (phone: 742-5415) for more information on the route. (Also see *Special Places* in THE CITY.)

Return to Joy Street, following it back to Mt. Vernon, then make a right. The *Nichols House Museum* (55 Mt. Vernon St.; phone: 227-6993) is an early Bulfinch mansion. Under the terms of the will of Rose Standish

Nichols, the last resident, it remains a private museum that provides visitors with a rare look at the interior of a gracefully furnished home of a Beacon Hill Brahmin. Among its many interesting features are a spiral staircase, portraits of Nichols family ancestors, and a console table that belonged to John Hancock. Open Tuesdays through Saturdays, June through August; Wednesdays and Saturdays at other times; closed December through February; admission charge.

Now head back to the State House, following Mt. Vernon Street to its beginning. Pass under a carport where the governor's limo sometimes waits to whisk its high-ranking passenger to his next official visit. Beyond the carport is an entrance to the right; enter for a tour of Bulfinch's most famous Boston building.

Some of the more important features of the State House interior are the Doric Hall, with its busts, statues, memorials, and paintings of famous Americans (join a guided tour, or pick up information for a self-guided tour); Memorial Hall (or the Hall of Flags), which displays an impressive collection of regimental flags from the Civil War, the Spanish-American War, and both world wars; the House of Representatives, where hangs the historic Sacred Cod (a symbol of the state's economy, donated to the legislature by an early member, and an outstanding example of early American folk art); and the Senate Chamber and Senate Reception Room. The State House is open weekdays; no admission charge (phone: 727-3676). Also see *Special Places* in THE CITY.

Exit through the doors on Mt. Vernon Street (where you entered) into the new Ashburton Park, which was a parking lot until recently. Here the Beacon Hill Memorial Column stands on the former site of the warning beacon, which blew over on a particularly windy night in November 1789. The present column was erected in 1898. Sixty feet were sliced off this hill in 1811 to provide earth to fill in the old Mill Pond, a project that added 50 acres to the northern edge of Beacon Hill.

Pass through the gate and across Bowdoin Street, to No. 122, where a wiry young John F. Kennedy established his untidy office and Boston residence after winning a seat to the US Congress in 1946.

Diagonally left from Ashburton Park is the John W. McCormack Building, home to an alphabet soup of commissions and departments characteristic of Massachusetts state government. Few visitors to Boston (or Bostonians, for that matter) are aware of a series of conference rooms on the building's 21st floor that offer an ideal aerial view of Beacon Hill on one side and the financial district, harbor, and North End on the other. No one will bother you if you act as if you belong there.

Follow Bowdoin Street south to the *Golden Dome Pub* (150 Bowdoin St.; phone: 227-7100) on the left. This boisterous joint always seems to be pushing the maximum capacity limit of the fire code. Known in some circles as the "State House Annex," it is used by press and pols as a news exchange. It's an ideal venue to leak stories to the press and exchange gossip since nobody — including (occasionally) your companions — can hear a thing you're saying. If you're looking for a tavern with real Boston ambience, this is it. It serves great ale, too.

The best stop on this Beacon Hill historical walking tour has been saved for last — the *Boston Athenaeum* at 10½ Beacon Street. An independent library, art gallery, and museum, the *Athenaeum* is a legacy of Boston's aspirations to be the "Athens of America."

The *Athenaeum* features a collection of George Washington's books on the top floor, periodic exhibitions by acclaimed artists in the gallery on the second floor, and a scenic view of the Old Granary Burying Ground out the rear windows. Look for a book written by Oliver Wendell Holmes, a former member of the *Athenaeum*, that has been edited in spots with a pen. The author, it is said, made a couple of later-than-last-minute corrections while leafing through the volume on a visit to the library. Asked why a visitor to the city should come here, a library administrator said it all: "Because it's just so darned Bostonian." Tours (no charge) are given on Tuesday and Thursday afternoons; reservations are necessary (phone: 227-0270). Also see *Special Places* in THE CITY.

A final note: Just a block down Beacon Street, on the way back to Boston Common, is a great delicatessen. Despite its name, a visit to the *S&M New York Deli* (14 Beacon St.; phone: 523-8776) is a pleasurable experience — the corned beef on rye is the best this side of New York City's *Carnegie Deli*.

Walk 6: Downtown

The important thing to remember about Boston is that, according to reliable lore, there was never any attempt to organize the city's downtown streets (Back Bay is a different matter). Paved-over paths trod by cattle as they wandered about freely on the Boston peninsula, they just evolved. But Bostonians have never seemed to mind that their downtown streets are just glorified cowpaths. As Ralph Waldo Emerson observed, "We say the cows laid out Boston. Well, there are worse surveyors." The legacy of this bovine school of city planning is that even native Bostonians sometimes get gloriously lost. They would be the first to admit it.

The jumble of streets that gives Boston its charm and Old World feel is no more evident than in the city's cradle, the downtown area, which now consists of the *Faneuil Hall Marketplace,* Government Center, and the financial, retail, and waterfront districts. The walking tour of downtown (allow up to 5 hours) begins at the corner of Park and Tremont Streets, site of the Park Street Church and Park Street *MBTA* station, where the *Red* and *Green Lines* intersect (see *Walk 5: Beacon Hill*).

Face Tremont Street, which runs north and south (remember the harbor is directly ahead), and proceed north past the Park Street Church to the Old Granary Burying Ground, named after the public granary that stood on the church site in the 1700s. Established in 1660, this cemetery is the final resting place of many Boston patriots. Among the worthies buried beneath the linden and oak trees are Samuel Adams, John Hancock, Paul Revere, the victims of the Boston Massacre, and many others. (Look for the grave of Mary Goose, thought to have been Mother Goose.)

Although a large memorial to the parents of Benjamin Franklin dominates the burial ground, most of the tombstones are small and stark. Few of the markers, in fact, are actually assigned to their correct graves. Tidy gravekeepers have, unfortunately, uprooted gravestones, using them to edge new paths throughout the cemetery. Pass through the Egyptian-style granite archway and stroll around the Old Granary, enjoying its remarkable tranquillity while Tremont Street bustles just yards away. The burial ground is open daily.

Continue down Tremont Street — formerly a hillside row of the mansions and terraced gardens owned by the colonial aristocracy — to its intersection with School Street, shaded by the skyscrapers of the financial district. Amid this jungle of high-rises, King's Chapel, one of America's oldest churches (phone: 227-2155), is a welcome sight across the street.

King's Chapel was the colony's most fashionable parish before the American Revolution — though not much liked by the colonists, since it was primarily a place of worship for British officers. The royal governor and his entourage worshiped here. The brownish, rough-hewn exterior of

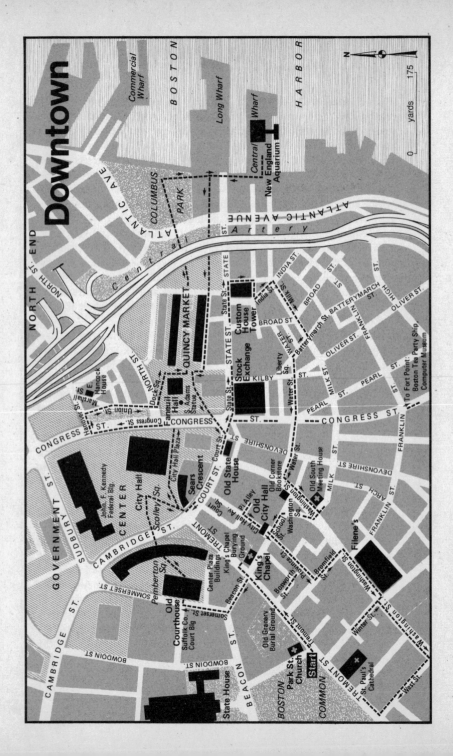

the building makes the freshly painted white walls and woodwork of the interior seem even brighter. Notice the Governor's Pew, banished from the church in 1826 as "an undemocratic reminder of a bygone era," then restored a century later after some historical distance from the British crown was gained. The ideal time to visit the chapel is just after noon, when concerts — anything from chamber music recitals to Appalachian dulcimer performances — are presented on Tuesdays. The church has been Unitarian since 1785. (Also see *Historic Churches* in DIVERSIONS.)

Next to the chapel is the King's Chapel Burying Ground. Established in 1631, it is the city's oldest cemetery and contains the graves and tombstones of many revered old Bostonians, including John Winthrop, the first Governor of the Massachusetts Bay Colony; William Dawes, who was Paul Revere's companion on his famous ride; and Mary Chilton, the first woman Pilgrim from the Plymouth Colony to go to Boston. Along the first path to the right is the grave of Elizabeth Pain, a Puritan woman who was tried for the murder of her child. Although she was acquitted, she was considered a notorious woman; her story is thought by some to have been the inspiration for Nathaniel Hawthorne's tragic masterpiece, *The Scarlet Letter*.

Backtrack a few yards and turn right, uphill onto Beacon Street. Another right on Somerset Street will bring you to the Old Courthouse, also known as the Suffolk County Courthouse.

Walk around to the rear of the building, noting its neo-classical design, which is reminiscent of the *Louvre*. Then walk toward the crescent-shape row of office buildings ahead. This is the rear of Government Center. The escalator that cuts through this wall of buildings was installed in the late 1960s, in conjunction with the construction of the new City Hall. In exchange for allowing developers to build over a little street that had connected Old Scollay Square (where you're going) to Pemberton Square (where you've just been), the city required that the developers provide escalator service between the two squares "forever."

Across Cambridge Street (ahead as you step off the escalator) is an endless sea of bricks and concrete, culminating in a top-heavy cement structure that one Boston native justifiably said looks like "the box that *Faneuil Hall* came in." This is City Hall.

It wasn't always this way. Completed in 1968, City Hall sits smack-dab in the middle of what was Old Scollay Square, the mere mention of which brings a faint smile to the faces of those old enough to remember. In its prime, Old Scollay Square was either rollicking, rowdy, or just plain raunchy, depending on one's point of view. It was a jumble of London-style buildings known in every port on earth for its roaring nightlife, tattoo parlors, short-stay hotels, and pawnshops. In the thick of it was the *Old Howard,* a building that no longer exists but deserves mention here, since the story of its downfall mirrored the demise of the once-respectable district where it stood.

The *Old Howard* was originally a church, built by the Millerites (a religious sect that predicted the exact day the world would end in 1834 and quickly disbanded when that day passed uneventfully). The building subsequently became the *Howard Athenaeum,* a theater with a very proper Bostonian name featuring classy plays and opera. In the ensuing years, the *Howard* began to decline, playing host to vaudeville, then burlesque, and finally, striptease acts. Its last act was with a wrecking ball to make way for the new City Hall. There is a plaque where the *Old Howard*'s stage used to be, near the Sears Crescent building.

Walk across the vast red brick City Hall Plaza, which, when stiff winter winds blow in from the harbor, can seem like the coldest spot in the city. There is no reason why one should go inside City Hall except maybe to pay a parking fine, for which this city is notorious. On the right facing City Hall is a curving row of buildings known as the Sears Crescent, built in 1816. Next door is the smaller Sears block, built around 1846. This row features Boston's most beloved sign, a large, gold, steam-spewing teakettle, which hangs in front of the coffee shop on the corner of Tremont and Court Streets. The 227-gallon kettle's human capacity — tested in the late 1800s — is eight small boys and a rather tall man.

Another amusing Victorian street sign — a large, smoking pipe — hangs in front of *David P. Ehrlich & Sons* pipe and tobacco shop (32 Tremont St.; phone: 227-1720), a short walk down the street to the right as you face City Hall. A brief visit inside this aromatic shop can be an olfactory delight, even for a nonsmoker.

Return to City Hall Plaza, passing just to the left of the teakettle. Continue on to City Hall's south side and down the several flights of steps that lead out onto Congress Street. Across the street is historic *Faneuil Hall,* with *Quincy Market (Faneuil Hall Marketplace)* in tow. A statue of Revolutionary War hero Samuel Adams greets visitors to this popular part of town. But resist the temptation to cross for now. Instead, turn left and follow Congress Street along the east side of City Hall to Hanover Street. From here, cross Congress Street for a look at Boston's oldest commercial district.

Turn right onto Union Street, then make an immediate left onto Marshall Street. At 10 Marshall Street is the Ebenezer Hancock House, former home of John Hancock's brother. John owned the building from 1764 to 1785 while his brother actually lived there. As paymaster of the colonial troops, Ebenezer kept in the basement the 2 million silver crowns sent by France to help pay the revolutionary troops (a deal artfully crafted by Benjamin Franklin). The house is now a law office and is not open to the public.

Across from the Hancock House is the Boston Stone, a millstone imported from England by a colonial painter. Originally used to grind colored powder into paint, it became — like its counterpart, the London stone — the official point from which all distances from Boston were measured.

Return to Union Street and visit the *Union Oyster House* (41 Union St.; phone: 227-2750), the city's oldest restaurant and a true Boston institution. At night it's impossible to miss the red neon sign atop the building; it's as much a landmark as the beacon atop Beacon Hill was in earlier centuries. If the smell of salt water has piqued your appetite, a plate of oysters on the half shell and a frothy ale may be in order. Think of it as a historical reenactment — it's said that Daniel Webster, the silver-tongued senator himself, often hunkered down at this very establishment to polish off a dozen plates of oysters, accompanied by more than a few pints, in a single sitting. A bastion of Boston seafood, the *Union Oyster House* boasts 18 varieties of lobster dinners.

Passing British troops used to yell for the hanging of the patriot who once lived on the second floor of the *Union Oyster House* building: Isaiah Thomas, publisher of a revolutionary newspaper, the *Massachusetts Spy*. Thomas smuggled his press and type out of Boston 3 days before the confrontations in Lexington and Concord. From Worcester he published the first official reports of the opening battle of the revolution. About 25 years later, the restaurant's second floor sheltered the exiled and impoverished French King Louis Philippe, who gave French lessons to Boston merchants and their daughters here before he returned to France to claim the throne as the "Citizen King."

Now walk toward *Faneuil Hall Marketplace*. En route, you'll pass *Bosworth's Boston Baked Beans* (37 Union St.; phone: 248-0880), a small restaurant and gift shop that sells authentic Boston baked beans with the traditional accompaniments: a piece of brown bread, a hot dog, and Indian pudding.

A pleasant little tree-fringed park running parallel to Union Street has several inviting benches as well as two statues of James Michael Curley, the renowned Boston politician who was accused of everything but bench sitting during his lengthy political career as alderman, mayor, state legislator, governor, and US congressman. The quip "Vote often and early for James Michael Curley" says it all about this scholarly rogue who had a profound influence on 20th-century Boston politics. (Spencer Tracy played the Curley-based character in the film version of Edwin O'Connor's *The Last Hurrah,* the last word on Boston politics of the time.)

This route approaches *Faneuil Hall Marketplace* from the northwest, through Dock Square, the former location of the town dock and site of the colony's first waterfront settlement. Just up North Street is the *Bostonian* hotel (phone: 523-3600), a 152-room establishment that has been surprisingly well integrated into this ancient block, a cherished remnant of 17th-century Boston. The *Seasons* restaurant and the *Atrium* lounge (beware, drinks have been known to cost as much as $7 at both places) occupy the hotel's first 2 floors and are fine places to observe the area's robust activity, particularly the "power breakfasts" among the city's movers and shakers for which *Seasons* is famous.

Faneuil Hall was built in 1742 for Peter Faneuil, a French Huguenot merchant prince who donated the building to the city in an early example of American philanthropy. The building became a public meeting place, one that patriot James Otis would call "the cradle of liberty." It was here, on the second floor, that the leaders of the revolution mounted increasingly blistering attacks on King George III and the British Parliament. It also was here in 1772 that Samuel Adams proposed that the city form a Committee of Correspondence and invite the other 12 colonies to do the same, a gesture encouraging the disparate colonies to unite in action. Later, this same hall became famous for the oratory heard here, including anti-slavery speeches and Daniel Webster's 1826 eulogy in honor of John Adams and Thomas Jefferson, both of whom had died on *July Fourth* of that year.

Before continuing on to the *Quincy Market* building, glance up at the grasshopper weather vane proudly perched on the *Faneuil Hall* tower. Nobody is quite sure why it's a grasshopper (rather than an eagle or rooster), but the most plausible explanation is that the grasshopper was part of the family crest of a deceased friend of Charles Bulfinch, who rebuilt the structure in 1806, and that the weather vane is a memorial to him.

Behind *Faneuil Hall* is *Quincy Market,* a long building with an impressive portico fortified by four stout, granite columns. At lunchtime and on weekends, street performers often entertain crowds perched on the market building's wide stone steps, and the area between the two buildings takes on the air of London's *Covent Garden.* Once Boston's premier meat, poultry, and produce market, *Quincy Market* and the adjacent warehouses were restored and transformed into a bustling, trendy marketplace in 1976, with dozens of shops, restaurants, fast-food concessions, and bars.

A note about terms: Strictly speaking, *Quincy Market* and *Faneuil Hall* are two historic buildings in the renovated marketplace known as the *Faneuil Hall Marketplace.* However, the terms *Faneuil Hall, Faneuil Hall Marketplace, Quincy Market,* and *Quincy Marketplace* are all used — often interchangeably — to refer to the entire marketplace. Also be aware that there's a smoldering controversy about how the word "Faneuil" is actually pronounced, even among Bostonians. Some contend it's pronounced *Fan*'l; others claim it's *Fan*-yool. The merchant's gravestone doesn't offer much insight. It reads "Funel," leading some historians to conclude that the name was pronounced to rhyme with "tunnel." If you don't have a favorite, just call it the "historic meeting house near *Quincy Market.*" You'll be understood.

Take a walk through the center aisle of *Quincy Market,* an alley-like building that has become a runway of fast foods from around the world. Dozens of concessions offer a cornucopia of gustatory delights. There are enchiladas, crêpes, daiquiris, cheese, oysters, bagels, hot dogs, brownies, fresh peanut butter, fruit salads, frozen yogurt, fudge, ice cream, salads, cookies, pastry, teriyaki, roast chicken, "designer" coffee, and gyros — and that's just a small sampling. Visitors make their purchases at the individual concessions and then search (often in vain) for an open table in the rotunda. Weekday lunch hours are particularly maniacal, as workers pour out of the adjacent office buildings to forage. On the sides of *Quincy Market* are two glassed-in malls, where vendors sell a plethora of trinkets, souvenirs, and accessories from pushcarts.

The two rows of buildings flanking *Quincy Market,* the *North* and *South Markets,* also have been upgraded considerably from their once lowly status as warehouses. The shops they house now include a mixture of the highbrow and the informal, the traditional and the bizarre. Shops are constantly being added and subtracted; the directory in the *Quincy Market* rotunda should help. Two of the market's more unusual shops are *Boston Scrimshanders* (*South Market*; phone: 367-1552), which specializes in scrimshaw jewelry (best described as whale-tooth and bone art, a New England specialty; since the use of whale tooth has been outlawed, carvings are now done on mammal ivory and fossil walrus), and *Hog Wild* (*North Market*; phone: 523-7447), which sells only items with a pig or hog motif. (There is also *Purple Panache,* a store with an entirely purple stock; another shop, *Have a Heart,* carries . . . well, you get the idea.)

Be sure to pay a visit to *Durgin-Park* (*North Market;* phone: 227-2038), a restaurant featuring traditional New England food that is so quintessentially Boston that it's in danger of parodying itself. The sharp-witted waitresses like to give patrons a rough time (it's partly an act), the portions are enormous, and the roast beef, chowders, Indian pudding, and baked beans are hearty, if not always tasty. Try as they might, nobody in the history of the place — including Cabots and Lowells, Kissingers and Kennedys — has succeeded in reserving a table, so be prepared for a short wait.

Just down from *Durgin-Park,* at the end of the *North Market* building, is *Lord Bunbury's* (phone: 227-7004), a British pub and restaurant named after a famous 18th-century caricaturist. *Bunbury's* centerpiece is a solid mahogany bar that was once in an English pub; it was disassembled, shipped overseas, and reassembled here (like Arizona's London Bridge). The pub is the ideal place to sip a pint of stout, served, as in bonny old England, at room temperature.

At the end of the marketplace is *Marketplace Center,* a small row of newer buildings that house still more stores and food concessions.

Now take a minute to look back over the marketplace. The view of the city, with the old (*Quincy Market, Faneuil Hall*) juxtaposed against the new (City Hall and Government Center), is gorgeous. Then turn around and walk out of the market and underneath the behemoth Central Artery overpass, to Columbus Park and the waterfront.

The pier directly ahead is Long Wharf, originally built in 1710 to provide Boston Harbor with deep-water mooring. It is considered the greatest construction project of Boston's colonial period. British troops embarked here for the Battle of Bunker Hill. Today, the pier is known as the site of the *Marriott* hotel (phone: 227-0800); the rustic *Chart House* restaurant (phone: 227-1576), which serves award-winning clam chowder; and the offices of F. Lee Bailey (at 66 Long Wharf in the granite Custom House Block), the famous trial attorney. Central Wharf, immediately to the south of Long Wharf, is the home of the *New England Aquarium* (phone: 973-5200), which harbors a spectacular array of fish — more than 2,000 species in all. Of particular note is the 4-story saltwater tank, girded by a spiral viewing ramp from which visitors can view the resident sharks, sea turtles, moray eels, and wide variety of fish. Penguins cavort in a pool at the base of the tank, and seals and dolphins perform in a floating pavilion next door. Whale watches depart from here, April through October; call for schedule information (phone: 973-5277). Open daily; admission charge. (Also see *Special Places* in THE CITY.)

Backtrack to *Faneuil Hall Marketplace*. This time, stroll along the shops of the south side, doffing your cap to the statue of the legendary Red Auerbach, former coach, general manager, and now president of the Boston *Celtics,* whose bronze, cigar-smoking likeness relaxes permanently on one of the benches.

While heading back to Congress Street, notice a tiny kiosk near the entrance to the marketplace. This is the office of *Bostix,* an establishment that sells same-day discount tickets for concerts, theater performances, and other events.

Follow Congress Street left a block or two, along the Freedom Trail, to the Old State House, one of the highlights of this walking tour. Dwarfed by the skyscrapers of investment banks and insurance companies, the Old State House remains a proud reminder of America's colonial past. The present building was built in 1713, but this was also the location of the Town House, Boston's first Town Hall, which was built in 1657; town meetings were held here as early as 1634. Boston's development began at this meeting place — homes and gardens were established nearby and roads struck out, by man and by cow, to connect them.

Since the Old State House served as the council chambers of the royal governors sent from England, as the conflict between England and the colonies became more pointed, so did the goings-on about the Old State House. When edicts and proclamations were read from the east balcony, the colonists would adjourn to local taverns to work themselves into a fury and then return, emboldened, to protest. In front of the east side of this building also was the site of the Boston Massacre, which occurred in March 1770, when a patrol of British troops panicked and fired into a mob of angry colonists, killing five men. This rash act did little to stifle the rebellious colonists' ire. A circle of cobblestone under the East Gable of the building marks the spot where the men fell. Reproductions of Paul Revere's lithographs of the incident, which were distributed throughout the colonies, can be purchased at the National Park Service visitors' center across the street (15 State St.; phone: 242-5642). The center also can answer any questions you may have. Completely restored last year, the Old State House is home to the *Bostonian Society,* which has a museum and library with many mementos of Boston history.

From here, visitors have the option of embarking on a side trip to the *Boston Tea Party Ship and Museum* and the *Computer Museum,* both located along Fort Point Channel, a brisk 10-to-15-minute walk straight down Congress Street.

The *Brig Beaver II,* a full-size working replica of one of the three original Tea Party ships, is moored just about where the original vessel, owned by the British East India Company, had her heavily taxed cargo jettisoned one fateful evening in December 1773. It was one of the first unique acts of defiance leading to the American Revolution. Abutting the ship is a museum, where visitors can enjoy a cup of tea while perusing the exhibits that recount the event. As a parting shot, hurl overboard a crate (which is provided) and pretend it's a bale of tea in belated personal protest. Don't be too concerned about tainting Boston Harbor. Bostonians mucked up the harbor in 1773 and have been polluting it ever since. Besides, the crate is attached to a rope for easy retrieval. Open daily March through mid-December; admission charge (phone: 338-1773).

Just over the Congress Street Bridge and left at the big milk bottle is the *Computer Museum.* Even non-"techies" usually spend a couple of hours here. Among the hands-on and interactive exhibits are terminals that allow visitors to test a variety of programs, voice-activated computers, robots, and a walk-through computer. Families may want to stop at the *Children's Museum,* also on Museum Wharf. (Also see *Special Places* in THE CITY.) Just beyond is *Venus Seafood in the Rough,* the city's only clam shack. Since its seating facilities are picnic tables under a tent, it's only open mid-April through mid-October (48 Sleeper St.; phone: 426-3388).

The weary who balk at the suggestion of a side trip may instead head down State Street, toward the water, for a loop through the Custom House District before resuming the tour with a walk through Boston's most historic block, near Washington Square, and on to the retail district.

For a spectacular aerial view of Boston from a sophisticated setting, locals and visitors alike go to the *Bay Tower Room* (phone: 723-1666), at the top of the 60 State Street building just across from the Old State House. Though it is a private club and a favorite of the working lunch crowd, the elegant restaurant and piano bar on the top floor are open to the general public after 4:30 PM. The menu features creative American cooking; the baked stuffed lobster is especially succulent. A jacket is required for men.

The monstrous building at 53 State Street is the home of Boston's stock exchange. It stands on the site of the historic *Bunch of Grapes* tavern, a favorite meeting place of patriots prior to the revolution that reputedly served up the best bowl of "punch" in town. The plans for the present structure originally called for a replica of the old exchange building to replace the real McCoy. In response to vocal protests by preservationists, a compromise was reached whereby an L-shaped façade of the original structure was spared and incorporated into the new design. There are many projects like this in Boston, the result of ongoing combat between developers and preservationists; opinions are mixed as to who will ultimately triumph. The aptly named *Stocks and Bonds* restaurant (53 State St.; phone: 723-8505) is located in the basement and is a favorite of Boston's financial crowd.

Farther down State Street — King Street before the revolution — is an imposing tower, which poet Walt Whitman once called "one of the noblest pieces of commercial architecture in the world." It is the Custom House Tower, built between 1912 and 1917, which for decades was New England's tallest structure (the older building at the base of the tower was completed in 1847). Before Atlantic Avenue was built, the building was so close to the waterfront that the bows of boats would bump the windows facing the harbor. The Custom House's 22-foot-wide clock was repaired and refurbished recently, and for the first time in years all four faces tell the same time. At night the building is awash in colored light. US Customs has decamped for more modern offices, and the city of Boston, which bought the building, is planning to convert this property into a luxury hotel by leasing the land to developers. It is hoped that the tower's 25th-floor observation deck, which offers a panoramic view of the city and the harbor, will be reopened one day.

Turn right just beyond the Custom House, then follow India Street just as it begins to dogleg left. On the left is the Flour and Grain Exchange, a distinctively handsome Romanesque building that houses, not at all coincidentally, the offices of a number of architectural firms.

Make a right on Milk Street and another right on Batterymarch Street. Walk straight ahead to Liberty Square. From the square, turn left onto Water Street heading west, back to its intersection with Congress Street. In a building on the northeast corner, William Lloyd Garrison began (in 1831) publishing *The Liberator,* an abolitionist newspaper dedicated to the end of slavery. Stay on Water Street one more block until you reach Washington Street, in the middle of Boston's most historic block.

The Old State House is 2 blocks north on Washington Street. However, make a left on Washington Street, an ancient thoroughfare that linked the Old State House with the town gate on the neck of the peninsula (when

Boston was a peninsula). The Indians who used to inhabit this area called the road Shawmut, which is why Boston-area banks, streets, and businesses bear this name. At the end of the block, on the right, is the *Old Corner Bookstore,* now called the *Globe Corner Bookstore* (phone: 523-6658). The building that first stood on this site belonged to the family of Anne Hutchinson, a religious dissident whose unorthodox beliefs became so popular in the 1630s that she was banished from the colony by an intimidated Governor Winthrop (he later conceded that he was about the only one in town who didn't like her opinions). The present building was constructed in 1718 after the Hutchinson home was destroyed in the Great Boston Fire of 1711. For years, it was the office of Jamie Fields, a luminary in early American publishing who attracted such names as Emerson, Holmes, Hawthorne, Thoreau, Lowell, and Longfellow to his stable of writers. Fields's office was a center of literary discussion. Today, the building houses an excellent bookstore with volumes and guidebooks about New England on the first floor and travel literature and maps on the second.

Across Washington Square, at the intersection of School and Washington Streets (anything in Boston is called a square as long as it has a park bench), is the Old South Meeting House, a structure steeped in history. Formerly the Old South Church, it was here that an overflowing crowd of colonists met in December 1773 to discuss what to do about three British tea ships docked in the harbor. The multimedia presentation "In Prayer and Protest" re-creates the deliberations prior to the Boston Tea Party. On Saturday evenings in the summer, you can watch costumed players reenact a town meeting. Open daily; admission charge (phone: 482-6439).

Just around the corner, at 17 Milk Street, is the site where Ben Franklin was born in 1706. His devout father bundled Ben up at the tender age of 3 hours and took him around the corner to the Old South Church to be baptized.

Now return to School Street and follow it up to the Old City Hall building on the right (there's a statue of Benjamin Franklin on its west side). Old City Hall, an intriguing granite building erected in 1865, was for years the undisputed domain of James Michael Curley (he served four 4-year terms as mayor between 1914 and 1950). He referred to his office on the southeast corner as "Agony Corner." The building is now home to *Maison Robert,* an elegant restaurant serving fine French fare. A more moderately priced café is downstairs (phone: 227-3370 for both).

Ramble along City Hall Avenue, a charming alley on the Josiah Quincy statue side (east) of Old City Hall. Just after passing the Kirstein Business Library is Pi Alley, evidence that the phalanx of streets in this area, though arbitrarily placed, were not arbitrarily named. A jumble of great American newspapers and magazines got their start in this area, thus the alley was named "pi," a printer's term for a jumble of type. (Other street-name trivia: The nation's first schoolhouse building was located on School

Street; an old courthouse stood on Court Street; Court Street was called Prison Lane when a grim jailhouse, said to have once held Captain Kidd, stood here.) Pi Alley is now home to a motley assortment of vendors. *Ties Only,* with many silk ties for under $10, is worth a look. Backtrack to School Street via City Hall Avenue and walk in the direction of Washington Street. On the right is Province Street, at one time called Governor's Alley because it ran behind Province House, the official mansion of the royal governors. The granite steps leading up to Bosworth Street connected the mansion to its garden, stables, and coach house. There's an intimate and traditionally Boston restaurant and bar, appropriately called *Governor's Alley* (42 Province St.; phone: 426-3333), across the street. Try the scrod or the lobster pie.

Just up the steps on Bosworth Street, a picturesque lane that looks a little like the French Quarter in New Orleans, is the *Marliave* (10 Bosworth St.; phone: 423-6340), an eating establishment that dates back to 1875. French Huguenots, fleeing religious persecution, built a small church at the corner of Province and School Streets in 1707, and this area was a French enclave when the *Marliave* gained fame as a French Bohemian–style hotel and dining room. Today, the restaurant serves Italian food that is quite good. There's a glass-enclosed patio overlooking Winter Street in the rear.

Continue down Province Street, taking a left on Bromfield, which leads to Washington Street. After weathering Boston's past, reward your efforts with some very modern-day shopping in the city's retail district. Turn right onto Washington Street; *Filene's* is at the end of the block, on the left. "The World Famous *Filene's Basement,*" as the sign says, is below. *Filene's* (426 Washington St.; phone: 357-2100) is a fine department store; *Filene's Basement* (phone: 542-2011) is an unforgettable shopping experience.

Those who shop religiously will find it fitting that Boston's first church, the "Old Brick," was located just about where *Jordan Marsh,* New England's largest department store (450 Washington St.; phone: 357-3000), now stands. The blocks branching out of the intersection of Washington and Winter Streets are closed to automobile traffic, forming a pedestrian shopping area known as Downtown Crossing. The area is known for its footwear stores.

Walk up Winter Street to Winter Place, about mid-block on the left. Sitting in the corner, reserved and proud, is the *Locke-Ober Café* (phone: 542-1340), a legendary Boston restaurant with traditional ambience and extremely traditional (read "conservative") values. It has a private club, *Yvonne's,* in the rear. Only recently have women been allowed to dine unaccompanied by a male in the exclusive *Men's Grill.* The painting of a nude that hangs above the L-shaped mahogany bar is draped in black when Harvard loses to Yale. Don't enter without a fat wallet and (for men) a jacket and tie. But if you do go, try the lobster bisque or the chicken Richmond under glass.

Return to Washington Street and turn right at the corner. Two blocks down on the right is West Street. The 3-story, early-19th-century row house at 15 West Street was the home of Elizabeth Peabody, an educator, bookstore owner, and the city's first female publisher. She published the *Dial,* a literary magazine for which Ralph Waldo Emerson served as editor and Henry David Thoreau as assistant editor and writer. Peabody also was responsible for publishing Thoreau's essay "On Civil Disobedience." Her home was a gathering place for the authors and intellectuals of the time. The building now houses *Cornucopia* (phone: 338-4600), a multi-storied restaurant that features "new American" dining. *Fajitas 'n' Ritas* (25 West St.; phone: 426-1222) serves up *fajitas* and margaritas that are remarkably good for New England; it even lets patrons scribble on the walls when they're feeling poetic.

The *Brattle Book Shop* (9 West St.; phone: 542-0210) is unquestionably Boston's best secondhand bookstore. Spend some time perusing its shelves, which reach to the ceiling, and leafing through its impressive collection of vintage *Time* magazines, old and rare books, and autographs. The books on the racks outside are $1 apiece.

Follow West Street to its intersection with Tremont Street. Ahead is Boston Common, the visitors' center, and the end of this walking tour of downtown Boston.

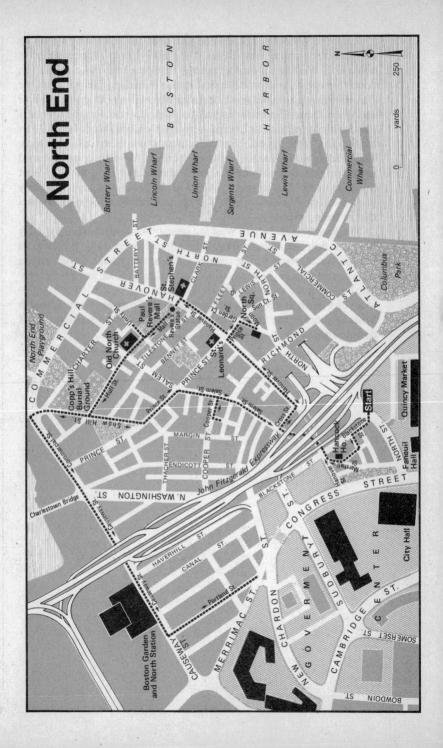

North End

B O S T O N   H A R B O R

Battery Wharf

Lincoln Wharf

Union Wharf

Sargents Wharf

Lewis Wharf

Commercial Wharf

Columbus Park

N

250

0   yards

North End Playground

COMMERCIAL STREET

HANOVER STREET

BATTERY ST

COMMERCIAL

ATLANTIC   AVENUE

CHARTER ST

CLARK ST

NORTH ST

FLEET ST

LEWIS ST

NORTH ST

SUN CT ST

Paul Revere's Mall

St. Stephen's

Old North Church

Unity St

Hull St

SALEM

Revere's Statue

TILESTON ST

BENNET ST

PRINCE ST

HANOVER ST

Garden St

Moon ST

North Sq.

RICHMOND ST

NORTH ST

SNOW HILL ST

Copp's Hill Burial Ground

St. Leonard's

Prince St

Cooper St

Salem St

Cross St

MARGIN ST

THACHER ST

COOPER ST

ENDICOTT ST

Salem St

Hancock Ho

Marshall St

Blackstone

Hanover St

Start

NORTH ST

Quincy Market

Faneuil Hall

Commercial St

Charlestown Bridge

PRINCE ST

N. WASHINGTON ST

John Fitzgerald Expressway

BLACKSTONE ST

CONGRESS   STREET

NEW   GOVERNMENT   CENTER

City Hall

Boston Garden and North Station

HAVERHILL ST

CANAL ST

Portland St

MERRIMAC ST

CAUSEWAY ST

CHARDON ST

SUDBURY ST

CAMBRIDGE ST

SOMERSET ST

BOWDOIN ST

Walk 7: North End

Any thoughtful Bostonian will admit that there is more to the North End than heaping bowls of linguine with white clam sauce and cup after tiny cup of espresso. They'll say there's also cannoli, calzone, calamari . . .

Bostonians (and this includes area suburbanites as well) are guilty of literally feeding the stereotype that everything in the North End revolves around its Italian restaurants. Most non-residents visit the North End only to assuage their cravings for some of the finest Italian food this side of Firenze. But after the last cappuccino, they head in the direction of Boston's glistening skyline and disappear into the night.

The habits of these itinerant diners suit North Enders just fine. They come, they spend, and they leave. It is the "guest" who doesn't leave that has the North End's predominantly Italian population mildly concerned.

This section of Boston, the city's oldest, has suffered what is known here as gentrification. This phenomenon is best defined as the movement of the upper middle class professionals from the suburbs into the heart of the city. In the process, townhouses are restored and condominiums are carved out of formerly ethnic-owned buildings. The result for the locals: higher property values, but also rents that sometimes price longtime residents right out of the neighborhood.

Perhaps North Enders went wrong when they let word get out that their neighborhood is the city's safest. Although the close-knit community certainly helps keep the crime rate down, many Bostonians would attribute the neighborhood's safety to a certain family-run organization that likes to keep an eye on things in this part of town.

Despite all the Italian restaurants, and signs, and the groups of swarthy men discussing the latest soccer matches in rapid-fire Italian, the present ethnic stronghold all over the North End is only the latest of several such dynasties. The North End is, after all, Boston's oldest residential neighborhood. The Puritans were the first to arrive, making their way from Charlestown, when they found the water was contaminated there. The area was home to clergyman Cotton Mather, Paul Revere, and later, was a meeting place of Samuel Adams and the Sons of Liberty.

After the upper crust moved to Beacon Hill, and then to the brownstones of Back Bay, the North End became primarily a commercial center. Mariners disembarked from its nearby wharves. In the mid-1800s, wave after wave of immigrants came ashore here to find housing and jobs. In chronological order, the North End became home to Irish, Jewish, and Italian immigrants. But while the Irish and Jewish communities eventually moved on, the Italians have held their ground here for more than 60 years.

The North End walking tour (it will take about 3 hours) begins in the Blackstone Block, Boston's oldest cluster of buildings, dating from as far back as the 17th century. Just north of *Faneuil Hall,* the block is best reached by turning left in an alley just west of the swank *Bostonian* hotel on North Street. The Haymarket stop on the *MBTA*'s *Green Line* is a short distance from here. On Friday mornings and Saturdays, this area looks like a Turkish bazaar, thanks to *Haymarket,* a farmers' market held on nearby Blackstone Street.

Walk straight on the Blackstone Block; a rather skimpy exhibit outlining the history of the block is on the right. Farther on is Marshall Street and, to the right, set into the foundation of what is now a shop of kitschy souvenirs, is the Boston Stone. The 3-story red brick building just across from the stone was built by John Hancock for his younger brother, Ebenezer, a paymaster for the Continental Army. The house was one of four that Hancock built along what used to be a creek, which made the North End an island in the early days. (See *Walk 6: Downtown.*)

Walk along Marshall Street to Hanover. Turn right on Hanover, then walk a short block to Blackstone Street. This is typically a malodorous little thoroughfare, home to several slovenly fish markets and a grubby pizza joint, littered with spent vegetable or fruit crates with rotting contents, and made even more unpleasant by the central artery rumbling loudly and spouting noxious exhaust fumes overhead. Blackstone Street is best avoided except on market days — when it becomes a Garden of Eden. There are colorful displays of plump, dirt-cheap vegetables and fruit, presided over by portly merchants who tout the virtues of their produce and fully expect to haggle over price. Watch out: They don't let you choose your own produce. So even though the fruit on display looks great, newcomers often walk away with a bag of rotting goods. On Saturday nights, all the refuse from the market is swept into giant heaps, wonderful scavenging sites for those so inclined. Two well-dressed women recently were spotted scaling the heap and extracting edible heads of lettuce with what sounded like victory cries. (For all their pretensions and the mystique of old Yankee wealth, Bostonians can be real penny pinchers.)

At the end of Hanover Street, walk across Blackstone Street. Be on the lookout for the whimsical bronze sculptures of *Haymarket* debris imbedded in the street. There are apples, vegetables, a fish, a banana peel, even the front page of the *Boston Globe.* The work is known as *Asaroton,* from a Greek word meaning "unswept floors."

Follow the Freedom Trail, marked by a red line, into a grim tunnel under the Fitzgerald Expressway, or Central Artery. Fortunately, the days of the eyesore above you are numbered. After years of bureaucratic wrangling, the groaning beast is finally being buried — literally. The Artery will be replaced by an underground highway 8 to 10 lanes wide and 7 miles long, in a project that will take a decade. Imagine the waterfront free of the ugly green monster that consumes so much space and causes such a racket, and restored to the beautiful and bustling area it once was. Enjoy the thought of this scenario. With the dynamics of federal funding, you'll probably be paying for it.

After passing through the tunnel and a parking lot, follow the Freedom Trail to the right, down Cross Street to Hanover. Even if the Italian grocery stores on Cross Street hadn't tipped you off, you'd soon know you were in the North End because of the dramatic change in ambience. Suddenly hand gestures are more animated, oregano permeates the air, pistachios are sold by the huge bag, and buildings are bunched closer together. But most noticeable is the energy. The North End bristles with it.

As you forge your way up Hanover Street, notice the church at the bend far in the distance. That is St. Stephen's, Boston's only remaining church designed by Charles Bulfinch. There'll be time for a closer look later.

There are a number of points of gustatory interest along Hanover Street. The *European* restaurant (218 Hanover St.; phone: 523-5694), on the left, is known for its tractor-tire-size pizza, exhaustive menu, and late hours. Most locals, however, swear by the crunchy, crusty pizza down the street at *Circle Pizza* (361 Hanover St.; phone: 523-8787). Next to the *European* is *Paolo,* which serves northern Italian fare in an elegant little subterranean room (216 Hanover St.; phone: 227-5550). Across the street is the cozy *Mother Anna's* (211 Hanover St.; phone: 523-8496). Nearby, *Ristorante Nicole* (54 Hanover St.; phone: 742-6999) serves heavenly homemade pasta dishes. If you just want a demitasse of espresso and a tasty sweet, stop at *Caffè Dello Sport* (307 Hanover St.; phone: 523-5063) or *Caffè Roma* (241 Hanover St.; phone: 723-1760). Farther up Hanover Street is the *Daily Catch* (323 Hanover St.; phone: 523-8567), formerly known as the *Calamari Café* (the old sign is still up), a petite, moderately priced closet that is the ultimate in intimate dining. Its specialty is (what else?) calamari (squid) with various sauces. Similar in spirit but less well known is *Giacomo's* (355 Hanover St.; phone: 523-9026). Another nearby restaurant is *Ida's* (3 Mechanic St.; phone: 523-0015), a small, home-style eatery noted for a fiercely loyal clientele and for authentic Italian dishes cooked to order.

On Fridays, Saturdays, and Sundays during the summer, Hanover Street and its environs are the site of Italian street festivals, each honoring a saint (the *St. Anthony Festival,* usually held on the last weekend in August, is the largest). The festivals mix religious custom (there is a procession in which statues of the honored saint and the Virgin Mary are carried through the streets) with the usual trappings of an outdoor fair: food concessions, musical performances, craft booths, games of chance, and a generally exuberant air.

Turn right on Prince Street. On the northwest corner of Hanover and Prince is St. Leonard's, New England's first Italian Catholic church. The next intersection is Garden Court Street. The house two doors down on the right (No. 4) is the birthplace (in 1890) of Rose Fitzgerald, later Kennedy — wife of Joe Kennedy, Sr. and mother of JFK, RFK, Teddy, et al.

Rose's father, John F. "Honey Fitz" Fitzgerald, is a North End legend. His father was a grocer on Hanover and North Streets. The Fitzgeralds, like the Kennedys, had fled the Irish potato famine in the mid-1800s for Boston, settling in a North End that was predominantly Irish at the time. Honey Fitz lived in this house for 8 years in the late 1800s; here he built a political base that took him first to the US Congress and later to the mayor's office in Boston's City Hall.

Honey Fitz always called his home base the "dear old North End," and his North End followers "dearos." He could be seen along these very streets around campaign time, performing the "Irish switch" — shaking the hand of one person while talking to another — and talking rings around everyone on most any topic. His gift for gab was so well known that he inspired a new word in the lexicon of Boston politics: "Fitzblarney." Continue walking down Prince Street to North Square. This was home to Boston's most impressive mansions during the late colonial period. One such mansion was owned by Royal Governor Thomas Hutchinson. In 1765, when the then lieutenant governor was suspected of supporting the Stamp Act, angry colonists pillaged the place, smashing furniture, draining the wine cellar, and scattering pages of his history of Massachusetts, a work in progress. Hutchinson was later the colony's last royal governor.

To the right is the Paul Revere House (19 North Sq.; phone: 523-1676 or 523-2338), a popular North End attraction. This medieval-style home was built just after the great fire of 1676. Its design — an overhanging upper floor, shingled roof, and lead casements in the windows — predates what is generally thought of as colonial architecture and gives the building a brooding feel.

The tour of the house is self-guided, but the knowledgeable caretakers are happy to answer questions. Revere bought the house in 1770, shortly before the Boston Massacre. He owned the place for 30 years but lived here for just a decade, later renting it to others. Ninety percent of the structure's framework is original.

Try to imagine the night of April 18, 1775, as Revere, after getting the nod from Joseph Warren in Boston that British troops were moving, quietly slipped into his house (British troops had mustered in North Square) to change into his boots. From here he was rowed by friends across the Charles River, within sight of a British gunship. Borrowing a horse from Deacon John Larkin in Charlestown, the silversmith-cum-patriot galloped off on the ride that earned him a permanent place in American history. William Dawes and Samuel Prescott also rode forth with the news (as did many other area patriots). Although Revere completed his mission, which was to bring word to the town of Lexington, he decided to ride on to Concord; on the way he was captured by the British, questioned, then released. Although he was only one of many, Revere is nevertheless remembered as *the* midnight rider, thanks in large part to the poem by Henry Wadsworth Longfellow. But Revere — Son of Liberty, friend of Samuel Adams, master silversmith, creator of church bells and cannon, artist, messenger (he rode to New York and Philadelphia to tell of the Boston Tea Party), and family man (he had 16 children) — would have been a noteworthy patriot even if Longfellow had not immortalized him in *The Midnight Ride of Paul Revere*. Open daily except Mondays during January and February; admission charge (phone: 523-1676). Also see *Special Places* in THE CITY.

Next to Revere's home is the Pierce-Hichborn House, one of the city's oldest brick buildings. Built about 1715, it was owned by a cousin of Revere's. Open 12:30 to 2:30 PM for tours; closed Mondays. Admission charge (phone: 523-1676).

Past Paul Revere's home on the way back to Prince Street, the Mariner's House is on the left. This is an inn for seamen and merchant marines with stopovers in Boston; there often are a few ancient mariners dawdling out front as they attempt to regain their land legs.

Across the square, at the corner of Sun Court Street, is the Sacred Heart Italian Church rectory. Here Methodist minister Edward Taylor once preached to sailors. A former seaman himself, Taylor was so dramatic and eloquent that sailors spread his fame around the world. Charles Dickens insisted on attending one of his services during a visit to Boston; he and the poet Longfellow were ushered to side aisle seats by a one-eyed, lame mariner (the center aisle was reserved for sailors). Ralph Waldo Emerson called Taylor "the Shakespeare of the sailor and the poor."

Two of the more peculiar incidents in Boston history happened nearby. On an unseasonably warm day in January 1919, a 4-story silo of molasses ruptured on Commercial Street, sending a 50-foot wall of molasses flowing down the street at a rate of 35 miles an hour, destroying buildings and crushing bridges in its path. All told, a dozen people died and many more were injured in the incident. The horses of mounted police that wandered into the morass became so inextricably stuck that they had to be shot. North Enders swear that on hot days they can still detect a hint of molasses in the air.

On the east side of Moon Street, just ahead, was a dwelling owned by a sea captain who was put in the stocks in 1673 for "lewd and unseemly conduct." The infraction apparently occurred when the captain kissed his wife on his doorstep after returning from a long voyage at sea.

Return to Prince Street, walk back to Hanover, then make a right. Two blocks up Hanover on the right, at the corner of Clark and Hanover Streets, is St. Stephen's Church, built by Charles Bulfinch in 1804. St.

Stephen's has been a Catholic parish since 1864. It was restored to its original appearance in 1965, regaining its plain glass windows, white walls, chandeliers, red carpet, and gilded organ pipes.

Across from St. Stephen's is the Paul Revere Mall, a.k.a. the Prado. The centerpiece of this quiet neighborhood park is Cyrus Dallin's lively equestrian statue of Paul Revere. There are a number of plaques on its south side that recount the lives of famous North Enders.

Ahead is the Old North Church (193 Salem St.; phone: 523-6676), Boston's oldest house of worship, built in 1723. Before visiting this landmark, however, notice the 3-story brick building on the left at 21 Unity Street. This is the Ebenezer Clough House. The home of a mason who helped build the church, the house (ca. 1712) is the only survivor of its era in the North End. It is not open to the public. A similar brick building, the only property Benjamin Franklin ever owned in Boston, once stood next door (now the courtyard behind the church). Franklin's sister lived there.

The Old North Church — officially called Christ Church — is best known for the fabled lanterns Paul Revere arranged to have hung in the church's steeple — "one if by land, two if by sea" — to warn the people of Charlestown of British troop movements. (Church sexton Robert Newman, who actually hung the lanterns and was jailed by the British for his efforts, is honored with a plaque in the garden on the church's north side.) The most famous steeple in the American Revolution toppled over in a gale in 1804. Its replacement stood stolid until it, too, was blown down in 1954. The steeple you see now was put up at that time. It contains the first church bells cast "for the British Empire in North America," according to their inscription.

Once inside the church, look for the nation's first memorial to George Washington, located in a niche near the altar. Also note the brass chandeliers that were made in England in 1700, the oldest clock still running in an American public building, and the brass nameplates affixed to the high-sided box pews, indicating former ownership. (Also see *Historic Churches* in DIVERSIONS.)

The next stop, following the Freedom Trail up Hull Street, is the Copp's Hill Burying Ground, Boston's second-oldest cemetery. Named after its first eternal occupant, William Copp, a shoemaker from England who had his house here, this is the highest point in the North End. Oddly enough, the oldest gravestone here dates back to 1625, 5 years before the Puritans came to Boston. The discrepancy is due to the fact that the remains (and apparently the gravestone) of Grace Berry, who died in Plymouth in 1625, were brought to Copp's Hill by her husband when he moved to the North End sometime later. Also buried here are the Mathers — Increase, Cotton, and Samuel — a succession of ministers who held sway over religious conscience in the heyday of Puritanism. Their tomb can be found about 20 feet from the Charter Street gate. Some of the Copp's Hill gravestones retain the marks of musket balls, scars from the days when Redcoats stationed nearby used them for target practice. The shooting appears to have been indiscriminate, with the exception of Captain Daniel Malcolm's gravestone, which took a heavy pounding. The marker reads, "A true son of liberty."

Leave the cemetery from the Snowhill Street side. Just over the rooftops, the rigging of "Old Ironsides," docked in Charlestown, can be seen.

At this juncture, the tour offers a choice of two (equally pleasant) alternatives: a visit to *Boston Garden* and a well-deserved ale in a brewery/bar nearby, or a stroll through the heart of the Italian neighborhood via a network of small streets and narrow byways.

Those who opt for the Italian neighborhood walk should head south (away from the water) on Snowhill Street to Prince Street. Turn left on Prince, then right on Salem Street down to Cooper Street, then turn right again into a tangle of interlocking streets that have an authentic feel of Italy. When you have finished exploring, return to Salem Street, turn right, and head straight across Cross Street and back through the tunnel under the Central Artery.

Sports fans with a hankering to see the fabled *Boston Garden* should descend Snowhill Street to the north, to Commercial Street, near the water. Proceed left on Commercial Street (which turns into Causeway Street after 2 blocks). Pass under the Fitzgerald Expressway; *Boston Garden,* home of the *Celtics,* and the famous parquet floor, and the *Bruins,* is on the right. (Also see *Quintessential Boston* in DIVERSIONS.) Tours are offered during the off-season (phone: 227-3200). The final stop on the tour is the *Commonwealth Brewery* (138 Portland St.; phone: 523-8383), for some of the finest beer in New England. Continue past the *Garden,* then turn left on Portland Street to Merrimac. Just a peek at the mammoth brass beer tanks, visible from the sidewalk, makes one a little parched. The proprietors brew about 11 different types of beer in their continuing effort to uphold their noble motto: "Let no man thirst for lack of real Ale."

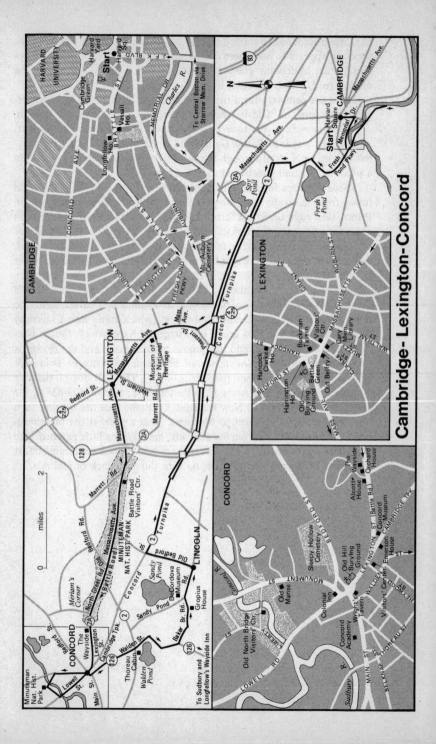

Cambridge-Lexington-Concord

Drive: Cambridge, Lexington, Concord, and Lincoln

Concord and Lexington may sound like familiar names, places you learned about in your eighth grade American history class. The site of the battles that started the Revolutionary War took place here in 1775; today, the towns take such pride in their history that plaques abound, and stories about the legends — the midnight ride of Paul Revere, the Minutemen, the shot heard round the world — still echo through the streets.

But there's much more to this area than a lesson in history. This drive will appeal to anyone who appreciates classic New England towns, period homes, and rural landscapes. We start outside Harvard Square in Cambridge, on a street of historic Tory mansions, and travel west to the snug little town greens of Lexington and Concord, with their white churches and colonial homes. Several of the old structures have been restored to period house-museums, giving a visitor a quick insight into all the glory — and grittiness — of colonial times. By the 19th century, the fighting men of Concord were gone or subdued, replaced by creative talents whose works spoke louder than cannon. Long after Paul Revere had stabled his horse, this became the home of Emerson, Hawthorne, and Thoreau. Walden Pond, Thoreau's famous woodland retreat, is on this tour, as is Louisa May Alcott's home, which was the setting for *Little Women*.

The drive begins in Cambridge at Harvard Square, the spiritual heart of these four areas. A singular center of learning and culture since 1636, when Reverend John Harvard set aside 400 pounds sterling to found a "schoale or colledge . . . to advance learning and perpetuate it to posterity," today the square is a center of singular traffic jams, where pedestrians delight in weaving among cars in a death-defying game. Driving here is definitely hazardous to your health. Better to park at a safe distance (the *Charles* hotel has an underground garage) and explore on foot.

Harvard Square is a loosely defined area emanating from the *Out of Town News* kiosk. On one side is the Harvard University campus; on the other sides are shops, movie theaters, restaurants, coffeehouses, and, especially, bookstores — about 3 dozen of them at last count. Worth noting are *Schoenhof's Foreign Books* (76A Mt. Auburn St.; phone: 547-8845), which boasts the largest collection of foreign books in New England, and the Schlesinger Library at Radcliffe, one of the country's foremost libraries on women and women's history. Brochures outlining a walking tour of

Cambridge may be picked up at the *Cambridge Discovery* kiosk near *Out of Town News.*

If you prefer to avoid the hassle, start this drive on Memorial Drive, at the intersection of JFK Street. The Larz Anderson Bridge is on the left, the hustle and bustle of the square is just a short block to the right. Drive northwest on Memorial Drive. This curving, tree-lined section of roadway was slated to be a major highway in 1963, but a group of citizens, led by Edward Bernays, the father of public relations, staged a save-the-syca-more-trees protest; the city took note and the scenic, narrow roadway was preserved.

At the rotary, follow the signs for Route 2, which curves to the right. At the large intersection with Mt. Auburn Street, take the right fork (*not* the sharp right turn), which continues out Route 2, or take one of two interesting detours. The first is the Mt. Auburn Cemetery (580 Mt. Auburn St.; phone: 547-7105), the country's oldest garden cemetery; its 170 acres are a beautiful spot for strolling and bird watching. (You also can drive through the cemetery; bikes and motorcycles are prohibited, however.) This is the final resting place of Henry Wadsworth Longfellow, Oliver Wendell Holmes, and Mary Baker Eddy; if you want to find their graves, ask for a map at the cemetery entrance. To get to the cemetery, turn left on Mt. Auburn Street, then left again to the entrance. After a stroll among the headstones, rejoin Route 2 by turning left out of the cemetery entrance, a right on Aberdeen Street, right on Huron, then left onto Route 2.

An alternative is to take a side trip down Brattle Street, one of the country's first mansion-lined streets. In colonial times, it was known, scornfully, as Tory Row, since most of the rich and famous residents were British supporters. Take a right on Mt. Auburn Street, then a quick left and right again to reach Brattle Street. Most of these fine old homes are privately owned, but their exteriors are worth a look. Two open to the public are the Longfellow House (No. 105) and the Hooper-Lee-Nichols House (No. 159).

Built in 1685, the white Georgian Hooper-Lee-Nichols House is the oldest home in Cambridge. Its low-slung frame now has a discernable sag and, in the interior, a huge central hearth, low ceilings, and wide-planked floors are all graceful indications of its age. Now home to the *Cambridge Historical Society* (which gives tours on Tuesday and Thursday afternoons year-round and on Sunday afternoons from May through October; admission charge; phone: 547-4252), it is more interesting for its architecture than any collection of artifacts; do look for the antique dollhouse and the circa-1850 wallpaper.

For 9 months in 1775, the yellow clapboard Longfellow House served as General George Washington's headquarters. Built in 1759 by John Vassall — a wealthy Tory who fled for his life during the Revolution — the home was bought in 1843 by Henry Wadsworth Longfellow's new father-in-law and given to Longfellow and his wife. Longfellow lived here until his death in 1882, writing many of his poems, most notably *The Midnight Ride of Paul Revere,* from this house. On display are Longfellow's books, furnishings, and art collection as they were when he lived here. Open daily; guided tours are available; admission charge (phone: 876-4491).

Other homes worth noting are the Vassall House (built in 1746), at the corner of Hawthorne and Brattle Streets, which was built by Henry Vassall, the uncle of the owner of the Longfellow House. The house was the center of the Army Medical Corps during the American Revolution.

Close to Harvard Square is the Dexter Pratt House (built in 1808). Pratt, the village blacksmith, was immortalized in Longfellow's poem. Both the tree and the smithy are gone; the building is now owned by the Cambridge Center for Adult Education, which runs the *Blacksmith House* bakery (56 Brattle St.; phone: 354-3036) on the first floor.

Finally, the modest yellow frame house at 42 Brattle Street was originally owned by William Brattle. In this city of zealous patriots, it's odd that the street retains his name: Brattle was the commander of all British troops in the colonies.

To rejoin Route 2, go west on Brattle Street, turn right onto Lexington Street, then left again onto Huron Avenue. Drive 3 short blocks and turn right onto Route 2, or Fresh Pond Parkway, as it's called here. Follow the road as it curves alongside the Fresh Pond Reservoir, which supplies much of Cambridge's water. Continue following the signs for Route 2 for about 2 miles (and through three rotaries). Then relax — the road becomes a highway and the driving gets easier.

The first stop is downtown Lexington, which was founded by a few farmers from Cambridge in the late 17th century and was called, appropriately enough, Cambridge Farms. By 1713, it had a population of 450 and was incorporated as the town of Lexington.

About 4 miles after the road widens to eight lanes, take the exit for Route 4 and Route 225. Turn right off the exit ramp to Pleasant Street. Follow this street north as it turns into Massachusetts Avenue. Continue north about 1.5 miles past the Route 4/Route 225 exit to 2A (or Marrett Road) to the *Museum of Our National Heritage,* a modern brick museum erected in 1975 by the Masons (open daily year-round; no admission charge; 33 Marrett Rd., Lexington; phone: 861-6559 or 861-0729). The museum has changing exhibits on American culture and "Let It Begin Here," a permanent exhibit that is a good introduction to local history. The title echoes the words of one Captain Parker, commander of the American Minutemen at Lexington Green on April 19, 1775. On the evening of April 18, 1775, a British force began a march out to Concord to seize the stores of weapons held there and possibly to capture patriots and rabble-rousers John Hancock and Samuel Adams. But some 77 Lexington Minutemen assembled on the green to meet them. As the British approached, Captain Parker told his men: "Stand your ground. Don't fire unless fired upon. But if they mean to have a war, let it begin here." The British were also under orders not to start firing, but somehow, someone fired the first shot — just who it was remains a mystery — and so the war began. Parker's quote is now inscribed on a plaque on the town green and included in a narrated 6-minute slide show at the museum. Accompanying exhibits are peopled with cutout characters that illustrate what life was like in colonial times.

On leaving the museum, return to Mass. Ave. and continue north through the center of Lexington. After passing several blocks of shops and restaurants, you'll come to the Village Green, the site of the first pre-war skirmish in 1775. If you're lucky, you may even walk into the fray. Every April 19, the townsfolk don red coats and colonial garb and reenact the famous battle. The ritual starts at 6 AM, when a Paul Revere character rides through town, yelling (what else?), "The British are coming."

The first thing you'll see as you approach the green from the south is the statue of Captain Parker, a.k.a. The Minuteman. On its base are inscribed the words spoken by Samuel Adams on April 19: "What a glorious morning for America." Boston embraced Adams's sentiments, and continues to celebrate the date as *Patriots Day*. A statewide holiday, it is more stirring today because of another competition: The *Boston Marathon* is held on the weekend closest to that date. Fans by the thousands line the city streets or cheer the runners on from windows and decks. Any way you look at it, it's a great day to be in Boston, but a lousy day for anyone hoping to drive through town.

Park near the Village Green, also called Battle Green, for a short walk to the major sites in the area. (There's some on-street parking available and a municipal lot around the corner on Meriam Street.) Stop first at the visitors' center (open daily, year-round; phone: 862-1450) and look at the diorama of the battle on Lexington Green; they also offer brochures and maps.

The handsome yellow house next door is *Buckman Tavern*. It was here, on April 19, that nervous militiamen waited for the British, who, as Paul Revere told them, "were coming" (the actual ride occurred at 2 AM, but the annual reenactment takes some liberties with the timing for the sake of everyone's sleep). The tavern has been restored to its original state (today it's strictly a museum, not a working tavern). Open daily from April 19 through October 31. Guided tours are available; admission charge (phone: 861-0928).

Walk north from *Buckman Tavern* up Hancock Street. A Minuteman Memorial sculpture, with the gunmen carved into a rock, is on the right. Farther up the street is the *Hancock-Clarke House*, built around 1698. Here Revere alerted patriots Samuel Adams and John Hancock that the British were on their way and warned them that they might be taken prisoner. The two escaped and lived to harass the Brits another day.

Today, the house is a museum of the Revolution. Open daily, April 19 through October 31. Guided tours are available; admission charge (phone: 861-0928).

Walk back toward Battle Green and turn right onto Harrington Road. One block over is the stately Harrington House. History (or legend) records that Jonathan Harrington, the fifer of the Minuteman corps, crawled back to his home after being wounded in the battle and died on the doorstep — in front of his wife. It is now a private home.

As you may have surmised, the people of Lexington are quite proud of their history and their beautiful town green with its two churches and its well-spaced, historic homes. But as you walk along Harrington Road, you may notice a small plaque that points out that it wasn't always so. As the plaque reveals, it wasn't until 1956 that a historic district was created to preserve the stately homes surrounding the green. In fact, it wasn't until the *Centennial* celebration, on a snowy day in 1875, when 100,000 people from all over the country led by none other than President Ulysses S. Grant, descended on Lexington, that its citizens realized the historical significance of their town and recognized the need to create facilities for visitors. Things have changed. The *Historical Society* was formed in 1886, and today, the town plays host to more than 80,000 visitors a year. Emblazoned in gold letters across the front of the massive flagpole in the middle of the green (which was erected for the *Bicentennial*) is the phrase: "Birthplace of American Liberty."

Follow Harrington Road just past the green to the Old Burying Ground on the right. Here you can find the grave markers for Captain Parker and for a nameless British soldier who died in *Buckman Tavern*. The oldest gravestone here dates from 1690.

Return to the green and note the small obelisk marking the graves of the Minutemen. Erected in 1799, it is the oldest Revolutionary War monument. Toss a penny on their gravestone, like so many others have before you, and read the stirring words praising this courageous fight by many so heroic Americans.

Continue around to where a path leads up the hill to an authentic-looking reproduction of the Old Belfry, whose bells roused the townsfolk on that fateful morning. It's well worth the 5-minute climb for the view over the green.

Across the street is the Cary Memorial Library, with its portraits of George Washington and Paul Revere, both copies of the Gilbert Stuart works, and a painting of the *News of Lexington* by Emanuel Leutze. Also here are reproductions of the engravings of Amos Doolittle recounting the battles of Concord and Lexington. Done in 1775 and based on eyewitness accounts, these engravings have served as a key source for historians trying to re-create the battles.

The municipal parking lot is just across Mass. Ave., but before going back to your car, enjoy a pleasant suburban phenomenon. Step into the street in a crosswalk and watch the cars come to a screeching halt. Ahh. You're not in Boston any longer.

Before driving on, you might want to make a stop at one of the many restaurants in the town center. *Le Bellecoeur* has classic French food (10 Muzzey St.; phone: 861-9400); *Sweet Peppers* is a sophisticated, Italian bistro (20 Waltham St.; phone: 862-1880); *Bel Canto* serves great deep-dish pizza and wonderful calzone (1709 Massachusetts Ave.; phone: 861-6556); and the *Food Emporium* makes tasty sandwiches and salads to go, if you're hankering for a picnic (1768 Massachusetts Ave.; phone: 862-0326).

For all the local hoopla about the Minutemen, it's easy to forget that they lost that first skirmish. They were badly outnumbered — some 77 to 700 — and completely unable to put up an effective front. After a few shots were fired and the field became confused with gunpowder smoke and the cries of the wounded, the Minutemen retreated. With a whoop, the British continued their march to Concord. But the significance of the accidental battle came later, when the militia from surrounding towns converged on Concord, seeking revenge.

By the time the British got to the town, the assembled populace — some 300 to 400 — were ready for a fight. They stopped the British forces at the Old North Bridge in Concord (more about that later) and the British began a retreat to Boston. It was here that the Brits' luck really ran out. Harassed by townsmen all along the road to Boston, they met their match at Meriam's Corner, where the Americans attacked and killed eight of their men. The retreat ended with some 73 British dead, 147 wounded, and 26 missing, from a total force of 1,800. On the American side, an estimated 3,500 men took part at some point or another — almost all the able-bodied men in the area. Of that number, some 49 were killed, 41 wounded, and 5 missing.

Be aware that this "history" was recorded by Americans, not British, so it emphasizes the courageous patriot action and the retreat of the British soldier. The present day Minuteman National Historical Park surrounds several miles of the roadway that the British traveled. To reach it, rejoin Massachusetts Avenue on the north side of the Lexington Green. Follow it west, for about 2 miles, going over Route 128. When it dead-ends into Marrett Road (Route 2A), turn right until you see the signs to the park. The first sign is for a turnoff to Fiske Hill, which has a parking lot, picnic tables, and a standing map of prospective sites in the area. From here, a nature trail leads to the remains of the Ebenezer Fiske House.

The Battle Road Visitor's Center is just ahead on the left in a land-scaped park, complete with picnic tables (open mid-April through mid-November; no admission charge; phone: 862-7753). Besides the typical brochures, this center has several good exhibits and a short movie about the British incursion.

A half-mile farther up the road is a disquieting clash of legend and reality. A large stone plaque marks the site where Paul Revere was captured by a British patrol on the morning of April 19. His companions, William Dawes, who took a different route from Boston, and Dr. Samuel Prescott, who started his ride in Lexington, were both able to escape the patrol. Revere was detained and wasn't released until the next morning. While he was able to warn the town of Lexington, he never made it to Concord.

About a mile farther, take the right-hand turnoff that leads to Battle Road. This short detour leads along a narrow, wooded road, past two Revolutionary-era homes. Immediately on the right is the William Smith House, home of the captain of the Lincoln Minutemen. This restored home is a traditional New England saltbox, typical of a Revolutionary-era farming homestead.

Next is the Hartwell Hearth, which is nothing but a wood frame over a huge, central fireplace — the house burned down in 1968 — but it's worth a stop to marvel at just how huge and how central that 18th-century heating system was. Eight fireplaces and numerous nooks and crannies, including a basement storage area, are set in and around the brick structure, which seems to take up a quarter of the living space.

Farther along Battle Road is the *Hartwell Tavern,* an important watering hole in the late 1700s. The wood saltbox has a simple floor plan. An exhibit is open to the public during the summer months.

Continue along the curved, wooded road to 2A. Take a right and head for Concord (2A soon becomes North Great Road). At the fork, stay to the left, which takes you into Concord center. At the intersection of the Old Bedford Road is Meriam's Corner, the site of the Minutemen's first attack on the retreating British soldiers. Just before the intersection is *Willow Pond Kitchen* (phone: 508-369-6529), a classic seafood shack, where inexpensive seafood, sandwiches, and pizza are served in a no-frills setting.

About a half-mile from Meriam's Corner is the first evidence of Concord's past literary glory. On the right is the Wayside, a rambling yellow Victorian home with three huge chimneys and a large wraparound porch (455 Lexington Rd.; phone: 508-369-6975). It was the home of Nathaniel Hawthorne from 1852 until his death in 1864, and its subsequent owner, Margaret Sidney — author of *The Five Little Peppers and How They Grew* — kept Hawthorne's study intact. You can park in the lot on the left-hand side of the street. Tours are available April through October; closed Mondays. Admission charge.

Orchard House, the home of the Alcotts, is just a bit farther down the road (399 Lexington Rd.; phone: 508-369-4118). The Alcott family lived here from 1858 to 1877, and it is the home Louisa May Alcott described in *Little Women.* The rooms have been carefully preserved, capturing the life of the period. Louisa's father, Bronson, was a noted philosopher, a friend of Emerson and Thoreau, and a starry-eyed, irresponsible dreamer, which accounts for the family's frequent moves. Several of the family's city homes are noted on the Beacon Hill walk (see *Walk 5: Beacon Hill*). Bronson Alcott founded his school of philosophy at Orchard House, after an earlier attempt to found a Utopian community in Harvard had failed. Open daily April 1 through October 31 and on weekends in March and November. Tours are available; admission charge.

Next to the Wayside is the yard of the Grapevine Cottage, where you can see the original grapevine of the Concord grape. The headquarters of Welch's — the jam and juice company and the biggest promoter of the local fruit — is in Concord. The house is not open to the public, but a plaque on the fence briefly describes grape harvesting.

About a half-mile farther, the *Concord Museum,* a red brick Georgian house, graces the triangle of land created by the fork of 2A and Cambridge Turnpike. Take the small cutoff to the left before the fork, or make a sharp turn to reach the museum's parking lot on Cambridge Turnpike. The museum's core is the 1,500-piece collection of Cummings E. Davis, a poor tailor who moved here in 1850 from Brooklyn, New York — and began collecting other people's unwanted furniture, tools, and other items. One of the first to recognize the value of preserving these artifacts, he opened a museum in 1858. Davis donated his collection to the city of Concord in 1886; following this bequeathal, the local antiquarian society was founded. Today, the museum has more than 30,000 pieces, and an addition to the building has doubled the exhibition space. Be sure to look for the "two if by sea" lantern, one of the rustic lanterns with a single candle that hung in Old North Church and provided Revere with a warning signal. Ralph Waldo Emerson's study is here, preserved intact, as are many of Henry David Thoreau's artifacts. (While you're in town, do as the locals do and just refer to him as "Henry David.") Open year-round; closed Mondays. Tours are available; admission charge (phone: 508-369-9609).

Walk across the street to *Emerson House,* the writer's home from 1835 until his death in 1882. Today, it houses many of his books, personal effects, and furniture. Open Thursdays through Sundays, mid-April through mid-October. Tours are available; admission charge (phone: 508-369-2236).

Leaving the museum parking lot, turn right onto Lexington Road and continue another 0.4 mile into Concord Center. Halfway there, look for the Visitors' Information Booth on Heywood Street (on the left); it offers maps and brochures during the summer months. In the winter, the same information is available at the Chamber of Commerce office, housed in *Wright Tavern,* just 1 block farther at the intersection of Main Street (phone: 508-369-3120).

The huge white church next to *Wright Tavern* is the third incarnation of the First Parish Meeting House. The two earlier structures were destroyed by fires. The First Provincial Congress of 1774 was held in the original building and, with John Hancock as president and William Emerson as chaplain, it's not surprising that the delegates to this historic meeting voted to resist British tyranny. The town of Concord had little sympathy for Tories. On January 10, 1774, every man in town and five women affixed their signature to a letter to the city of Boston agreeing to support them in their ban of the East India Company's tea. On September 26, 1774, the town voted to raise two companies of men, willing to stand at a minute's warning in case of alarm. Thus the term "Minutemen."

Across the street, you'll notice a hill dotted with gravestones. This is the Old Hill Burying Ground, where several Revolutionary families are interred. In early Concord, except for going to and from church, graveyards were the only places "proper" families walked on Sundays. Since so many families wandered the graveyards, tombstones tended to be decorative and carried suitable moral messages. The raised tombs with large flat stone slabs on top had space for the longest messages, and so were reserved for ministers, deacons, or magistrates. The earliest stones have death heads with wings on them, which, far from being morbid, denote immortality.

You are now in the center of town, as marked by the flagpole and the small green strip of land. Park your car and walk along Main Street and see the many unique shops, selling everything from jewelry to toys. If you arrive in the afternoon, stop in at the *Colonial Inn* (48 Monument Sq.; phone: 508-369-9200) for tea, complete with scones and silver service — you'd think the Tories had never left. The original part of the inn was built in 1718. Today, it has 54 modern and moderately priced rooms decorated in simple colonial style. Traditional (and moderately priced) American fare is served in the dining room, or stop in the atmospheric pub. A parking lot is at the rear of the inn.

From the *Colonial Inn,* you can take a side trip to Sleepy Hollow Cemetery (open weekdays; phone: 508-371-6280), the final resting place of some of the town's leading literary lights: Louisa May Alcott, Thoreau, Emerson, and Hawthorne have graves on "Authors' Ridge." To reach the cemetery, turn right onto Bedford Street from Monument Road, which runs in front of the *Colonial Inn.*

The Old North Bridge is about three-quarters of mile from here. Depending on your energy and the weather, walk or drive north on Monument Street for about a half-mile to the Old Manse, the home of Concord's early ministers, notably one Reverend William Emerson, leading patriot and grandfather of Ralph Waldo. From its windows, Emerson, Sr., watched the battle of Old North Bridge. Nathaniel Hawthorne once rented the house for about 3 years (open April 19 through October 31; closed Tuesdays; tours available; admission charge; Monument St.; phone: 508-369-3909). If the weather permits, a pleasant way to explore the surroundings is to rent a canoe from the nearby *South Bridge Boat House* (open April through October; 496 Main St.; phone: 508-369-9438); the Concord River flows right behind the Old Manse.

Just past the manse, the parking lot on the right is the starting point for a short walk to Old North Bridge. It was here, on this small wooden structure over the Concord River, that the British expeditionary force met with the American Minutemen for the second time, on April 19, 1775. The British had set fire to stores in the center of Concord and traveled on to the bridge, because they thought, quite rightly, that more guns were stored in the fields beyond. The local militia, on the west side of the bridge, saw the flames and, imagining their town burning, approached the oncoming forces. The British fired over the river and the patriots returned fire, with a "shot heard round the world." At the old bridge today, you can see Daniel Chester French's famous Minuteman statue, and a battle monument. When the weather is good, talks are given here on the area's history. You can continue by foot across the bridge to the North Bridge Visitor's Center (174 Liberty St.; phone: 508-369-6993), or drive around by continuing along Monument Street and turning left onto Liberty Street. The center features exhibits and a short film that illustrate the North Bridge battle. Its hilltop location also affords visitors a splendid view of the bridge. You can picnic in the shade of its great trees. Open daily year-round.

This route now heads to Walden Pond, Thoreau's famous retreat. From the visitors' center, turn left onto Liberty Street, then left again onto Lowell Road, which brings you full circle to a flagpole. Turn right onto Main Street. If you're a Thoreau fan, you'll want to visit the Thoreau Lyceum (156 Belknap St.; phone: 508-369-5912) before you leave town. To get to Belknap Street, turn left off Main Street; the street is just past the snug white clapboard buildings of Concord Academy, a proper New England prep school, which counts Thoreau as one of its early graduates. (Less often noted is that he also taught here for under a year, resigning in protest after being forced to beat several students.) The Lyceum, an unremarkable shingle house on an unremarkable street, is the international headquarters of the *Thoreau Society* (open daily, March through December; admission charge). If you're not a transcendentalist, just be glad you weren't visiting in July 1991, when the town was crowded with an international conference of Thoreau-ists.

If you want to go directly to Walden Pond, go to Main Street and make a quick left onto Walden Street. Follow that for about a mile, past the intersection with Route 2, and you'll see the signs for Walden Pond. In the summer, the clash between past and present couldn't be greater. A replica of Thoreau's small house sits in the parking lot of this state park, which is usually jammed with screaming kids, strutting teenagers, and sun worshiping singles. It's a far cry from his solitary, wooded home, where he went to "live deliberately, to front only the essential facts of life and see if I could not learn what it had to teach . . . to drive life into a corner and reduce it to its lowest terms." Now, the contest seems to be to drive as many lives into a corner of the pond as possible, where the beach rests. For a bit of solitude, take the second path to the right and look for the cairn that marks the original site of Thoreau's cabin. Continue around the pond on the wooded path and hope to find an unoccupied inlet.

On the way home, we recommend a stop at the *Gropius House* and the *DeCordova Museum,* for a one-two punch of modern life. At the exit of the Walden Pond parking lot, take a right onto Route 126 South to Lincoln. After 0.7 miles, make a left at Baker Bridge Road. In a half-mile (on the right) is the dramatic white *Gropius House* (68 Baker Bridge Rd.; phone: 259-8843). This was the first American project of architect Walter Gropius, head of the Bauhaus in Germany from 1919 to 1928. After he emigrated in 1937, he built his home from materials from catalogues and building-supply stores. The clean, modern lines — revolutionary at the time — dramatically illustrate the Bauhaus philosophy of form following function. Open Fridays, Saturdays, and Sundays from June through mid-October and on the first weekend of the month from November 1 through May 31. Admission charge.

To go to the *DeCordova Museum,* turn right out of the *Gropius House* driveway. Turn right again at the dead end; the museum entrance is on the left. Though it showcases one of the area's best collections of modern and contemporary art, the museum's most appealing feature is on the outside. The turreted red brick mansion sits like a medieval bastion amid 35 acres of rolling gardens, among which are scattered 20 to 30 pieces of sculpture. There are great, expansive arcs of steel, twisted bronze shapes, and rounded pieces of concrete; most are abstract shapes, some are recognizable objects, and all blend remarkably well with the rolling hills and landscaped gardens.

To return to Boston from Lincoln, turn left out of the *DeCordova* driveway. Take the first left at Old Bedford Street. At Route 2 (the first major intersection) turn right. Head east to Fresh Pond, then to Memorial Drive. Instead of going to Harvard Square, return directly to Boston via Storrow Drive.

A COLONIAL NIGHT	If you want to spend the night in colonial country, a short detour to the

west leads to *Longfellow's Wayside Inn,* just off Route 20 in Sudbury (phone: 508-443-8846). The inn has just 10 rooms, beautifully furnished with authentic antiques, and priced under $100 a night for a double room (reserve well in advance). Or just stop by to visit the restaurant, which serves moderately priced New England fare. Stop in at the mini colonial village that was assembled by auto magnate Henry Ford in the 1920s. The *Old Bar* tavern was built in the 1680s and, almost 200 years later, was Longfellow's favorite watering hole. The poet would tell stories here that later became part of *Tales of a Wayside Inn.* Among the memorable lines were (you guessed it) "Listen my children and you shall hear, of the midnight ride of Paul Revere." To get here, go south on Route 126, past Walden Pond. After about 5 miles, turn right on Boston Post Road (Route 20). Signs for the inn will appear after about another 5 miles.

Index